# Here's what some of sk
## are saying about

"Claudia's efforts to educate women in skiing provide a great value. Her preaching align with our continuing commitment to build top performing skis designed specifically for women by women."
— Stuart N. Rempel
Olin Skis Vice President

"As women become more savvy purchasers (of ski products), they search for better, more in-depth information. Claudia has been one of the early pioneers in making a call-to-conscience for resorts and manufacturers as to the specific needs for women in skiing."
— Jeanne-Marie Gand,
Vice President, Rossignol

"At long last, a book that will help women stand up on their skis and get involved with the sport. When I started skiing, it took a unique and feisty woman to be recognized as a knowledgeable skier. It still does. But, this book will help women claim their fair place on the slopes."
—Anna McIntyre, First woman officer of the U.S. Ski Association and first woman Chief of Alpine World Cup Races in the world

"*WomenSki* addresses the frustrations that prevent so many skiers from reaching their potential. Claudia empowers the reader by breaking down intimidating barriers, providing insightful tips and crusading for the athlete in all of us."
—Dee Byrne, PSIA Demo Team member
Instructor, Beaver Creek Ski School

"*WomenSki* has my full attention! Claudia covers crucial issues that are barriers to improvement that I had to overcome in my own skiing and that I see constantly as a ski instructor and coach. Coming from a true love of skiing, Claudia is telling women skiers NOT to settle for LESS and how to do so."
—Carol Levine, former PSIA Demo Team member & Staff Trainer, Beaver Creek

"If you are female and you ski, this is essential reading. If you are male and want to understand women who ski, likewise."
—Diane Slezak Scholfield
Executive Editor, *Skiing America*

## Dedication

*To John*
*who started it all by teaching me to ski*

*To my children*
*— Susan, David, Michael, Kathleen, Nick,*
*and the newest generation,*
*Amanda, Madi, Galen and John Dylan —*
*the constant joys of my life*

*And to all women who ski*

# WOMEN™
# SKI

*by Claudia Carbone*

**World Leisure Corporation**
Hampstead, NH • Boston, MA

Distributed to the trade in USA by
LPC Group, Login Trade, 1436 West Randolph Street, Chicago, IL
60607; (312) 733-8228, (800) 626-4330.

Distributed to the trade in Canada by
E.A. Milley Enterprises, Inc., Locust Hill,
Ontario L0H 1J0, Canada, tel. (800) 399-6858.

Distributed to the trade in U.K. by Roger Lascelles,
47 York Road, Brentford, Middlesex TW8 0QP Tel. 0181-847 0935.

Mail Order, Catalog and Special Sales by
World Leisure Corporation, 177 Paris Street, Boston, MA 02128.
Tel. (617) 569-1966, fax (617) 561-7654, e-mail wleisure@aol.com
ISBN: 0-915009-55-2                                  *second edition*

# Acknowledgments

To my brilliant publisher, Charlie Leocha, for "thinking like a woman" in order to appreciate the value of this book in the skiing world and bringing it to life.

To my gifted editor, Julie Hutchinson, for her guidance, her encouragement, and her delightful enthusiasm. Thank you for making our sessions so pleasant and mutually enlightening!

To Diane Scholfield—Thelma to my Louise—for her friendship, encouragement and keen editor's eyes.

To Warren Witherell, who kept my writing technically correct and provided me with a huge boost from the ski industry side.

To Dee Byrne and Carol Levine for the inspiration.

To Janet Spangler, Debbie Voigt, Diane Stone, Jay McGarry, Peggy Spangler, Tricia Hohl, Martie Irish, Kathy Ryan, Leslie Glaysher, Maggie Loring, Ashley Fischer, Nancy Luke, Patricia Simmons, Barbara Kester, Peggy Sax, Lisa Feinberg Densmore, Brenda Buglione and Mermer Blakeslee for their willingness to share their expertises.

To Edna Dercum for being an amazing role model for women skiers.

To everyone who took time to talk with me about my favorite subject.

Especially, to all the women who eagerly shared their skiing experiences, good and bad.

# Table of Contents

# About the Author

*Claudia Carbone started skiing during the '50s, when only
a handful of ski areas existed in her native Colorado.
High school friends took her to the top of Winter Park and
urged her to follow. She has skied nearly every season
since. Claudia writes a weekly ski column in Englewood
and a "WomenSki" feature on the internet at Yahoo's
AMI Recreation News Website. She has been published in
numerous magazines and newspapers. She has received
the North American Ski Journalists Association's highest
award for excellence and was named 1992's Freelancer
of the Year by Colorado Ski Country USA. WomenSki was
honored for "Outstanding Achievement" by Colorado Ski
Country and named "Best Ski Book for Women" by
Denver's* Westword *magazine.
Claudia lives and works in her mountain home above
Breckenridge, Colorado where she is visited regularly by
her five children and their families.*

# WOMEN™
# SKI

# Introduction

*"I would like to ski more so I can be more confident.
I would enjoy taking a class so I could look like those
skiers on TV ads for ski resorts. I would also like to
read a book with tips."*
— Amanda, age 23 from Colorado

*"WomenSki helped me realize it's OK to ski the way
I ski ... as long as I'm enjoying it! I'll improve when
I'm ready."*                — Ginger, age 33 from Colorado

*"Claudia's work is helping to get women out on the
slopes, and I thoroughly endorse it! WomenSki brings
the whole sport into a more workable,
understandable occasionn."*              — Sally, on-line

We've come a long way, baby.
     The winds have shifted, the tide is in. If you are a
woman who skis or who wants to ski, the time is *now!*

Attention to women in this sport, which had received
scarcely a nod prior to the 1994 publication of *WomenSki*,
has swelled to an obsession in the ski world.

In this industry where change often occurs with the
speed of a glacier, momentum is building toward a
revolution against the testosterone tyranny of the skiing
domain. Manufacturers of ski equipment, retailers, ski
resorts — virtually anyone involved in skiing — have
heard the buzz: *Women are different from men.* They have

different needs, desires, and expectations on the slopes, and unless somebody out there listens to them, the increasing dropout rate will become even more severe.

Michael Berry, president of Denver-based National Ski Areas Association, has identified women as a market on which the industry must focus if it expects to survive the aging of the baby boomers and the lack of new skiers.

"Women," he said, "are the gatekeepers of the children. We must bring back women to skiing." (While I don't like the notion of courting women for the sole purpose of reaching their children, I am in favor of getting them back, whatever it takes.)

Researcher Nolan Rosall of Boulder, Colo., wrote in NSAA's September, 1995, newsletter, "Clearly, future skier candidates abound in the marketplace. Among them are women ... A focused and cooperative effort ... is necessary to attract and retain more (women) skiers."

One of the first concrete signs of a shift toward women came in Beaver Creek, Colo., at the 1995 Ski Industry Week, the annual gathering of skiing's big guns — those who run the industry. Discussions revolved around building demand and connecting with the customer in a flat industry. One such seminar was a panel discussion on the women's market.

A year before that, it never would have happened. A year before, the industry turned a deaf ear to women's needs in this sport. A year before at this same gathering, I attended an all-male round-table discussion on ski equipment, and my suggestion that manufacturers design *real* products suited to the female anatomy (not just marketing gimmicks) was all but laughed at.

Since then, a myriad of significant events have taken place to put the industry on notice:

• The publication of *WomenSki*, the first book to spill the proverbial beans from the tightly sealed jars of equipment makers and bring to light factors other than lack of ability that can account for women's difficulties on the slopes.

• Long overdue recognition of the pioneering work of Jeannie Thoren, Carol Levine and other women (which I will discuss in this book).

• National media coverage recognizing women as skiers and athletes.

• The successful debut in 1996 of National Women's Ski and Snowboard Week. NWSSW was the first joint effort by three areas — Winter Park, Colo.; Stowe, Vt.; and Mammoth Mountain, Calif. — to focus a national spotlight on women's snow sports. The inaugural event, hosted simultaneously at all three resorts, included week-long lessons and off-slope seminars on women's issues in skiing and snowboarding.

• The first comprehensive study of the women's on-snow market in 1996 by Ski Industries America, the national trade association representing ski, snowboard, and on-snow manufacturers, distributors, and suppliers.

SIA sent a survey to 1,500 randomly selected women skiers. Of those, 748 responded. This 50 percent response rate is considered excellent for the six-page mail-in questionnaire. Throughout this book I will refer to the SIA Women's Skier Study, as well as my own written subjective survey of 1,000 women whom I've met personally at ski resorts, ski shops, and ski shows throughout the country.

• The founding of the Snow Sports Association for Women in June of 1996. As one of its founding members, I am particularly proud of this groundbreaking event. The stated purpose of the group is "to be the leading resource dedicated to expanding participation in winter sports." What this means to recreational women skiers is they now have friends in the ski industry who will act on their behalf. SSAW will lobby for women-specific equipment and instruction, more services and programs for women and their children at ski resorts, and a more woman-friendly environment in the ski industry overall. Eventually, SSAW expects to form a consumer branch of the association.

• The incredible performances of female athletes at the 1996 Summer Olympic Games. Thanks to Title IX, little girls of the '70s have blossomed into women athletes of the '90s. Clearly, the outstanding showing of this athleticism proves that women and girls are ready, willing and definitely able to play and excel in sports.

• Concrete proof that physically active women possess greater energy, better health and more positive self-esteem. A 1996 survey from the Women's Sports Foundation says 70 percent of American women consider themselves active in sports and fitness. More than one in five consider themselves "extremely active" or "very active." The survey, sponsored by Colorado-based Coors Brewing Co., further found that active women hold themselves in a more positive light than those who don't exercise or play sports. They also are more likely to see themselves as "competitive, fashionable, assertive, goal-oriented, energetic and sexy" than their sedentary peers, the survey said.

The 1996 Nike ad campaign based on studies of active women brings tears to my eyes and says it all:

> If you let me play
> I will like myself more
> I will have more self-confidence
> I will suffer less depression
> I will be 60 percent less likely to get breast cancer
> I will be more likely to leave a man who beats me
> I will be less likely to get pregnant before I want to
> I will learn what it means to be strong
> If you let me play sports.

## From the beginning

In interviews after *WomenSki* came out, the question people asked most frequently was, "What inspired you to write the book?"

The genesis, as I explained in the introduction of the first edition, was a revealing conversation I had with a reader of my weekly newspaper ski column. This Colorado native admitted she wanted nothing more than to be a skier. But unpleasant experiences on the slopes — and years of trying — had killed her enthusiasm. She felt guilty that she couldn't live up to the image of her home state.

Her testimony started me thinking about the conflicting attitudes women hold toward the sport. Obviously, because I wrote this book, I believe women have a rightful place in the world of alpine skiing. But I've met so many women who have tried to ski and have been terribly frustrated — convinced they're not strong enough, athletic enough or confident enough to be good skiers.

Believe it or not, I think that much of their alpine angst is caused by the ski industry itself.

Bob Gillen, one of the founders of National Women's Ski and Snowboard Week and a veteran marketer of the ski industry, acknowledges it has been male-dominated and macho since its beginning. "We must eliminate barriers to women in this sport," he says. "It's just not fair and it's not good business."

Harry Campbell, inventor of the Campbell Balancer used in ski shops for alignment evaluation, sympathizes with countless women struggling to stay with this sport. "Skiing was designed by men, for men, for their own pleasure," he says.

This strong statement rings true when you consider women until very recently have had no choice but to use ski equipment made for men and to be expected to perform on the slopes with the same reckless abandon as men.

Unable to do either, many women get complacent and settle in the intermediates' rut. They become experts at negative self-talk but secretly wish for more confidence and less fear. Women will stand frozen atop a steep mogul field, their mates and male friends yelling, "Ski down the fall line," and then blame themselves because they can't.

Before we examine why, let's look at another fact: The women's ski population has been declining.

The National Skier/Boarder Opinion Survey of 20,000 skiers in the 1994/95 season shows that women comprised fewer than half of all skiers — 41.2 percent, down from 42.8 the previous year and down significantly from 46.2 percent in 1992/93. However, the 41.2 percent stayed the same for the 1995/96 season, and that same year recorded an increase in women skiers on the East Coast. That's the good news.

Here is the bad news: Even though women comprise 60 percent of first-time skiers, they tend to *stop skiing after only two years,* according to Jim Spring, president of the Boulder, Colo.-based research company. Of all first-timers, only 63 percent of women say they'll continue to ski compared to 71 percent of men.

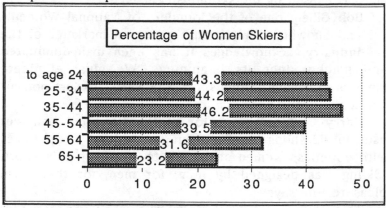

The truth is sad: *Many women who can't get comfortable on the slopes would rather just quit.*

People in the U.S. ski industry would like to know why. They want the potential business these women represent. To get it, industry leaders are beginning to pay attention to women as skiers. At last, ski-clothing and equipment manufacturers are acknowledging, just like disposable diaper makers did, that male and female bodies are different!

The idea that women skiers bring different needs to the sport is viable enough to warrant the formation of the first national Women's Education College of the Professional Ski Instructors of America (P.S.I.A.). Its founder, Vail ski instructor and supervisor Carol Levine, also serves as a P.S.I.A. Rocky Mountain Division clinic leader and examiner and was selected to the prestigious (and mostly male) P.S.I.A. Demo Team.

The focus of the inaugural meetings in 1993 was understanding anatomical differences between men and women and their impact on skiing performance. Long-term goals include providing suggestions for teaching women based on physiological, psychological, and social influences in skiing. While the mechanics of skiing are the same for both sexes, their *attitudes* about the sport are vastly different.

"Women like a more stylish approach to skiing rather than the kamikaze approach," says Annie Vareille Savath, director of the ski school at Telluride Ski Resort and a pioneering founder of ski programs taught for women by women.

Indeed, wanting to perfect technique and look smooth and graceful were mentioned most as a skiing ideal in my survey of more than 1,000 women. But the style, beauty and grace of skiing have been overshadowed by machismo: push the envelope, skate on thin ice, ski on the edge. This is how skiing is perceived today.

No wonder many women are saying, "No thanks!" to skiing.

Janet Spangler, executive director of Women's Ski Experience at six resorts in the Northeast, reminds us not to lose sight of what skiing is all about. "We are bombarded all the time with various media lines like 'stretch your limits' and 'go the distance,'" she says. "Skiing is a fun activity. It's rewarding — physically, mentally and emotionally. 'Fun' does not have a limit or a distance. We are free to create exactly what we want to achieve in this sport of snow sliding."

I encourage you to embrace this sport and *enjoy* it as much as your mates, sons, fathers, brothers and friends do. Recognizing the physical and mental uniqueness of women, this book presents evidence that *there are forces against women which may have more to do with inhibiting their skiing than lack of ability or courage.* In this book, I'll teach you to break barriers that prevent you from achieving your best and show you how skiing can be safer, as well as more *fun,* and more *satisfying.* Testimony from other women skiers will inspire you. Discussions on confidence will motivate you. Lessons in fear and injury prevention will calm you.

You'll learn to enjoy your days in the sun and on the snow by choosing and using the right equipment, clothing and accessories, and taking measures to stay healthy on the slopes.

Top female instructors will teach you to ski in control — the No. 1 concern expressed by women and the key to skiing with confidence. They also offer tips on skiing moguls, steeps, gates, powder and ice. The need to expand comfort zones and move in and out of comfort levels in order to improve skill and build confidence will come up often. They'll show you how to achieve this necessary — albeit scary — ingredient to better skiing in less-threatening terms.

You'll learn why women-teaching-women classes provide a learning atmosphere that breeds success. And you can choose a women's ski clinic that's right for you from a list of North American ski areas offering these programs.

I wrote this book for women skiers — beginners, experts, dropouts, terminal intermediates and, especially, wives whose husbands ask them to take a long lunch so they can do some *real* skiing. Men, too, should read this book to gain insight into the frustration women experience on the slopes and learn ways to encourage them.

A male colleague of mine, Byron Klapper, told me he thinks the book should be required reading for *everyone* who skis.

My intention is not to bash male skiers or ski instructors. And I'm not suggesting women shouldn't ski with men. My purpose is to bridge the gender gap by showing women that they can ski on a par with men — or better!

Only when women learn all they can about their skiing will the industry take us seriously. If we show that we're ready to be players instead of cheerleaders, if we demand equipment that will enhance our performances, if we prove that technique, not brute force, makes a strong skier, we will profoundly change the rules of this sport.

Says Winter Park's Kirsten Matule, "Women are no longer interested in the fru-fru aspect of skiing. They really want to become accomplished in the sport and enjoy it."

I, for one, want to see the dreams of a 13-year-old Nebraska girl fulfilled. "I wish my body would be smooth and graceful coming down the hill," she wrote in my survey. "I wish that someday the curls would stay in my hair in cold weather. I hope someday I'll be the very best skier I can be."

## How to read this book

Each chapter deals with a specific topic. To get the full flavor of the book, read the chapters in order the first time, especially the first four chapters. After that, refer to sections for information as you need it.

My goal for this book, more than anything, is to share what I've learned in 30-something years of skiing the United States, Canada and Europe. I'm not a psychologist. I'm not a ski instructor. I am what you could call a clinic junkie. I have a backpack full of valuable tips from my years of attending clinics and taking lessons, as well as from my own considerable trials and errors.

I've been frustrated up there on the slopes. I've been scared and cold and I've fallen flat on my fanny in front of long lift lines. I've broken bones and pulled knee ligaments and even slammed into a tree. I skied through five pregnancies and left my own skiing on the back burner for years while my children learned. Now, as I pass along the joys of skiing to a new generation of skiers in the family, I *still* work on my technique.

I want to share with you the tricks that have gotten me here. My work as a ski journalist has provided me opportunities to learn industry secrets that will surprise you and help you.

*Everything* I've learned helps me ski better. With each little improvement, I enjoy skiing more than I ever thought possible. Let me know if these tips help you, too. And, if you've discovered some secrets you'd like to pass on to other women. Let's get a dialogue going. Together, we can change the climate for women in skiing from cool to HOT!

Write to me: PO Box 3023, Breckenridge CO, 80424; email: ccarbone@colorado.net. You can find my column "WomenSki" at http://www.aminews.com on the Internet. Have fun reading and *keep skiing!*

Claudia

# Chapter  One

# *Girls just want to have fun*

*"Skiing isn't totally about the sport. It's more about the experience than if I functionally ski well. Am I with people I like to be with? What kind of day is it? It's more about attitude than anything else."*
— *Ginger, age 33 from Colorado*

*"I get tired of being pressured to ski more difficult slopes and conditions. My ability is directly related to how I'm feeling. I'd rather focus on the sheer joy and beauty of skiing rather than on my fear and inadequacies."* — *Jill, age 42 from Colorado*

Several times a year, Mary accompanies her husband, Jim, on ski trips to Vail. Every December, Jim participates in Pepi's Wedel Weeks, a week-long coed ski clinic, to get primed for the upcoming season. Meanwhile, Mary patiently practices her turns alone on the bunny hill at Beaver Creek, 10 miles west. Jim buys new equipment every year. Mary accepts hand-me-downs from her daughter. Jim shows marked improvement with each lesson, becoming powder-proficient in Vail's back bowls. Mary plods along on the green slopes, never venturing from familiar terrain because she's afraid of going too fast and skiing out of control. She says she's "not good enough" to join the clinic. Jim calls his ski day "fantastic." Mary calls hers "terrifying."

The worst part of this scenario—Deep down, Mary *wants* to ski freely and fearlessly with her husband. She yearns to be part of what appears to her as a secret society of skiers. Heck, she just wants to have *fun!* But Mary has succumbed to the belief that she cannot. Kept in the dark, she thinks she has no choice but to accept her second-class status or give up completely, as many women do.

Author Clarissa Pinkola Estés, in her best-selling book *Women Who Run With the Wolves,* (Ballantine Books, $23) reminds us that we all carry a taste of the Wild Woman within us ... "wild" meaning not out of control but the natural life force in all women.

She writes: "The memory is of our undeniable and irrevocable kinship with the wild feminine ... buried by overdomestication ... or no longer understood. ... Without her, women are silent when in fact they are on fire."

Women are expected to approach skiing with the same bravado and no-guts, no-glory attitude that their male counterparts bring to the sport. Some women can. But the majority, confused and uneasy with such expectations, feel faltering, even foreign, in the skiing world. When women need her most, their Wild Woman escapes them.

I encountered my Wild Woman as a high-school student, one winter afternoon in 1956 in my native Colorado. A fledgling on the bunny slope, I was nesting in the warming house at Winter Park with friends from the Eskimo Ski Club. Just as I was beginning to doubt I'd ever really ski, Josephine burst onto the scene, like a movie star greeting her fans.

Unquestionably the prettiest and most popular girl in the freshman class, Jo skied so much better than any of the girls that boys *allowed* her to ski with them all the time. Later that afternoon, as Jo and the boys approached our table, she brushed snow from her hair with a dramatic sweep of her hand and announced, "It's snowing *up top.*"

*Up top.* Those words became a metaphor for what I seek to this day every time I ski — the melding of mind and body, the elegance when it all comes together, the soothing of my soul in the beauty of winter. My Wild Woman compels me to go up top, to look for peaks beyond, to aspire higher. And I have learned to do it *my way.*

## For men only?

Masculine traits always have set the standard for skiing: power, innate toughness, brute strength, competitiveness, aggressiveness, and a downright cocky attitude about athleticism. Telling a woman she "skis like a man" is considered a compliment by both sexes; telling a male he skis like a girl is taken as an insult. A woman who skis well is admired; a man who skis well simply is living up to expectations.

One man from Pennsylvania expressed this arrogance in a letter published in *Powder* magazine. He said he thinks the new wide-bodied powder skis, like the short beginner skis of the past, have "ruined skiing ... making it possible for fat housewives and their wimpy, accountant husbands to wedge gracelessly into my lines ... Skiing was better when it was elitist and an adventure. Trying to make it a sport for everyone ruins it for everybody."

Slap this man! Tell him that, just because he has entered the kingdom, he cannot close the gate behind him. Skiing is not *just* about speed, catching air, jumping cliffs and venturing into the unknown. Skiing is wonderful, but it is not to die for.

There is more than one way to ski. The ultimate experience does not have to be a steep, fast, frightening run down back-bowl slopes. Some people experience exhilaration and satisfaction from a seamless sequence of perfectly carved arcs, a wintry waltz through fresh powder, or smooth 'n' easy gliding on a brilliant crisp day.

You are not alone if you like to *caress*, rather than *attack*, the hill. You do not need to hide on intermediate slopes if you prefer to *flow*, rather than *bash*, through bumps. If you concentrate on skiing with *finesse* instead of *force*, it does not mean you are a wimp!

Study the skiing of women instructors. Like ballet dancers, their technical mastery produces graceful moves that make skiing a thing of beauty.

"When it all clicks," says Geri, 44, from Vermont, "it's a wonderfully sensuous experience. I feel like I am truly dancing in harmony with the mountain."

Ski technique requires coordination and balance, agility and flexibility, endurance and strength — none of which lie beyond a woman's capability. Given the same mechanical advantages that men enjoy in skiing, there is no reason women, too, cannot own this sport!

Clearly, in ski racing, they do. U.S. and Canadian women racers have won four times more Olympic and World Championship alpine medals than men.

Says Tom Kelly, vice president of communications for U.S. Skiing: "Our female athletes are outstanding across the board." Picabo Street, Hilary Lindh, and Donna Weinbrecht consistently rack up wins for the American team. This proves the point: *When the playing field is level, skiing itself is not gender-based. Only attitudes make it so.*

## Gender differences

Let us look at the differences between men and women and how they apply to skiing. Psychologist John Gray, in his book, *"Men Are from Mars, Women Are from Venus"* (HarperCollins, $23), says a man's sense of self is defined by the ability to achieve results. "Martians [men] value power, competency, efficiency, and achievement," Gray writes. "They are always doing things to prove themselves and develop their power and skills.

"Instead of being goal oriented, women experience fulfillment through sharing and relating. They value love, communication, beauty, and relationships," he writes. "Involved in personal growth, they spend a lot of time supporting, helping, and nurturing one another."

In a compelling report on ABC News (Feb. 1, 1995), reporter John Stossel explored yet another factor that contributes to the differences between men and women: hormones. These glandular secretions, Stossel said, actually make men's and women's brains different, affecting behavior. This biological difference transcends societal influences, he said.

How do these biological and psychological differences show up in skiing? Instructors will tell you that in ski classes, men want to learn a maneuver and go right on to the next — moving quickly toward that goal. They often misinterpret power for skill, using strength to turn instead of technique. They ski aggressively and physically.

Men love competition. The following senerio is a perfect example: One afternoon, I found myself the only woman skiing with four guys. After three lengthy bump runs, the guys decided they had enough of the technical stuff. Success in bump skiing is measured subjectively. They wanted — no, needed — a more goal-oriented challenge. They needed a contest. They chose a long, smooth course for our next run, then set the rules: only three turns allowed. It reminded me of hearing as a kid, "The first one down, wins." Wins what? The right to boast of course.

Being the first one down and the last to leave the mountain earn bragging rights among men, but mean little to most women.

Women prefer doing it right and being in control more than taking risks and chancing a fall. Women *must* develop good technique to ski well because they simply do not possess the physical strength required to muscle a turn. They enjoy skiing *with* friends, not *for* them. The tremendous success of women-only ski clinics confirms their supporting and nurturing qualities. Attempts at male-only clinics bomb. "Most men consider seeking help a weakness when they can solve a problem themselves," Gray says. If it's not broken, their instincts tell them to leave it alone.

"Men and women have totally different views on skiing," observes Glynis, 47, from England. "Men want to get to the bottom as fast as possible, whereas women want to improve their technical skills."

One woman I met while skiing told me she thinks men always are trying to prove something. "When I ski with my husband, I have better technique, look better, and I'm more in control," she said, "but he always thinks he has to be faster and better. Maybe it's just part of being a man."

She added, "Men risk more. Women have more brains when it comes to safety. We know, if we hurt ourselves skiing, it won't be easy to take care of the house and the kids. But men have secretaries to help at the office and their wives to take care of them at home."

Another woman said when she surpassed her husband, who started skiing at the same time, he lost interest. "It was a real problem for him," she said. "Not only could I ski better, but I could also ski faster. Males are determined not to let you get ahead of them."

Nineteen-year-old Shawna from Colorado sounded a bit miffed when she wrote: "The men I ski with always leave me behind because they want to 'kill' themselves."

Other survey participants said the following about the differences between men and women on the slopes:

• Ego, a 23-year-old Japanese woman, said, "My brother likes to go fast and get air. I try to put more style and grace into my skiing instead of just going fast and out of control."

• Shelley, 50, from England, said the men she skis with like challenges. "I don't," she says. "I enjoy skiing where I *can* ski; they make an effort to ski where they don't think they can."

• Patricia, 47, from Colorado, says, "I ski with more control and without a desire to go as fast and do as many runs as possible in a day. But I can keep up with them when I want to!"

• "Men like going full out, straight down," said Katie, 23, from England. "I'd rather go down trying to get style and rhythm, rather than going top to bottom without stopping."

• Twenty-seven-year-old Mindy, from Ohio, notices men ski beyond their ability. "Like in corporate America, they just go for it, whether they're going to get themselves killed or not!" she said. "I tend to ski within my ability and stretch my limits in increments."

• Madlyn, 52, from Michigan, said she dislikes the "pressure to achieve a higher level of skiing," which men find so important.

• Andrea, 33, from Mexico City, thinks her husband "looks more secure" when he skis.

• Forty-six-year-old Margaret, from Australia, told me about the time she skied a run with her son. At the bottom, he said, "Mom, there were some great jumps on that trail!"

"Really?" She replied. "I didn't see one."

They went back and did it again. The run turned out to be infested with moguls. Margaret's son had taken them as opportunities to catch air while she had seen them as obstacles to ski around!

While these illustrations demonstrate the different approaches each gender takes toward skiing, they do not prove that either approach is right or wrong. I agree with John Stossel when he concluded, "Recognizing differences shouldn't lessen equal opportunity. *Why not celebrate the differences?*"

## Like father, like son

To understand how gender differences in skiing are reinforced, let's peek at a typical children's ski-school scenario: Brother and sister Sammy and Sally enter the children's center with Mom and Dad on the first day of the family ski vacation. Turning them over to an instructor, Dad lands a gentle punch on Sammy's shoulder: "Go get 'em, Tiger. Tear up that mountain, buddy boy!"

When Mom shows apprehension, Dad admonishes, "Leave him alone; he'll be fine." A high-five with Dad and Sammy's off with a clear message.

To his daughter, Dad warns: "Be careful, princess."

Mom and Dad bend down to give Sally hugs and kisses.

"Bye, bye, sweetheart," Dad says.

"If you get cold, be sure to come in," Mom adds.

On some days Sammy goes to class alone because Sally goes shopping with Mom. It's acceptable for girls to take a day or two off but the men need to rack up that manly vertical.

Twenty years later, Sam meets a friend at the top of a double-black-diamond run.

"Hey, big guy, how's it going?"

Sam answers, "I'm *tearing* up the mountain, man. Just jumped off that cliff. I was outta control but pulled it out. Wanna do this run, Dude? Last one down buys the beer.

"Go get 'em, Tiger," Sam says, punching "Tiger" on his arm. Sam spits and pushes off, straight down the middle.

Meanwhile, Sally skis carefully on the green slopes. She would love to ski with her husband but will not move to more difficult runs because she fears getting hurt.

"My feet are killing me and my hands are numb," Sally confides to friends over a hot-chocolate break. "And some kid almost ran into me with his snowboard. I think I'll quit early and go shopping."

Todd Williams a supervisor of children (age 6-12) at Golden Peak Children's Center in Vail, notices a strong cultural emphasis for boys to be strong and girls to be protected, even in skiing. Around age 7, boys begin to get aggressive on the slopes. "They don't worry about speed. They just go straight down, whereas girls want control," he said.

"Girls also demonstrate more concern for their friends in the classes than do boys. When we switch the kids to different classes, girls get very upset because they don't want to leave their friends. But boys don't care."

I witnessed this behavior in my own five children, all of whom started skiing at age 4. My two girls were "pretty" skiers. They loved to bring their friends, meander along favorite trails and take long hot-chocolate breaks.

My three boys constantly were darting into the trees, then shooting out on the trails. They skied steep moguls the same as flat, groomed runs — straight down. Never satisfied to just ski, they either raced each other or were flying off jumps. In the 1970s, my young sons copied the back-flips of the hot-doggers of the day, many of whom landed in the hospital with broken backs. The boys assured me they were not flipping, but I knew the truth.

Williams notices fathers pushing their sons in skiing. When boys are placed in a slow group, often dads come unglued and demand a stronger ability level, but when this happens to daughters, dads do not complain as much.

Gracie Goodwin, the manager of the Vail children's center, says she has noticed that girls who grow up in ski towns ski more on a par with boys.

"Skiing on Vail Mountain is like the swing set in their backyard," Goodwin said. "Girls here grow up athletically feminine."

*Athletically feminine.* These words pack a powerful punch for those who want a woman "to ski like a man." Sports like gymnastics, ice skating, horseback riding, even tennis, allow women to express themselves in an athletically feminine way. Yet in skiing, women are expected to perform *athletically masculine!*

I believe this is why most women hold themselves in such low regard as skiers.

"All my children have surpassed me in ability," says Paula, 44, from Minnesota. "Except the four-year-old. It's just a matter of time!" she laments.

Another woman, thinking about how she looks when she skis, wrote on my survey form, "Style? I have no style." Then, in very small letters she printed, "I'm also a bit wimpy."

In the National Skier/Boarder Opinion Survey, 75 percent more women than men said they would ski more often if only they could ski better! In my survey, women said they need to beef up their courage, self-confidence and aggressiveness in order to ski as well as they would like.

Let us explore how to do this. Because more courage and less fear rank high on the list, I have devoted Chapter Thirteen to fear. We will examine self-confidence and aggressiveness in the next chapter.

---

### Chapter Summary

Skiing has always been defined according to male standards. The pressure to "ski like a man" and be more aggressive causes many women to suppress how they really want to ski — smoothly and gracefully. Athletically feminine.

In this chapter we reviewed genetic differences between men and women and how social conditioning perpetuates these differences on the slopes.

Chapter  Two

# *Ski with an attitude*

---

*"To be the skier I want to be, I need a personality change. Then I would be one of those skiers who goes straight down and never hesitates or traverses looking for an easier way."*
— Anne, age 29 from Colorado

*"I'd like to look and feel confident, glide down the mountain and bomb past the guys. I would rise and fall gracefully and jump when needed."*
— Geri, age 44 from Vermont

*"I need more self-confidence so I don't freak out so easily when I get in a tough situation."*
— Mary Ellen, age 47 from Oklahoma

---

*P*lease understand there is no depression in this house and we are not interested in the possibilities of defeat. They do not exist. — Victoria, Queen of England.

Self-confidence is acquired, not inherited. So says Judith Briles in her book, *"The Confidence Factor"* (MasterMedia Ltd., $12.95), which is based on *The Keri®️ Report: Confidence and the American Woman*, a nationwide survey of 6,000 people. The 1990 book explores why women lack self-confidence and prescribes a list of Ten Commandments to improve self-image and enhance self-respect.

---

The Keri Report suggests that confidence "comes to women through their risk taking, crises, even failures, and their ability to bounce back from these events," Briles writes. "Confidence is strengthened by difficulties — not rose gardens."

My experience has shown me that this is indeed true: Confidence in skiing is acquired by overcoming challenges, striving to be comfortable on one skill level, then moving on to the next. Each success provides encouragement to try again and again. Women with no physiological barriers (we'll discuss that in Chapters Three and Four) *can* build confidence steadily as they add new skills and advance to more difficult terrain and snow.

First, let's look at women who possess self-confidence in spades, and learn what motivates them.

## Nurturing self-esteem

In skiing, no one encounters more challenges than members of the ski patrol. At Jackson Hole, one of the United States' steepest, toughest skiing mountains, five of its 47 patrollers are women.

Their job starts before dawn when they ready the mountain for skiing. It is pitch black and bitter cold. While you and I sleep, these women ride to the top of the mountain where, in snow past their knees, they throw bombs to force slides down any of 142 avalanche-prone spots. When they are not bombing, the women haul crates of explosives, shovel snow and debris, set up poles, fencing and signs, and remove rocks from runs — all before the lifts open.

During the day, they respond to calls from injured skiers, administer first aid, check barricades, and police runs for reckless or out-of-control skiers and "powder hounds" slipping out of bounds. When the sun begins to set, the women help sweep the mountain for stranded skiers.

The scariest part of this job is "ski checking." In this snow-control procedure, patrollers monitor each other's solo crossings of snow fields, zig-zagging one by one, often in front of ominous cliffs that could thunder into avalanches at any moment. As they watch each other, the concern is always there: Can I move fast enough to save a life if the mountainside lets loose?

Each of these women acknowledges the influence of strong support from their mothers, which they believe helps to account for their positive self-perception. Each demonstrates a willingness to accept hard work and meet challenges. All share a love of skiing and the outdoors. The greatest satisfaction of the job is knowing they can do it.

"I need to prove to myself that I can do it," says Suzanne Hagerman, who admits to having been timid and afraid of heights as a young girl. "But I've always been strong-willed. That's what keeps me going."

Cindy Budge was told 20 years ago at a Utah resort that "girls" did not do well on the ski patrol. "This job has taught me what I'm capable of. You do not have to be a pretty skier to patrol, just strong. You have to be able to ski down anything pulling a rig. You need to know the mountain, have mountaineering skills and first-aid training. We feel strong, although the mountain is always humbling," she said.

Though they perform difficult and dangerous tasks, these women are not superhuman. They are mothers, wives, sisters, friends. Off season, they sew, garden, waitress, work in retail sales. *They are no different than you and I except they believe in their ability to handle the consequences of the risks they take.* Though their physical strength might not equal a man's, the intensity these women bring to their work makes up for it.

## Confidence in competition

Deb LaMarche, former director of athletic development for the U.S. Ski Team, says women racers exhibit mental toughness.

"There's a certain drive to be the best they can be," LaMarche says. "A lot come from families where daughters are considered important and as having as much potential as sons; where parents think daughters can do anything." Consequently, they excel at everything they do. The majority are also honor-roll students, she adds.

Patti Sherman, a two-time champion of the Women's Pro Mogul tour, found her family's support an important ingredient of her self-confidence and skiing success. "My family pushed us to do sports — not necessarily to win, but to build confidence and believe in ourselves," Sherman says. "I never compared myself to other women. I compared myself to whomever was out there. I didn't care if I was the best little girl. I just wanted to be as good as my big brother. Mentally, you've got to believe deep inside you can do it."

Speed skier Amy Guras, clocked at 126 mph on skis in 1993, agrees that mental conditioning is the key to confidence. "The fun in speed skiing is to go beyond what you've ever done," Guras says. "You've got to let your mind *think* your body has the ability. I think I can ski better than I can walk down stairs!"

Guras, who owns The Racer's Edge ski shop in Breckenridge with husband, Greg (also her technician) was one of only 30 women to clock their speed on a straight, steep course in Les Arcs, France, where speed skiing debuted as a demonstration sport at the 1992 Olympic Games.

Passing on the kind of parental support she received when she started skiing at age 3, Guras encourages her 7-year-old daughter, Alexandra, to do whatever she wants.

"Kids have no fear ... I'm not going to hold her back,"
Guras says. "When we're hiking, if she sees a big boulder,
I'll say, 'Go climb it.'" Alexandra, who skis straight down
in a tuck, says, "I like to go fast — just like you, Mommy!"

Kristen Ulmer is one of a handful of women gutsy
enough, and crazy enough, to enter and win extreme
skiing competitions on the gnarliest, nastiest mountains
in the world. Ulmer says in an article she authored for
*Skiing* magazine that it helps to be born with an invincible
attitude on which you can build.

"It takes the finest genetic makeup and years of
scraping by to become an ass-kicking skier," Ulmer wrote.
Also essential, she said, is a huge ego and a "superhero"
attitude. "With each new successful descent, cliff jump, or
stunt, that feeling becomes stronger," the extreme queen
wrote. "After a horrible [but] injury-free crash, you feel
like King of the Hill because you got away with it. You've
always gotten away with it!"

Confidence knows no age boundaries. Eighty-two-year-
old Colorado ski pioneer Edna Dercum still dons her
helmet every season to compete in the downhill on the
national and international Masters ski-race circuit. In
1993, Dercum added another gold medal to the hundreds of
trophies spanning a racing career that began in 1938.

Dercum, who once built and ran a ski lodge with her
husband, Max — a founder of Arapahoe Basin and
Keystone ski areas — says the key to confidence is
"learning good, controlled skiing."

She also believes skiing confidence is fostered by
parental involvement. "Skiing was a bond that kept us
close [with two children]. Skiing has made our
grandchildren more gutsy, more eager to try other things,"
she said.

When Dercum hears about women giving up skiing
because they think they are too old, she says she would
like to have introduced them to her mother-in-law who
took up alpine skiing at 65. At 90, she decided to switch to

cross-country because it was less demanding. She skied cross-country until age 98, and then lived to be 104!

For every "ass-kicking" woman skier out there, hundreds more are just looking for the nerve to point 'em a little straighter down the fall line.

To find out how to get it, let us apply Briles' "Ten Commandments of Confidence" to skiing:

*I. To your own self be true.*

Ski for thee! Kara Makata, a Winter Park ski instructor, says women often enroll in lessons because someone asks them to. "They hate it!" Makata says. "They're frightened. They don't want to be there."

Breckenridge instructor Jan Degerberg encourages women not to allow their husbands to make decisions about lessons for them. "And when you state your goals to the instructor, make them *your* goals," Degerberg says. "Remember, this is *your* experience."

Annie Black, a Keystone instructor, has seen enough of "analysis paralysis" in her 20 years of teaching skiing. "Sometimes men try too hard to get us to ski by tearing our skiing apart," she says. "Women should ski for their own sense of accomplishment," Black advises women to avoid "trying to get better than someone else," as men often encourage.

Black believes going fast does not measure success in skiing. She warns women not to set themselves up for failure by skiing faster than their comfort level allows. "Set a rule for yourself: You never need to go faster than you want," Black advises. "Skiing is supposed to be fun. If your husband or friend won't ski with you because you're too slow, find someone else to ski with."

Rhea, my friend who races cars, lives by this creed: "I never drive faster than my guardian angel can fly."

If speed is not your bag, reinforce other strengths and concentrate on them. Technical skills, such as running gates and skiing powder, make a strong skier.

My friend Barbara says she is happiest skiing with people who ski at her level. "I could ski just Northwoods at Vail all day and love it," Barbara says. "Then, we'll meet someone on the mountain and they want to ski something over my head. So, I go along. Then I get perched on the top of something I can't ski and I can't move. I lose my form and my confidence, and I start skiing uphill to control my speed instead of down."

"When you're planning your ski group, try to include at least one other person of your skill level," Black suggests. This way, if the pressure to go faster or ski a run that is too difficult becomes debilitating, you can hang back with each other.

Dorcas, 49, from Pennsylvania, has it figured out: "When I first started skiing, I always asked, 'How did I look?'" she says. "Now I realize I ski for my recreation, and if I enjoyed my run, I don't care how it looked to someone else. I ski for fun and I do not feel my skill level limits that enjoyment."

Wild Woman!

## II. Create positive thinking.

I witnessed a classic example of negative self-talk when I skied in a blizzard with two women friends. One saw the deepening snow as a rare opportunity to practice her emerging powder skills. The other woman, a competent enough skier, was not a happy camper. Though she was making nice, round, even turns and not falling, she kept protesting that she was out of her element. But by telling herself she couldn't ski powder and then retreating to the lodge, she missed the chance to continue learning.

Winter Park instructor Mary Moynihan says women should think about "tactical self-talk."

"Women know negative self-talk is not productive and they do not really *believe* positive self-talk," Moynihan says. By telling yourself you can do something, you are setting yourself up to answer, "No, I can't!" Moynihan suggests talking to yourself about ski *tactics* — things like keeping your hands up or your shoulders square to the fall line. This take-charge self-talk gets your mind off the confidence issue and focuses on the skiing.

"It's an attitude," says Shelley Scipione, a 24-year-old girls' ski coach from Vermont. "You just have to say, 'I'm going to do it.' When I was learning to do a helicopter [360-degree turn in midair], I thought, 'Ooh, this is scary!' I did it halfway the first time, all the way the next," Scipione recalls. "Now, every time I do one, it's still kind of scary. But I just say to myself, 'People don't die doing this. If somebody else can do it, why can't I?'"

Sugarbush instructor Ashley Fischer says most women need some attitude adjustment. When she asks women in the Women's Turn program if they remember their good turns or bad ones, nearly every woman says she remembers only the bad turns. "I teach them to *reframe* negative attitudes and look at themselves in a positive light," she says.

She asks her students, "How do you view the mountain? As adversary or partner? Do you fight it, holding on to each turn, leaning up the hill, not allowing gravity to help you?" Instead of thinking "woman versus mountain," she says, reframe that attitude to "woman with mountain."

"Enjoy being there," she says. "Let gravity pull you into your turns so you can dance with the hill instead of struggling with it. Now you are in harmony with your surroundings, not in conflict."

When people get into a mindset that says, "I can't," it keeps them stuck, says Denver psycho- therapist Mimi Kaplish. They get the idea they are powerless and not in control or able to make changes. "Words can change this attitude," Kaplish says. "Next time someone wants you to ski where you know you'll be in trouble, instead of saying, 'I can't,' use the words, 'I don't choose to.'

"This is a very empowering phrase," Kaplish says. "It means 'I have choices, and for whatever reason, I access my ability to make a choice and this is it.'" This leaves the path open to try another time.

Another phrase that undermines power is the negative "I-should" phrase. "This implies authority outside myself telling me what is right for me," Kaplish says. Once again, you become a powerless victim instead of an empowered person.

### III. You are not alone.

Trust me. Confidence is an issue with women — in skiing and in life. For example, in a 1993 survey of 151 women published in *First for Women*, 51 percent admitted that more self-confidence would make them happier about their self-image.

In my survey, self-confidence ranks second after technique as the answer to my question: "What is one thing in your skiing you would like to change or improve?"

Of the 1,000 women who filled out my written survey, plus hundreds more with whom I talked, many, mostly beginners and intermediates, feel a lack of confidence on the slopes. Even some instructors and self-described experts said they would like to feel more comfortable on difficult snow and terrain.

Again and again, I read admissions like this: "I really need more confidence in myself so I can grow in my abilities and evolve past this plateau I have reached." If you think this way, you are not alone.

### IV. Learn something new.

Mastering something — anything — builds confidence in any stage of life. Consider toddlers: After their first step, if they didn't have confidence to take another, then another, they would never learn to walk. Sports, especially individual sports like skiing, offer great opportunities for building confidence because the learning curve involves setting and meeting small, doable, measurable goals. With each goal mastered, you gain confidence to move forward and learn something new. Pretty soon, you have moved through the whole process and it becomes a matter of fine tuning. Do not take too big a leap at one time. You will set yourself up for disappointment. Anne, 40-ish, admits, "The one thing I would like to improve is my confidence level — it's hard to try new things when you're afraid. I need to build up confidence slowly."

Take lessons to learn new techniques. Learning to ski correctly in the beginning proves far better than trying to change bad habits later on that will hold you back. When you get stuck, you lose not only the ability to progress, but confidence, too. You need to keep learning!

## V. Assess the situation.

Women know how to do this well. They meticulously check out trails before they try them, approach difficult runs prudently, and ski cautiously on unfamiliar terrain. Ask any man and he will tell you women react *too* cautiously. "Timid" is used by a lot of men to describe women skiers. But they do not understand — We are *assessing* the situation!

So what about off the mountain? A reality check of your life can help you understand why skiing may be a source of diminishing self-confidence and frustration. A relationship with a controlling man, for instance, can cause lack of self-esteem. This will surely carry over to the slopes.

Responsibility for small children or aging parents, demanding jobs, extensive travel or any circumstance beyond our control can squelch the best of wintertime getaway plans. If you can't get away as often as you would like, do not beat yourself up when you finally do go skiing because your confidence has eroded.

Put it in perspective: Understand that one important factor in gaining assurance in skiing is mileage. When you build up vertical miles, you will build up confidence.

## VI. *Give yourself credit.*

We all know praise generates self-esteem. Yet women hesitate to make a big deal about little achievements in skiing. Men, however, find no such problem. For some, exchanging ski stories over beers at the end of the day can be as fulfilling as the actual feats.

A few years ago we visited my oldest daughter, Susan, when she was living in Utah. She's a high-energy, self-confident, do-it-all kind of woman. We coaxed her from a busy schedule to ski with us at Snowbird for a day. After she breezed down The Cirque (a huge bowl scooped out of a steep mountainside), we laughed about her chalking up yet another accomplishment. She had just become a mother, gotten a job, bought a new house ... *and* she skied The Cirque! Though we joke about it even now, I know it remains a source of pride.

Women like and need pats on the back, says ski instructor Annie Black. "If you can't get them from your husband or boyfriend, learn to give them to yourself."

## VII. *Aspire higher.*

Diann Roffe-Steinrotter, who captured gold for the United States in Super-G at the 1994 Olympics, credits her career wins, including a 1985 World Championship, to her need for improvement.

"At my first Olympics in '88, I realized that I was really good, that I was a woman, and that there aren't that many opportunities for women in sports," Roffe-Steinrotter says. "I knew people would kill to be in my shoes — to be an Olympian — and I was just kind of going through the motions. So I said I have got to settle down, get stronger, more concentrated. I gritted my teeth and said, 'OK, I'm going to get better at this.'"

A slow building process ensued. "I just worked on my confidence, year after year, day after day. I did everything I could to make it more difficult in training so the races would be easy. I tried to do everything right."

Roffe-Steinrotter won her first Olympic silver at Méribel, France in 1992 and retired a champ after Lillehammer in 1994.

"I had full confidence in all the work I'd done in my whole career," Roffe-Steinrotter says. "The minute I had any preconceived ideas of how good I was, I stunk! So I tried to stay humble and work on what I had to do to ski fast."

Her advice to women is the following: Be realistic about your ability ... then gradually inch away at getting better. Your confidence will build and you won't even know it.

### VIII. Get some feedback.

Women-only clinics offer great opportunities to women for skiing feedback. Constructive criticism delivered in a gentle, non-threatening manner by understanding women instructors proves a powerful tool in ski teaching and confidence-building. (In Chapter Fifteen, I discuss women's ski seminars and list ski areas with such programs.)

Often, women do not get the encouragement and support they need from husbands, boyfriends or family member. One man said to me, "Sure, I *let* my wife go skiing. But I always tell her when she walks out the door that if she breaks a leg, she'll still have to take care of the kids and drive them to school every morning."

Imagine this woman skiing all day with that message playing in her head: Don't break a leg. I cannot believe she has much fun, or that she will advance.

During the 1994 Olympics, it was not hard to figure out why a Russian cross-country skier told *USA Today* that she did not want to phone home. "Every time I call, my husband tells me to come back," she told the newspaper. "He's getting impatient." Knowing what he was impatient for, she added, "I don't *like* cooking. I'd rather go eat at my mom's place."

## IX. *Take care of yourself.*

In upcoming chapters, we will talk about taking care of equipment: your body and your ski gear. Now, let us talk about the care and feeding of your psyche.

On ski vacations, most women bear the responsibility of the children, described in my survey as one of the "hassles" of skiing. According to the National Skier/Boarder Opinion Survey, more women ski with children (62 percent) than do men (53 percent). Further married men with children are more likely to ski with their buddies than with their families.

Amy, a friend of mine, recalls: "It was always my responsibility to ski with the children. My husband would meet us for lunch and maybe take one run with us. Once the children got better than I was, they went off on their own. It got pretty lonely skiing by myself." She has come close to quitting many times.

Let *him* ski with the children sometimes. Or, ski together as a family. But do not make yourself sole caretaker on the slopes.

Treat yourself to some expert coaching. Multi-day clinics can be fun mini-vacations, as well as great opportunities for breakthroughs in your skiing. Take lessons with your husband or boyfriend only if your relationship is supportive and non-competitive.

In an early-season clinic I attended at Copper Mountain, a husband and wife (psychologists who should have known better) showed the rest of us how not to find marital bliss on the slopes. He relentlessly berated her in class on her techniques, especially her tendency to ski with stiff legs. But he got his due when, during the group video critique, our instructor pointed out the very same mistakes in *his* skiing as the ones for which he was harassing his wife.

When my young friends Kent and Beth married in their early 20s, Kent's skiing ability far surpassed Beth's. He easily could have said, "See ya!" and skied off with the guys. But he figured spending a season to help and encourage Beth on the slopes might ensure lots of togetherness later on. Today, the couple telemarks in the high country around their log cabin in Summit County, Colorado — a perfectly matched couple. (No, he does not have a brother.)

### X. Keep in circulation.

• Ski as much as you can.

• Hang out with skiers; join a ski club. To find a club in your area, ask your local ski shop.

• Buy a home or time-share condo at a ski resort if you are considering a second home.

• If you live close to a ski area, drive up regularly with friends or sign up for weekly bus trips. Or, start your own group and charter a bus.

• Take at least one ski vacation a year. Read *Skiing America* (World Leisure, $18.95) or *Ski Europe* (World Leisure, $17.95), guidebooks by Charles Leocha, for an annually updated, insider's scoop on everything from ski schools to sushi in America and Europe's major resorts.

• Subscribe to a ski magazine: *Snow Country*, *Ski*, *Skiing* or *Powder*. *Skiing for Women*, which debuted in 1994, and the new *Sports Traveler* (1995) have found an instant audience, because both target the women's market. Search your hometown newspaper for articles about skiing in the sports and travel sections.

## Aggressiveness

Ski instructors, usually males, constantly tell women to be more aggressive and let themselves get a little out of control. Society pulls us in the opposite direction. The notorious lady-in-the-parlor, whore-in-the-bedroom stereotype begs for attention, again.

Julie Woodworth Buniva, 32, a professional ski racer, says women need to step away from their submissive selves when they are on the slopes. "To reach the next level in skiing, you really need to be aggressive — not mean, just have more fight and feistiness," she says. But most women, especially those born before 1964, are as uncomfortable with the notion of getting aggressive in skiing as they would be robbing a bank. They cannot overcome years of socialization in two or three ski lessons, explains Denver psychologist Linda Lister.

"Aggressiveness may not fit with a woman's self-concept," Lister says. And those instructors and husbands who think they are helping when they tell women to "get aggressive" only intimidate them and make them feel worse. It is just not a command a woman immediately can respond to, such as "turn your shoulders," or "bend your knees."

Try this instead: Set a goal, then work out a system for achieving it, says Lister. If you want to ski faster or straighter, just call it that. Do not psyche yourself out by calling it "getting aggressive."

## "Just do it" — but do it in control

Becoming aggressive involves skill. Instructor Mary Moynihan remembers a student who struggled until she finally learned to ski in control. "Once she realized technique would control speed," Moynihan says, "she could do anything." Her confidence *and* aggressiveness improved dramatically. "That's the key," Moynihan says. "I do not think women are less aggressive, *they just need to be in control.*"

It all comes down to technique.

Alice, 53, from Connecticut, recalls skiing bumps at a resort in New England. She was linking perfect turns in the fall line, she says, when a man from the chair lift had the nerve to yell, "Go faster!" A woman on the same lift, enraged, yelled back, "She looks fabulous. Leave her alone!"

I have skied with Alice. I would not describe her as aggressive, but she does ski bumps with precision and authority because she knows how to control her turns. That man on the lift should be so lucky! (Tips on skiing in control are found in Chapter Fourteen.)

## Rock-a-bye-bye bumps

No matter how much aggressiveness you do bring to the slopes, do not be surprised if it goes on maternity leave once you become a mother. It's amazing how you instinctively take the edge off your skiing when you have the responsibility of children. Just about every skiing mother I know — instructors included — admits to toning down her risk-taking. Even men notice the taming effect of motherhood on the women around them.

Society does not regard hard-core skiing as part of motherhood and apple pie. I remember skiing with friends of my teenage son at Steamboat. Trying to build enough speed to propel myself over a knoll, I got in a downhill tuck. As I took off, I heard one of the boys say, "Wow! Mike's mom *tucks!*"

After Mike blew out both knees playing football in high school, I heard one of his buddies ask if he would still be able to ski.

"Sure," Mike said. "I'll just have to ski like my mom."

Kay, another woman who took part in my survey, said she remembers being nervous on ski slopes when her children were little. "I could never relax because these big men would come down like they were crazy and I was afraid they'd hit my little kids," she says. A mom's peripheral vision gets a workout on ski slopes.

A mother cannot separate herself, says Sharon, a Colorado skier. Recently, she was so preoccupied with helping her 7-year-old daughter get on the lift that she forgot to get on herself. The lift — and her daughter — went up without her! Interestingly, she never worries about her 10-year-old son. "He skis in control and can stop on a dime," Sharon says.

If motherhood has curbed your assertiveness on the slopes, be patient. It will come back.

I wouldn't trade skiing as a family for anything. Though I skied with much less boldness and attention to my own skiing when my children were little, I was able to witness the development of *their* skills and confidence. I knew the time would come when I would be chasing their tails!

## Push yourself — gently

I found practical, compassionate advice about "letting go" in skiing from Dave Merriam in a video featuring Merriam and fellow Professional Ski Instructors of America (P.S.I.A.) Demo Team members, Dee Byrne and Nancy Oakes, teaching the art of carving turns. Merriam compares pushing yourself in skiing to balancing on a fence.

In this excerpt from the video, *"The Signature of Excellence"* (Driscoll Communications, $19.95), Merriam explains this balancing act:

I call it the 'Risk Fence.' The better your skills, the wider the fence and the easier it is to balance on it.

On one side of the fence is frustration — the area that represents the feeling of holding on, the time when you do not let go ... On the other side lurks catastrophe — the zone you may fall into if you push it too far ... if you do not have the skills or know your personal limits.

*Walking on the fence is the essence of the sport.* It's exhilarating: this is your peak performance. ... You might have to jump on the fence to grow as a skier. If risk-taking becomes necessary, do it intelligently:

• Know your abilities, the limits of your equipment and the condition of the slope.

• Be aware of how you respond to pressure; only then can you make good decisions.

• Be aware of your environment; do not focus inward.

- Choose uncrowded runs and those relatively easy for you.
- Ski the trail a few times so you know it well.
- As you gain comfort with a skill and decide to push it a little more, do it when you won't endanger anyone else.
- Be warmed up physically and mentally. Pay attention — do not let your mind wander.
- Quit when you're tired, or find less demanding terrain or snow.

To risk wisely, it's imperative you are aware of all elements and consequences of your actions. By taking *calculated risks*, you may find sources of strengths and finesse you never dreamed existed. By pushing yourself intelligently and stretching your abilities, you may find you come closer to reaching your potential as a skier.

Ski smart, ski safe, and ski in control.

In the remainder of this book, we will learn to do exactly that.

## Chapter Summary

You learned ten steps to building confidence in skiing. You also learned that internal motivation — rather than aggressiveness, which is external — is a more natural way for women to develop mental toughness. Aggressiveness may not fit with a woman's self-concept. There are other ways to ski with authority. Learning to ski in control is the key.

Finally, extending your limits in skiing is like balancing on a fence. Dave Merriam shows how to push yourself wisely to reach your full potential.

## Recommended:

*"The Signature of Excellence"* To order, write Driscoll Comm., P.O. Box 1197, Stowe, VT 05672, or call (800) 424-0033.

**Check out these national all-women's ski clubs:** Skiyente Ski Club, based in Portland, Ore. (503-245-3742) and Women's Ski Club, based in Huntington Beach, Calif. (714-842-4148).

# Chapter  Three

# Why can't a woman ski like a man?

*"I've been skiing for 36 years and I never get any better. There must be a little trick I'm missing. My biggest problem is my knees get in the way."*
— Judy, age 56 from Colorado

*"I'm terribly disappointed [in my skiing] because I have always been athletic and been in all types of sports."*
— JoAnne, age 46 from California

*"My ex-husband would get very frustrated with me because what he'd suggest to improve didn't ooze right out of my body — especially my legs and feet."*
— Jane, age 41 from Colorado

D o not be misled by this chapter's title. I am not suggesting women should ski like men. This title refers to the biomechanical obstacles that prevent many women from learning and progres-sing in skiing as readily as men.

From the chair lift, it is easy to spot women on the slopes below. And it is not because they are wearing tight stretch pants or purple boots. It is because of their form — bent at the waist, butts out, knees together, skis splayed.

Why is it so much easier to pick out other women's flaws than to correct your own technique? And when you see a man skiing as though his skis are an extension of his feet, do you wonder if there is something he knows that you do not? And why, you also may wonder, are you skiing at the same level after all these years?

If you cannot find the answers, you will be happy to know that lack of ability may not be what separates you from the skier you want to be. *You can blame it on your female body!*

## The Q angle

The anatomical characteristic that makes our bodies ideal for having children — our pelvis, or hip bones — also creates problems for us on the ski slopes. The broad central cavity of the female pelvis is designed for carrying babies. At the lower part of this bony framework are ball-and-socket joints to which the thigh bone (femur) connects. These joints allow the legs to move in many directions and bear all the weight of the trunk and upper body. Because a woman's pelvis is wider than a man's, the points where the femurs attach are farther apart. And with the female femur also shorter, a pronounced "V" is created from the hips to the knees.

Now, if you draw two imaginary straight lines, one down the femur and the other up the tibia (large bone of the lower leg), the angle created by the intersection of those lines in the mid-patella region (knee) is what orthopedic doctors and physiologists call the "Q angle." (Fig. 1.) Q angle is medical shorthand for the angle of the *quadricep* tendon. It was developed as a measure of how the knee cap tracks.

## Why should we care about the Q angle?

Any skier, male or female, must have good *balance*. In fact, in their book *The Athletic Skier* (The Athletic Skier, Inc., $24.95), ski teachers-authors David Evrard and Warren Witherell say good balance is not enough — it has to be *perfect.* "You must strive for perfect balance ...

---

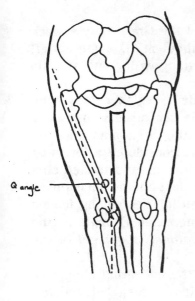

Q angle

**Figure 1**

Imperfect balance inhibits performance," they wrote, "No other issue is more important to your progress as a skier." Perfect balance requires perfect alignment — this is the overall principle in ski instruction. "Proper alignment allows you to do anything you want on skis," says Annie Vareille Savath, Telluride's ski school director. "It makes you agile and quick," she says. "When you are out of alignment, you are not going to be ... technically correct."

Picture how the pole of a carousel pony passes through its center as it moves up and down in the same spot. We want to maintain an imaginary pole from the tops of our heads through our centers. Proper alignment continues that vertical line as *straight* as possible down the legs and over the ankles and feet.

But, thanks to the Q angle, this is not the normal skiing stance for many women. The wider the hips, the more crooked the legs.

If you have ever been told you run like a girl, this means you run with your lower legs kicking to the side, or knock-kneed — a position created by the Q angle. When you ski, this position (affectionately called The Virgin Clutch by male ski instructors) creates an A-frame from your knees to your skis. All this body geometry — the A frame, the Q angle, the V femur — adds up to plain old bad alignment for skiing.

One woman who read my book expressed her frustrations in a letter to me: "I desparately want to ski better ... I thought I never would learn to ski parallel," she wrote. "Why did it take the rest of the family only a week to manage it? If only I'd known about my Q angle earler! Men seem to be able to do everything wrong and still ski better!"

Cindy Suplizio, a biomechanical engineer, has long believed that an excessive Q angle can make skiing more difficult for women. While at the Steadman-Hawkins Sports Medicine Foundation in Vail, considered a foremost center of research and education in sports-medicine orthopedics, she embarked on a fact-finding mission to learn about the Q angle's effect on injuries among female skiers. She concluded that, "An increased Q angle at the knee joint results in *less than optimal alignment* of the femur and tibia."

Remember Pipi Longstocking, the endearing children's literature character, with her braids sticking out and her knock-knees above her rumpled socks? Pipi would have major problems trying to ski, not because of lack of ability, but because her knees do not line up over her feet. It is biomechanics. Pipi and the skiing sisterhood that grew up reading about her cannot help it!

## So what's a girl to do?

Not all women are cursed by a Q angle. And some are more "Q'd" than others. Take a look at the figure of your next female ski instructor. It is no coincidence that most top-ranked women skiers are built straight and narrow. Women with curvy bodies and pronounced Q angles usually do not make it to the highest levels of perfection in skiing. You are in luck if you have hips like a teenage boy's.

If you are not sure whether this applies to you and you haven't had much luck skiing, there is a good chance your Q angle could be part of your problem.

"If a woman has a very large Q angle, she is probably not going to enjoy skiing very much and will be more likely to quit," says Kacey Conway, a physical therapist and specialist in sports medicine. Conway spends a lot of time working as a ski guide in Colorado at Copper Mountain where she frequently encounters such women unable to perform basic maneuvers required to ski. "Excessive Q angle can be very self-limiting," Conway says.

Do this test right now while reading this book:

• *Stand with your feet pointed forward, about six inches apart, in your normal parallel skiing stance.* Look straight ahead, then drop your knees as though you were pushing on your boot cuffs to initiate a turn.

• *Look straight down.* Do your knees touch, or at the very least, go in? Can you see one or both of your feet peeking to the outsides of your knees? If the center of your knee is not over your big toe you are not aligned correctly for skiing.

• *Try to "edge," turning to the left.* Notice how far in you must pull your right knee just to roll your right foot over. Because of this, it is nearly impossible to get a strong edge set with that ski, so instead of carving, all you can do is slide.

• *Now, using your quad muscles, move your knees so they are centered over your toes.* Edge again in this position. See how much more easily you can roll to the sides of both feet, and how much farther you can lean on your edges? Imagine how dynamically you could ski with this extended range of movement. Bingo! This is the difference between slipping and edging, skidding and carving, intermediate and advanced skiing.

• *Now, try to edge as if you were turning to the right.* Like many women, you may have one knee that turns in more than the other. This could be the reason it is more difficult for you to turn this direction when you are on skis. (My easier-turning side, called "the chocolate side" by an instructor named Gabi, is not as crooked. You probably have a chocolate side, too.)

## Roll zee knees, pleeze

You should strive to have your knees pointing in the same direction. Telluride instructor Melissa Eddlestein says the knees should chase but never catch each other when you are in the skiing stance. Picture how a team of horses looks pulling a sleigh. The horses do not touch, but they trot alongside each other; in a turn, the inside horse is slightly ahead.

When he is teaching advanced ski clinics, extreme skier Eric DesLauriers demonstrates the proper position for the knees by placing his hands as if in prayer and sliding them between his knees. "Skiing is basically rolling your knees from side to side like this," he tells his students.

It is a simple enough premise. Everyone can roll their knees just so, right? But remove the hands from between the knees and, if you are a woman, your knees naturally want to greet each other like long-lost buddies. Men's knees, on the other hand, will hold in the correct position.

How many times have you heard your husband or your boyfriend or your son or your male ski instructor tell you to *drive* your knees into the turn, or pretend your knees are headlights, or *steer* with your knees? This is easy for them because their hips, knees and feet line up in the same vertical plane. When men "bend zee knees," zee knees usually bend right over their boots, which transmits the action to the ski. (Assuming they are wearing properly fitting ski boots. We will talk about the art of bootfitting in Chapters Four and Five.)

Men who try to help us improve our skiing do not understand why we cannot "Just turn!" Or "Ski straighter down the fall line!" Or "Go faster!" Granted, sometimes it is fear, but it is also because our hugging knees won't allow the one ingredient necessary to ski like that: edge control.

## Ride a flat ski

The starting point in skiing begins with both boots flat on the skis, skis flat on the snow. Your boot must be completely flat on the ski and your foot in a neutral position in the boot for you to roll your ski effectively from edge to edge. From there, the ski takes over. You apply pressure while on edge and the ski carves a perfect arc. The skill of carving turns rather than skidding is one of the differences between intermediate and upper-level skiers. Once you feel a truly carved turn, you will have advanced your skiing a notch. (Provided you know what you did and can do it again!)

You can tell if you are riding flat by studying the tracks of your skis. If the tracks are deeper on the insides, your knees, legs and feet are rolling toward the center. If your skis are tracking heavily on the outsides, you are probably skiing bow-legged, an affliction more common among men.

A friend with a good eye, or an instructor with a trained eye, can pick up your misalignments by watching your knees as you glide on a cat track or a flat slope. The obvious signs: knees rolled together and large A-frame below the knee. More subtle indications on a steeper slope are skidded rather than carved turns, A-frame stem turns, skis sliding out from under you and edges that catch. Some women even bruise the insides of their knees.

## Knock-knees = injury-prone knees

Skiing knock-kneed is not a healthy way to ski. Beaver Creek instructor Carol Levine says if a woman is extremely Q'd, with her knees touching, trying to roll the skis on edge probably will place the knees in an unsafe — not to mention inefficient — position.

"Knees are supposed to bend *forward*, not side to side," Levine says. With some experts beginning to suspect that women's ligaments are looser than men's, skiing under misalignment is risky business, Levine warns.

It is not just skiing that is risky. A 1995 article in *Sports Illustrated* cites startling evidence that women playing basketball, where there is a high degree of lateral movement as in skiing, are nearly four times more likely than men to suffer tears to the anterior cruciate ligament — one of two central ligaments that support the knee. And a study by Kentucky Sports Medicine, a private clinic in Lexington, shows an increased incidence of knee disorders and injuries in women athletes due to women's misalignment caused by excessive Q angle.

These revelations support my survey of hundreds of women that shows knee injuries — sprains, twists, pulls and tears — are the most common skiing injuries among women.

The significance of this kind of information, once it becomes common knowledge, will be far reaching. Women skiers around the world at high risk of knee injury — from beginner recreational types to elite racers — will benefit. As awareness of women's biomechanics and its effect on skiing grows, the industry will be forced to change the way equipment is manufactured and to alter the way women are taught to ski.

And what about young girls just learning to ski? Does the Q angle affect their technique? Denver pediatrician S. Andrew Tucker says all females are born with a Q angle; as a young girl enters puberty, the angle increases as her hips widen. Physical therapist Conway says it is at about this age when young girls begin to experience knee injuries, usually from sports. Before puberty, however, the Q angle is not much of a factor.

## Center of mass

The second female biomechanical factor that gets in the way of women's skiing is our low center of gravity.

A man carries his overall body mass in his upper body. Women, with their narrower shoulders and broader hips, carry the bulk of their body weight slightly lower. If your figure is pear-shaped, you know this all too well. To make matters worse for women, the weight of ski equipment further lowers the center of mass.

While men reposition their center of mass with their arms, women control their center of mass through lower-body movements. As a result, women tend to sit back on the tails of their skis, where most of their weight is concentrated. This is often called "skiing in the back seat." It makes the tips of the skis float — or worse, cross or shoot out from under them. When women are told to "get forward," they cannot do it as a man would. Because women do not have the leverage men have with their upper-body weight, women try to "get forward" by bending at the waist and sticking their butts out.

In addition, the majority of women ski in boots designed for men. Women do not possess the leg strength to bend the hard plastic cuffs. It's like trying to ski with a cast on your foot. While we need lateral support, we also need flexibility in the cuffs in order to bend our ankles and knees enough to get forward, centered and balanced over the arches of our feet.

Feeling your arches underneath you is key to being centered. Boots that are too stiff keep your legs straight, pulling the center of mass off the sweet spot of the skis. In this teetering stance, the slightest ripple in the terrain will throw you backward.

If a boot is too loose-fitting (another problem with wearing boots designed for men's bodies), the foot moves around inside, sacrificing the important foot-to-boot oneness needed for control. It is like trying to steer a car with a wayward wheel or ride a bike with loose handlebars. You can do it, but you lose precision and accuracy of movement.

## Hip mobility

Women can do a helluva hula, but bumps and grinds can get us into trouble on the ski slopes. Because we *can*, many women rotate their hips to turn, instead of using their legs to create efficient edging. This results in overturning the skis and leaning into the hill, dipping the uphill shoulder away from the fall line. Women have a foolproof way of knowing when they are doing this: Our bra strap falls down on the side we tend to dip!

## Bone length

Women are shorter than men. An average woman's tibia, or lower leg bone, measures 1.14 inches shorter than the average man's, according to Suplizio. Because most women wear ski boots that are really just smaller men's boots, the tops of the boots hit women higher on the legs, usually in the thick part of the calf. By grabbing snugly at the widest part of the lower leg, the boot does not allow the foot to drop into the footbed, where it must be for that important transfer of energy. Yet a boot big enough to fit around the calf may be too big everywhere else.

## Strength

Any woman who has been overpowered by a man knows all too well men are stronger. Men's strength makes them more able to use ski equipment to power through the snow. But women can make up for their lack of strength with properly fitting equipment. Bob Hintermeister, director of the Rehabilitation and Human Performance Laboratory at the Steadman-Hawkins Foundation, sums it up: "Given a man and woman of similar body size, the average woman will be weaker and more likely to suffer knee problems because of her wider pelvis and greater Q angle. Women can minimize these risks by optimizing their strength and getting equipment that fits and is properly aligned." I will show you just how to do this in the following chapters.

---

*Chapter Summary:*
In this chapter you learned that factors other than athletic ability can hinder a woman's skiing: the Q angle, a lower center of mass, greater hip mobility, less leg strength and smaller size. Some of these factors also increase risk of injury in sports requiring lateral movement.

Chapter **Four**

# *Solutions*

---

*"To become the skier I want to be would take 15 less pounds, cute clothes, new equipment, and a year's worth of lessons."* — Anne, age 40+ from Colorado

*"First, I need new boots — mine are like bedroom slippers. Second, I need more lessons. Maybe I really need 20-year-old knees!"* — Sue, age 52 from Colorado

*"I need to find the 'key' to help me loosen up at the knees so I can ski the bumps and look fluid and effortless."* — Jane, age 41 from Colorado

---

Now that you have learned how your body structure affects your skiing, take heart. With awareness, the right equipment and proper exercise, you can correct the unsound stance your genetic makeup creates.

## Body awareness

If you are a long-time skier, muscle memory rules your reactions. Changing it requires concentration. Crucial to this change is being aware of your body and how it moves.

Teaching the neuromuscular system to develop sensory awareness for learning a physical skill is the theory taught in a program based in Vail. Founded by physical therapist Margaret McIntyre, a former ski instructor, Integrated Skiing is the only ski seminar in the country that teaches the Feldenkrais Method. Named for the Israeli scientist and athlete who developed it, the process

---

improves body awareness and self-image through movement. His is the following philosophy: *Nothing is permanent about our behavior patterns except our belief that they are so.*

Guided by this, McIntyre's six-day sessions combine indoor exercise and awareness training with on-slope instruction aimed at changing habits that hinder smooth, effortless skiing — a kinesthetic approach. "The ability to sense is directly related to the ability to move," she says. "If you can't feel something, you cannot move it."

To create this awareness, you need to learn to feel. You have already taken the first step in becoming aware with the exercise measuring your Q angle. When you moved your knees to line up with your big toes and held them there, you used muscle and concentration to achieve alignment. This is what you must do when you are skiing. With repetition, it will come automatically.

One practice I found helpful on the slopes to prevent my inside knee from even thinking about turning in is to imagine the little toe of my inside, uphill foot touching the snow. When I lead into the turn with that foot's outside edge, my knees are more directed and both skis carve cleaner.

I have also learned to notice when I am cruising that a *breeze between my knees* means I am skiing dynamically and athletically, not knock-kneed.

Fore and aft alignment also ranks high on the list of important balancing techniques. In your skiing stance, focus on feeling the ball of your foot, then push on your arch, then press on your heel. Instructors will have you do this while skiing to make you think about the pressure points in a turn: the forefoot in the initiation, the arch in the belly of the turn, and the heel at the completion.

One woman who took part in my survey wrote, "I wish for feet perfectly parallel and close together at all times." That's fine, as long as she does not try to accomplish this by *locking* her knees. Skiing parallel and skiing knock-kneed are not the same sport.

If you learned to ski in the 1960s like me, you probably use the Stein Eriksen style: feet and knees acting as one limb, like a mermaid. It looks graceful, and for women it's more comfortable because our knees want to stick together. But it's not as stable as the wider stance taught today. Called "the athletic stance," this wider stance gives skiers more agility and quickness.

I used to be proud of how together I held my legs while skiing. But instructors have convinced me that independent knee action and a wider stance make for stronger, safer skiing.

In the mid-1980s, I skied with a coach of the U.S. men's ski team who kept telling me to open my legs. I did not have a clue how to ski like that, and he did not have a clue why I couldn't!

## Throw away your skirts

Denver physical therapist Bob Mathewson has a theory about why women keep their knees tight while skiing — Skirts!

Most of us probably learned the more lady-like position for sitting while wearing a skirt — crossing the legs at the ankles, knees primly locked. Girls learned that knees belonged together at all times.

Notice the sitting positions of musicians in a symphony orchestra. The men sit relaxed, legs splayed; the women present a picture of propriety.

Think about the daily functions we perform with our knees purposefully together: getting in and out of cars, sitting, standing, kneeling, climbing stairs, driving a car, going to the bathroom. No wonder we want to ski this way, too!

Social pressures have taught women habits that are ruining our skiing!

# Equipment modification

While women cannot restructure their skeletal system, they can compensate by modifying their equipment.

This is a good time to introduce Jeannie Thoren, a tenacious crusader for female skiers. When most women skiers were struggling with whether to buy in-the-boot or over-the-boot stretch pants in the early 1970s, Thoren was figuring out how to improve her skiing by messing around with her equipment. She knew something beyond her control was preventing her from skiing the way she knew she could.

"I knew skiing wasn't supposed to be a constant struggle or fight," Thoren says.

The culprits, she found, were overbuilt skis, binding locations out of position to the rear, and ill-fitting boots.

After finding the right combination of boot and ski adjustments, she became convinced she could help other women with bodies like hers — queens of the Q angle — learn to ski better. "It takes one to know one," she jokes. "Anatomy is destiny. If you have the right build, you'll go to the top. If you don't, there's hope — you can be fixed."

In 1990, Thoren parlayed her expertise into what she now calls Jeannie Thoren Ski Systems, ski equipment clinics for women. Each year, Thoren reports, participation in her clinics doubles. "I get doctors, lawyers — women who are successful in every other aspect of their lives and in other sports," Thoren says. "It's a mystery to them why they cannot do well in skiing. They tell me if I can't help them, they're out of the sport."

Helping women learn to ski better has been easy for Thoren. It was getting the equipment designers, manufacturers and sellers to support her that's been difficult. "Men, who control the industry, just didn't understand it," says an exasperated Thoren.

This sounds a lot like male obstetricians telling women what it feels like to give birth or how to breastfeed a baby. They can explain it scientifically, but they will never know what it's like because they do not live in a woman's body.

But skeptics can no longer ignore thousands of born-again skiers populating the slopes, and loving the sport, because of Thoren's tenacity.

"Like a canker sore, I have not gone away. They (equipment manufacturers) have made me smarter, have made me do my homework. Everything I have been saying has been true all along. They can't argue with the truth," she says. "If this worked only fifty percent of the time, do you think I'd be on my hands and knees, adjusting skis and boots?" she asks. "The success rate is overwhelming. I am in this business because the women keep me going. Their happy faces are implanted in my brain."

## Boots

Thoren's methods of boot adjustments for women, which now have become universally accepted, include installing custom-made insoles with heel lifts, laterally aligning the boot cuffs and tilting the boots with a wedge underneath (canting) for better balance and alignment.

### Custom insoles

Your first step in this alignment process should be a visit to a professional boot*fitter*, not just a boot*seller*. He or she will build you a pair of custom insoles, also called footbeds, which are the foundations of building a better stance. These replace generic insoles that come with ski boots.

Lee Kinney, a veteran Denver-based bootfitter, believes custom insoles are key to good skiing. "They're the single most important thing you can do for yourself to get you performing correctly on skis," Kinney says. "Assuming you have a reasonably good boot fit, custom insoles help that boot transfer energy to the ski. The best ski in the world is not going to perform as it should if you are not transmitting to the ski the way you can."

Custom insoles correct a foot's pronation, a tendency to roll inward, as well as supination, rolling outward. This insole helps the foot maintain a neutral position in the boot, creating a solid base. Heel lifts help balance the foot fore and aft, which further aids the overall alignment in women. *All skiers — novice to expert, men and women — should ski with custom insoles.*

### Shaft alignment

Aligning the shaft follows next. (This lateral adjustment of boot cuffs often is called "cuff canting" by manufacturers and retailers, causing confusion about what canting involves. The distinction: shaft alignment *centers the leg* in the boot shaft; canting *changes knee alignment.*) On more expensive boots with a cuff adjustment mechanism, this is done easily with a screwdriver. Many entry-level boots, however, aren't equipped with cuff-adjustment devices. They're made with the assumption that beginners, who only wedge or snowplow, do not need precise alignment.

But a beginning woman skier with a pronounced Q angle will find that poor alignment makes learning to ski harder. She, in particular, needs all the help she can get. Beginners with less misalignment probably won't need to think about cuff adjustments until they begin to parallel ski.

### Canting

Under-the-boot canting involves placing a strip of tape or a pad of thin, plastic material as a wedge under the binding in order to tilt the boot. When boots are canted in this way, it realigns your knee position and changes your Q angle when you are standing on a flat ski. When canted correctly, Warren Witherell says, you do not have to *force* your knees further in or further out. You can stand naturally, and with the slightest movements of your knees, get the ski responses you are looking for: the "breeze between the knees" and just the right amount of edging of your downhill ski.

*Do not try canting yourself.* It requires a professional ski technician and you'll need to go to a specialty ski shop to do it.

Because binding manufacturers indemnify shops from liability, you may encounter some shop owners that refuse to alter bindings in any way. But technicians, who follow specific guidelines set by binding manufacturers and companies that make canting materials, can cant your skis without affecting binding-release mechanisms.

If technicians try to convince you that the combination of custom insoles and cuff adjustment is all you need, without evaluating your knee alignment and canting needs, go to another shop. They *know* the additional help of under-the-boot canting can be highly effective in reaching your goal of ideal alignment. They are either too lazy and do not want to deal with it, or they have been living in an ice cave on a polar cap.

Warren Witherell has been canting skis since 1968. He firmly believes, "The great majority of skiers require some canting under the boot soles to provide the most efficient alignment."

Canting is not new. I remember it from the 1970s. It faded in popularity for recreational skiers in the 1980s when the liability issue came about. Now, it's making a comeback, and women, in particular, should be delighted. Canting is the frosting on the alignment cake.

Warren Witherell and David Evrard say in *The Athletic Skier* that canting as a final step can make the biggest difference. "The first 80 percent of correction provides a 20 percent gain in performance," they write. "The last 20 percent of correction provides an 80 percent gain in performance." The authors arrive at this conclusion through extensive backgrounds in ski coaching, physiology and biomechanics. Both enjoy outstanding careers performing sports as well as studying them.

Since canting came out of the closet in 1993 with the publication of *The Athletic Skier,* more skiers are requesting it. Evrard, a ski-boot technician, estimates eight to nine hundred shops across the country now provide canting services.

### Ideal alignment

Even the *slightest alteration* in finely tuned boots makes a difference in skiing performance. Think of how the steering in your car feels after the wheels are aligned: The car becomes more responsive, faster turning and better balanced.

*Depending on the degree of your misalignment,* you'll want to use one or all of these methods to reposition your knees in order to achieve ideal alignment. This, Witherell and Evrard say, is when the center of the knee lines up 1/4- to 3/4-inch inside the center of the boot. In most people this requires only a slight adjustment, but it makes a big difference.

This change in stance will greatly boost your ability to flex your boots and turn your skis on edge, the first step in carving turns. This also helps with angulation and a more flexible torso. These methods correct all types of misalignment, including bowleggedness, and work for men as well as for women.

Cindy Suplizio, the biomechanical engineer, believes poorly fitted boots contribute to those skiing injuries mentioned earlier. "Women just do not make the adjustments to their boots and equipment that males either know how to do or don't need," she says.

A word of caution — Tony Osborn, a British orthopedic surgeon, says corrections should be made with care. "Most Q angles are from 15 to 20 degrees in angulation," Osborn says. "If you try to correct the full 15 to 20 degrees, then you are going to stress your knees, especially the patella-femur joint. I think you have to adjust, to a certain degree. You can do five to eight degrees quite easily; once you start going over that, you are liable to get into trouble."

How do you know the extent of your Q angle? Scientific equipment, such as a *goniometer* used by physical therapists, take precise measurements of your tibia-patella-femur relationship from a long-leg X-ray or from bony landmarks on the body. Or a trained bootfitter can evaluate you by measuring the distance between your hip bones and the distance between your knees. But the best way to determine if you need correction is simply to ski.

Often the effects of knock-knees (or bow-leggedness) do not show up until you are in a dynamic skiing situation.

That's why at Winter Park's Performance Lab the very first evaluation takes place on the mountain with trained technicians looking for certain movements in the student's skiing. Only after the on-snow session do the technicians take measurements and make needed adjustments. Then they go out again with the participant to teach a private lesson with the new modifications.

The Performance Lab, the first of its kind at a ski resort, owes much of its success to this type of format. On-mountain alignment centers debuted for the 1995-96 ski season at Aspen, Buttermilk and Snowmass in Colorado.

In Chapter Seven, which deals with buying equipment, we'll talk more about canting. For complete information on canting, see Part II of *The Athletic Skier*.

## Getting the center of mass forward

Women cannot redistribute their center of mass, but we can get it more *forward* on our skis. According to the Thoren theory, three tactics can be used to do this:

• Install heel lifts in your boots, as mentioned earlier, for better fore and aft balance. Because women's heels are usually narrower than men's, they tend to float in the heel pockets. Heel lifts give your heels firm contact with the back of the boots so you can lever the tails of the skis in the finish of the turn. They also raise your leg in the boot for a better fit around the calf muscle, which tapers lower on women's legs.

Heel lifts go hand-in-hand with custom insoles. Boot technicians can build them into the insoles, or you can buy them separately at a ski shop and fit them in place.

• The second way to get forward and in command of your skis is to press your shins against the front of your boots. You learned this in ski school. But many women have trouble because their boots are too stiff and/or too loose. A lot of women ski in rear-entry boots that are more difficult to flex than mid- or front-entry.

Jack Mason, chairman of the Colorado-based National Ski Patrol, says women should keep their legs in the "position of strength" to prevent knee injuries. Also called the athletic stance, this is the centered, dynamic skiing position with knees flexed 15 to 30 degrees, positioning the *derrière* above the back of the binding.

If you cannot get this much bend in your knees by pressing the boot cuff forward, you risk injuring your knees. You are also more likely to be thrown to the back of your skis and lose control.

One instructor taught me to stand a ski pole perpendicular to the ground, against the toe of my ski boot. If I could easily touch the pole with my knee, the instructor said, I was getting sufficient ankle and knee bend.

If you think your boots are too stiff or too loose, replace them with easier-flexing boots that have lower cuffs — boots made for women. Make sure you get a snug fit with the help of a bootfitter. (More on this in Chapter Seven.) A temporary solution to a sloppily fitting boot is to add padding between the boot shell and liner.

• Finally, bindings can be mounted one to three centimeters closer to the front of the ski than ski-manufacturers' guidelines recommend. (All skis show a mark on the waist, which corresponds to a center line on ski boots, indicating where the binding should be mounted.) Placing the boot's center line just ahead of that mark moves the mass forward *en masse*. It also places the boot where it really should be. Think about it, the smaller the boot — when matched to the ski's normal mark (designed for a man's longer boot) — the more likely it will be placed too far back.

Women who have attended Thoren's clinics say this adjustment cures wandering ski tips and creates more controlled turns.

Before you drill holes in your skis, this is something you might want to try on snow, using demo skis with movable bindings. Or invest in an Ess binding, the only movable binding on the market that allows this kind of experimentation.

Suplizio suggests that body characteristics such as height, weight, bone structure and distribution of mass should be considered individually when relocating ski bindings.

Regard this tactic as part of a three-fold process of getting the mass forward. If you move your bindings, but continue to ski in ill-fitting boots that are too stiff and without heel lifts, you have only solved part of the problem.

As always, after you adjust the mechanics, take lessons to learn the technique to go along with the altered alignment.

## We are not little men

Does it make sense for women to use ski equipment designed for men's bodies, simply because they have no other choice? Until recently, manufacturers have not produced equipment designed for women because it is not profitable, they say. Essentially, the needs of women skiers have been ignored. In Thoren's words: "The ski industry regards women as little men."

Slowly, the industry is responding. Manufacturers are beginning to understand the need for boots that fit women's feet better and skis that respond to women's bodies.

Although changing your equipment may not solve all your problems, giving yourself these mechanical advantages is a good beginning. It's like hemming a skirt that's too long or getting prescription glasses to see better. Now, just do it with skiing!

## Exercise

The last, and most important, solution to knock-knees due to the Q angle is maintaining strong leg muscles, especially those that stabilize the knees. (Exercises appear in Chapter Twelve.)

You can adjust your equipment and align your knees. But if your legs are weak, you will tire easily, your knees will ache at the end of the day and face increased risk of injury while skiing.

---

*Chapter Summary:*
You learned that awareness, proper equipment, adjustments to equipment, and exercise can help compensate for women's biomechanics in skiing.

---

*Recommended reading:*
*The Athletic Skier* by Evrard and Witherell. To order, write to The Athletic Skier, P.O. Box 21315, Salt Lake City, UT 84121. Enclose your name, address and $24.95 per book, plus $3 for shipping and handling. Or call (800) 223-4448.

*For more information:*
**Margaret McIntyre's Integrated Skiing** — P.O. Box 342, Vail, CO 81658; (970) 949-5529.
**Jeannie Thoren Seminars** — 2501 Jefferson St., Duluth, MN 55812; (218) 724-5809.
**The Performance Lab** — Winter Park Resort, P. O. Box 36, Winter Park, CO 80482; (970) 726-5514.
**Aspen's Alignment Centers** — Aspen Skiing Co, P. O. Box 1248, Aspen, CO 81612; (970) 925-1220.

---

# Chapter Five

# *Giving women the boot*

*"I didn't select my own boots and skis. My male companion had them from a previous female friend — truly!"*    —Mary, age 52 from South Carolina

*"My feet hurt — they get cold, then numb. My boots are 10 years old, but I don't want to invest money in new boots because I'm not that good."*
— Jan, fiftyish from Colorado

*"I have a pair of boots that really fit well and immensely improved my skiing. I can't remember their name."*    — Lynette, age 40 from Colorado

Long-time Colorado ski retailer Steve Vorhaus believes "Everybody is searching for the Holy Grail in this business." How true! Nobody has been searching longer or harder than women. But we don't *know* we have been searching. That equipment could be a major barrier to our skiing has not occurred to us. Boots hurt? So what's new?

Sore feet are a regular part of life for women — like having cramps or bad-hair days. For generations, we have been squeezing our feet into disfiguring shoes and tolerating the pain. Why, we rationalize, should ski boots be different?

Some women tough it out. Others give up the fight. In Ski Industry America's (SIA's) survey nearly a quarter of the respondents who used to ski said they do not ski any more because *ski boots are too uncomfortable.*

Hello? Ski boot manufacturers, are you listening?

## In search of the glass slipper

Boots and feet are a ticklish subject. Because feet are as different as fingerprints, ski boot manufacturers face a monumental challenge in designing for the masses. With proper boot fit *crucial* to ski performance, the task becomes even more significant. Building boots specifically for women can mean the difference in whether they advance as skiers or stay home, as we see in the survey. Boots too stiff, too loose or too tall for women — which means most men's boots — make skiing a lot harder for us.

Not too long ago, ski shop salespeople told women just to add another pair of thick socks if their feet swam in ski boots. Now, they bring out boots with cushy liners that cradle the contours of our feet, and shells in eye-catching colors.

But contours and colors are not enough. Let me explain.

## Boot liners

What makes a boot a *woman's* boot? Most of all, it is the removable, pliable, soft liner, also called an innerboot. Bootmakers have put a lot of thought into making innerboots conform to women's feet, ankles and calves, which are different from men's. (The term for a foot mold is "last." Remember it; it is a key word in this chapter.)

Here is a look at how women's liners differ from men's:

• They feature a lower cuff and a wider opening with less padding, to accommodate a woman's *lower calf muscle*. Because the average woman's leg is shorter than the average man's, the shaft of the boot needs to be shorter, too. A female calf muscle is not only lower, it tapers gradually to the ankle; a man's bulges like a nodule on a tree trunk. The flared cuff of women's models takes this shape into consideration, thereby helping to alleviate pinched calves. There are exceptions: A tall, long-legged woman might find a shorter-cuffed boot won't provide the support she needs. And calves can be as different as feet or faces.

• They are lasted (formed) for a woman's foot, which tends to be *narrower* in the *heel, ankle* and *Achilles tendon* than a man's foot of the same length. A woman's *forefoot* is *wider*, and her *toebox, lower.* Her *instep* is *higher*, and the area from *heel to instep* is *longer.* In a boot liner, these areas are shaped for a woman's foot by adding or reducing the padding.

• They feature built-in heel lifts or higher ramp angles for *forward* lean. (Remember where our center of mass lies?)

• They feature footbeds designed for women's feet. (The last two features become irrelevant if you opt for custom footbeds with heel lifts. Alpina's women's boot comes with a footbed that can be custom molded.)

There are variations from one manufacturer to the next in the lasts they use, just as women's feet vary. But at least manufacturers are starting us off on the right foot by creating an interior shape uniquely for women.

"We sincerely believe we can do more (for a woman's fit) with the liner," says Lange's Director of Product Development Charlie Adams.

## Boot shells

The shell of women's ski boots is another story.

Two components make up the shell — the upper shell or shaft, and the lower part, which encases the foot. With few exceptions, differences between women's and men's shells exist in the *upper shell only.* In women's models, it is made of softer plastic and, like the liner, closes lower on the leg, with a flared cuff.

A less-stiff upper shell makes it easier for a skier with less leg strength to push on the cuff and flex it forward for better control. It also offers more comfort and shock absorption. Beware of an upper shell that's soft on the sides, though, because it severely limits edging ability.

The other component of the shell, which holds the foot, *is made from a man's last.* Manufacturers conveniently call it a unisex shell — an oxymoron, because we know a woman's foot is different. Unisex implies it is suitable for both and that there is no need for a woman-only shell.

But there is such a need.

## Shell sizing

When you buy boots, the bootfitter lifts the innerboot out (yes, it does come out), sets it aside and asks you to step into the hard, plastic shell. He (let us assume the bootfitter is a man) makes sure your toes touch the front of the inner shell while leaving room in the back. He adjusts the cuff until the space between the lower leg and shell is even all the way around. This is called "shell sizing." (Chapter Seven covers bootfitting in detail.) The idea is to get the shape of the shell to match the shape of your foot. Always. No exceptions.

*If the shell were not crucial to boot fit, sizing it would not be so important!*

Think of the shell as the Jell-O mold or the bundt pan into which we pour our feet. It should fit like Cinderella's glass slipper, not her coach-man's clodhoppers.

## Lifting and drifting

Even when you get the liner to fit well — snug in the heel, ankle, arch, shin, and wide enough in the forefoot — the inevitable occurs. Depending on how hard and how long you ski, and how much you walk in your boots, the liner "packs out" and conforms to the shape of the shell. It is like sneakers acquiring the shape of your foot over time, defining bumps you could not see when the shoes were new.

This may never happen to a woman who skis moderately, six to eight times a season, and buys boots every three years or so. But for someone who skis a lot — 20 to 30 times a season — liners can pack out in one winter and get trashed in two.

When I bought a pair of boots a few years ago, I took them to my bootfitter for fitting, custom insoles and heel lifts. He put me in tune with the boots and I loved how responsively they skied. At the start of their second season, I began to feel my heels slipping. It was subtle at first but gradually became worse. So did my bump skiing.

I also noticed I was needing to hook the buckles over my insteps one notch tighter. This, I later found out, cut off the flow of blood to my forefoot and was responsible for the lack of feeling in my toes.

Then one day, as I buckled my right boot, I felt shooting pain across my instep. Had I grown a new bone overnight? I had to quit skiing after a few runs. What was happening?

I went back to the bootfitter. Indeed, the liner had compressed like a flat tire. My foot had shifted, and the hole cut in the plastic of the tongue was no longer resting above my high instep. The material in the heel pocket also had compacted, allowing my heel to slide around in the shell. My bootfitter was able to pad the sides of the heel and cut a larger hole in the tongue. This helped. However, I knew the innerboot would soon break down to the point of no return.

"The inner will always seek the outer," explains Jeannie Thoren, crusader for women's equipment. "Until they design a woman's shell, it is not a *true* woman's boot." *When the shell is lasted for a man, even the best woman's liner eventually will become a man's.*

## If the boot fits...

In his work with shoe and boot manufacturers engineer and consultant Jay White has been building a database of foot shapes dating to the 1970s. The computers at his Foot Image Technology in Bend, Ore., hold more than a half-million images of feet, plus the dimensions of every ski boot model on the market.

Each year, White and his researchers compare the new crop of boots with those three-dimensional foot images. *So far, says White, they have not found a single boot that addresses all components of the female foot.*

"It is our job to find that boot, and we cannot point to one yet," White says. (As this book went to press, F.I.T. had not begun to compare data of the more than 400 models for 1996-97 season.)

Even with all the hype generated by the ski industry about boots for women and the slick ads of ski boot companies touting their "women's" models, White maintains, "Women's boots are adaptations of men's shells, at best. If a woman finds a boot that fits, it fits by mistake."

Ski boots (except for Daleboot) are made in Europe. Most manufacturers build shells to the likeness of a *European male's* foot — not the American foot, which, thanks to our casual, sporty lifestyle, is wider than the European's. To change boot size, they simply scale dimensions proportionately. But a downsized boot with smaller internal dimensions does not fit a woman's foot, which becomes wider and thicker as it gets smaller. In addition, scaling does nothing to account for a woman's narrower ankles and heels, higher instep and all the other peculiar properties of a woman's foot.

Jami Davis-Poisel, director of operations for Foot Image Technology, says women have never worn ski boots that closely resemble their feet. "Boot engineers think that women are more interested in colors than fit; and frills are more important than substance and performance," she says.

Instead of building a true woman's boot shell, bootmakers just add more bells and whistles, which they say will ensure a better fit. It seems as if they do

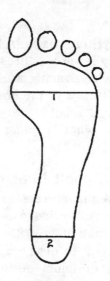

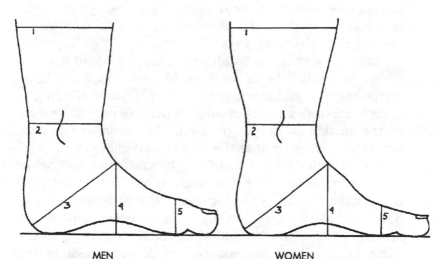

**MEN**
1. NARROWER FOREFOOT
2. WIDER HEEL

**WOMEN**
1. WIDER FOREFOOT
2. NARROWER HEEL

**MEN**
1. LESS ANKLE TO CALF TAPER
2. LARGER ANKLE DIAMETER
3. LOWER HEEL/INSTEP VOLUME PER LENGTH
4. LOWER INSTEP
5. HIGHER TOE BOX

**WOMEN**
1. MORE ANKLE TO CALF TAPER
2. SMALLER ANKLE DIAMETER
3. HIGHER HEEL/INSTEP VOLUME PER LENGTH
4. HIGHER INSTEP
5. LOWER TOE BOX

© FOOT IMAGE TECHNOLOGY

everything *except* build a shell from a woman's last. "They're not addressing the issue," Davis-Poisel says. "They're dancing around it."

But talk to the boot companies and you hear a different story. "Almost every company has its own philosophy about what is going to fit a woman's foot," Davis-Poisel says.

## Why won't boot makers go all the way?

Manufacturers are shooting themselves in the foot. They acknowledge women's feet are different from men's and that fit is critical to ski performance. Yet, they are reluctant to design a boot that will provide optimum fit — thus, optimum performance — for women skiers. Their reason is money, plain and simple.

The ideal situation for boot manufacturers would be to market a complete lineup of liners *and* shells sized and shaped for women, agrees Steve Kvinlaug, Alpina's product-development manager. "But as you might understand, that's a lot of molds, and ... it is a major investment," Kvinlaug says.

Mark Mahoney, product manager for Head Sports, maker of Head skis as well as Munari and San Marco boots, agrees manufacturers are reluctant, "Having a specific set of skis and boots that appeals to only 30 percent of the market is risky," he said. (The women's market was actually 40 percent at the time of that quote.)

Said Tecnica's Peter Knights: "It boils down to cost of manufacturing. In a high-end boot, you're talking $800,000 to $1 million worth of tooling cost....Out of 30,000 pairs of boots, should we make 10,000 of them ladies' and 20,000 men's? Or make 30,000, and whoever buys them gets the same boot and we do not get stuck with them in the warehouse?"

In 1986, Tecnica did break the mold by introducing the "first-ever ladies-lasted shell" in a rear-entry boot, says Joe Decker, a 19-year Colorado sales rep for the Italian company. "It was a huge hit — totally a fit situation," Decker says.

It lasted only six years. Why? Knights says the women's market didn't support it. Decker explains that the shell that replaced it, an overlap design, can decrease or increase volume, making it more suitable for both sexes. Because each shell comes with a woman-lasted liner, the company's position is that women can want no more.

"With the versatility of the overlap, you do not need to have a specific lady's shell," Decker says.

The dilemma over whether to design for women is clear. It is like deciding whether to get that two-seater sports car as a second car, or to buy a station wagon that will hold the whole family.

## Read my lips: no she shells

What will it take for manufacturers to make a complete ski boot? Knights notes, "Not unless racers demand an entire boot [woman's liner and shell] will recreational skiers ever see it."

But Knights isn't expecting that. He believes accomplished women skiers identify with hard-core skiing — skiing "like a man" — and would not buy a woman's boot because they would perceive it as less performance-oriented or, in other words, feminine.

"If I built a competition boot that was perfect for women in every way — with a lady's last and a lady's actual shell — the trendsetters, racers, PSIA women still will ski in a man's boot," Knights says.

Not so!

Every woman racer and instructor I talked to disagrees. "As a mechanical engineer, I would be one of the first to volunteer to test them," said Vail instructor Jean Richmond. "The reason I do not wear women's boots is they're too rinky-dink. They feel like a kid's boot."

PSIA Demo Team member Dee Byrne, one of the world's most beautiful and skilled skiers, says the issue of boots "is a huge frustration for us. Most of the instructors I know are in men's boots because women's aren't strong enough." She doesn't think there are that many "macho chicks" that would refuse a good woman's boot because of its image.

Women racers are concerned only about what will make them go fast, period. German national team member Martina Ertl, who won the giant slalom in the 1993/1994 World Cup finals at Vail, says, "Sure, I would try them if they would be faster than the other boots. Boots are the most important thing. They have to be *exactly* like your feet."

Shana Sweitzer, a U.S. Ski Team racer, agrees. "If it [woman's boot] were made to race, I think everyone on the team would try it."

Nine-year U.S. Ski Team veteran Edith Thys says she would wear a good race boot built for women. "If your feet are happy, you can put up with bad conditions and poor skis," she says.

So we end up with the chicken and egg theory: Elite women skiers wear men's boots because comparable boots for women do not exist. They do not exist because boot makers think elite women skiers won't wear them!

Some strong skiers even like a softer boot. Norwegian ski team member Jeanette Lunde says, "I used to ski on stiff boots. I got softer boots during the last few years because it is better for downhill. When you ski down you get more feeling.

"If Lange made them [women's racing boots]," she concludes, "I would try them."

## Shell shock

If ski and bootmakers want women to take them seriously and buy their products, they must take *us* seriously. Deb LaMarche, former U.S. Ski team coach, says racers do not put much stock in women's boots because manufacturers do not. "When manufacturers build boots for women that are the same quality as the men's, the women will go for whatever *fits and works*."

That's the bottom line.

As I see it, women skiers need to join forces. If we create a demand for boots that fit and help us ski better, manufacturers will realize the market potential.

It has happened in other sports. Brooks shoes created the first running shoe for women in 1987, after 42 percent of runners were women. In the early 1990s Lange (not the ski boot company) designed the first women's golf club when less than 20 percent of golfers were women. And recently fly fishing has captured the attention of women with neoprene waders shaped and sized for women's figures. Basketballs and softballs for women are smaller, hurdle heights lower, windsurfer sails smaller. As Jeannie Thoren puts it, "Skiing should not have a special dispensation for not making equipment for women."

How can we make a difference? By using our buying power. Start at your local ski shop. Tell the owner you will buy new ski boots when he can sell you boots engineered from the outside to the inside for a woman's foot. Until then, *nada*. Then, write or call the distributors. Tell them you are not interested in their product until they come up with a boot design that meets all the requirements of a woman's foot — in the liner *and* the shell. (Addresses, phone and FAX numbers are listed at the end of this chapter.) With the women's market on the verge of exploding, I believe you will not have to wait long.

---

*Chapter Summary:*
Women's feet, ankles and calves are different than men's, and ski boots made for men simply will not work for women. In this chapter, you learned that manufacturers recognize this fact by producing liners lasted for women, but so far have been reluctant to spend the money to make a complete women-specific boot.

*Product information:*
**Ski-Ki** — If you've had it breaking fingernails while buckling boots, use this palm-sized tool for better leverage when tightening and opening buckles on all types of ski boots. Under $5. To order, call (916) 926-2600; FAX (800) 926-0004.

*Ski boot distributors:*
**Alpina** — Steve Kvinlaug
Alpina Sports Corp., P.O Box 23, Hanover, NH 03755; (603) 448-3101; FAX (603) 448-1586.
**Dachstein** — Jim Fitzpatrick
KD Sports, Inc., P.O. Box 206, Banner Elk, NC 28604; (704) 898-4536; FAX (704) 898-6384.
**Dalbello** — Heinz Herzog
Dalbello Sports LLC, 519 Main St./Route 11, Andover, NH 03216; (603) 735-5650; FAX (603) 735-5651
**Dolomite** — Paul Angelico
Dolomite America, Inc., One Selleck St., Norwalk, CT 06855; (203) 852-1278; FAX (203) 855-1360.
**Dynafit** — Steve Patruno
Blizzard North America, Airport Industrial Park, 7 Commerce Ave., West Lebanon, NH 03784; (800) 654-6185; (603) 298-6000; FAX (603) 298-8643.
**Heierling** — Tom Slade
Heierling, 5415 Ridge Trail, Littleton, CO 80123; (303) 794-8935; FAX (303) 797-0546.
**Koflach** — David Donahue
Atomic Ski USA, Inc., 9 Columbine Drive, Amherst, NH 03110; (603) 880-6143; FAX (603) 880-6135.
**Lange** — Charlie Adams
Dynastar Skis, Inc., Hercules Drive, Box 25, Colchester, VT 05446; (802) 655-2400; FAX (802) 655-4329.
**Nordica** — Jens Bang
Nordica, P. O. Box 800, Williston, VT 05495; (800) 892-2668; (802) 879-4644; FAX (802) 879-1260.
**Raichle** — Hans Schiessl
Raichle Molitor USA, Inc., Geneva Road, Brewster, NY 10509; (800) 431-2204; (914) 279-5121; FAX (914) 279-4877.
**Rossignol** — George Couperthwait

Rossignol Ski Co, Inc., P.O. Box 298, Williston, VT 05495; (802) 863-2511; FAX (802) 658-1843.

**Salomon** — Mike Adams
Salomon North America, Inc.
Eastern Customer Service: 400 E. Main St., Georgetown, MA 01833; (800) 225-6850; (508) 352-7600; FAX (508) 352-7478.
Western Customer Service: 1311 N. McCarran Blvd., Sparks, NV 89431; (800) 654-2668; (702) 358-1075; FAX (702) 358-8299.

**San Marco, Munari, Tyrolia** — Mark Mahoney
Head Ski Division/Head Sports, 9189 Red Branch Rd, Columbia, MD 21045; (410) 730-8300; FAX (410) 730-8309.

**Strolz** — George D. Donovan
George D. Donovan and Sons, Inc., 243 Lowell St, Andover, MA 01810; (508) 475-5062; FAX (508) 475-5868.

**Tecnica** — Peter Knights
Tecnica, USA, 19 Technology Drive, West Lebanon, NH 03784; (603) 298-8032; FAX (603) 298-5790.

Chapter Six

# *A ski of her own*

*"I didn't know there was a difference (between men's and women's skis)."*

—Jill, age 39 from England

*Women's skis? Is there such a thing? Are they more expensive?"* — Carole, age 51 from Colorado

*"I don't know about women's skis. I would like to (find out). It might help!"*

—Lynne, age 38 from Massachusetts

The move toward ski equipment for women could have come sooner. Two years ago, Charlie Adams, director of product development for Dynastar Skis, explained the delay. "The materials and technology were there 10 years ago. It is more successful to do it now because we understand the need for products that will be better for women than their unisex counterparts," Adams says. "Everyone acknowledges the consumer thinks that way, so we are now marketing products that way."

The cavalier attitude of the male-driven equipment industry also has contributed to this decade of delay.

Volkl's Peter Knights explains that times have changed. "Twenty years ago, women really didn't want to decide," Knights says. "They wanted to be *told*."

David Currier, vice president of sales and marketing for Volant Ski Corp., agrees women's needs have been ignored. "It wasn't until women made themselves vocal and showed they were willing to spend money on ski equipment that companies began to pay attention," Currier says. In 1993 Volant jumped on the bandwagon with the FX2L, a high performance, all-mountain ski marketed to women.

Now that women have proven themselves with their pocketbooks, choices are being offered to them in an unprecedented variety of skis.

## Skis for her

Labeling skis as "women's" or "men's" conveys the impression they're as different as bikini panties from boxer shorts. But they're not. A 140-pound, intermediate male skier can ski very well on a so-called woman's ski. (In the industry, the term politely used is "ladies'" ski.)

The ideal ski for the average woman is softer, lighter, easier flexing. By lightening up materials and reducing mass, ski makers build skis that enable lighter-weight skiers to decamber the skis (bend them in the middle), carve and hold the edges in a turn. Some add binding placement marks approximately one centimeter closer to the front of the skis to place a woman's center of mass farther forward.

A unisex ski, designed to flex under the weight of a 200-pound man, often can be too much ski for a woman. It has little to do with ability.

"Weight is what matters," explains Adams. "The biggest difference between a woman's and a unisex ski is in the flex distribution. Unlike boots, which have anatomical differences, skis for women are not different in shape or sidecut," he says. "Being softer and easier to flex could work for men and children, too. It's a marketing decision whether you say 'Woman's Model' on a pair of skis. You can take any type of ski in our line. ...

All you have to do to make them better for women is soften them up. Anybody who says otherwise is creating a marketing story that does not exist."

Most women of average weight and up to advanced ability will be happy with a ski that is designated as suitable for women. Those who weigh more than average, ski hard and can work a stiff ski might do better on a "unisex" ski.

The initial crop of women's skis a few years ago proved to be too soft for women who were beyond beginner ability. So unimpressive were they that half of the respondents in Ski Industries America's (SIA) survey didn't even know women-specific skis existed. Now, nearly every company that makes women's skis (about 16 out of 20) produces at least one women's model in its high-performance category destined to be skied hard and fast with no loss of edge control.

Another significant step toward better skis for women is that manufacturers are beginning to use women in the design process. One such company is Olin. Its all-mountain ski for women, the DTv, unlike other skis built to a man's prototype of 200 and 205 centimeters, was prototyped in 190 and 195 centimeters, the average length for women. Women of the P.S.I.A. Demo Team tested the ski from beginning of construction to the end, determining optimal binding placement, location of the ski's waist, and flex pattern for all conditions and terrain.

"Right to the very end it has been their ski," says Olin rep Mark Lee. "This ski was built from the ground up for women. You can't beat it." The DTv targets strong, high-performance, recreational women skiers — a market previously neglected by ski makers — and ranks among the top-selling ski for women in the country. Do not expect to find it in large sporting goods stores. The Olin brand is carried by specialty ski shops only.

## Shapes for the shapely

For so many fruitless years we have been campaigning for women's skis. Just when manufacturers are beginning to see the light, albeit with squinted eyes, what could be the answer comes like a lightning bolt — shaped skis.

Also called parabolic, hourglass or super-sidecut, these dramatically different skis with their Q-tip silhouette trace their ancestry to three broad-based predecessors in the ski family tree: fat skis, snowboards and giant-slalom racing skis. Influenced by the flotation of the fat ski, the quick-to-learn carving of the snowboard, and the flared tip and tail of the GS, shaped skis evolved. The first short, radically shaped skis called SCX (for SideCuteXperiment) were introduced by Elan in 1991. At first, they were touted as nothing more than useful tools for teaching intermediate skiers to carve rather than skid their turns. Not a bad thing.

Looking back at that time, equipment editor Jackson Hogen wrote in *Snow Country*: "... surely no self-respecting expert would choose them as a daily ride ... Few skiers would have bet that they were looking at the future of skiing."

But soon, as more companies played around with the hourglass shape, the ski took on the appearance of a dieting woman by changing its profile in varying degrees. Less radical variations appealed to a wider range of skiers, and soon racers, adventure skiers and experts were having too much fun for the ski to be dismissed in their categories. Clearly, said Hogen, these skis could elevate even the most accomplished skiers and racers to unprecedented heights.

Even women.

Yes! These skis possess many characteristics women could ever want in a ski.

• They come in shorter lengths, as much as 20 centimeters shorter than conventional skis. The general rule of thumb dictates the deeper the sidecut, the shorter the ski. Since many women tend to get skittish with any ski over 180 cm, they should love the shaped-ski lengths, which allow them to maneuver more skillfully, initiate a turn more easily, and even schlep around more conveniently.

- They are not meant to be skied fast. Enough said.
- They are designed to produce controlled carved turns at slower speeds. Two desirable skills that often elude women can be mastered at once.
- They work better in a wide stance. Think wide hips.
- They force you to find your fore/aft balance point. Like the Tommy Tippy punching clown you played with as a child, your weight wants to settle in the center of the ski because that is where it *feels* best.
- They require less fore/aft pressure and energy to make a turn. When simply tipped on edge, their deep sidecut carves an arc for you. This no-brainer aspect shortens the road from theory to practice. Women who take lessons often say that having so much to remember about technique distracts them from simply having fun.
- They are identified by names rather than numbers. If you are mathematically impaired like me, you will appreciate this little detail.

One downside for women still remains: the old Q-angle again. You will hate them if you are knock-kneed. But, as you have read in chapter four, that problem goes away when you get aligned.

Do not slack off on your ski conditioning for strengthening your inner thigh muscles, warns Aspen instructor Tricia Hohl. While shaped skis turn with less energy, they require more muscle to hold the carve because there is more force coming back at you compared to a sliding turn on a flattened ski.

Also, these skis must be tuned often and correctly. If you are not used to frequent tunes with conventional skis, you'll need to change your maintenance schedule.

Whether you choose shaped skis or conventional ones, in the next chapter you will learn how to match your skiing style with the ski that will help you produce your personal best.

## If two skis don't work, try one

Women who have reached an impasse skiing on two skis might want to try a single ski. Think about it — You will never have to deal with crossed tips or skis drifting apart or problems with your Q angle. Instantly, you'll gain the form you seek because legs and feet must work together on one ski, making you look as fluid and graceful as a mermaid, all the time. Two legs working together prove stronger than when separate on dual skis.

In 1992, I had a chance to demo the prototype of World Ski's new monoboard (not to be confused with snowboard). A mono*board,* with its wider shovel, is a much-improved variation of the mono*ski,* popular in Europe but never big in this country. This new version makes monoboarding as effortless as power-steering your car.

Yes, I knew my feet would be locked in non-releasable bindings side-by-side on a single, wide ski. That scary thought proved harmless, I soon found out. The inventor, Kent Hunter, gave me a quick lesson, showing me how to use the outside edges. (The ski has no inside edges, remember.)

It didn't take long to grasp the feel of the new technique on the flats: more turning, no gliding. I even got comfortable enough to take it into the bumps and powder. With its wide shovel, it skims across powder and slush like a windsurfer.

The few spills I took consisted of nothing more than falls to the side of my butt — none of the yard-sale type I have experienced on two skis. By the end of the day, I had mastered a new, safe skill. Monoboarding's faster learning curve — for beginners as well as experts — eliminates many of the frustrations of skiing on two skis.

## "Ad-ing" to the confusion

If you are confused about ski equipment, you are not alone. Women in my survey indicate they really do not know what equipment is out there for them. Answers range from "I don't know anything about women's equipment," (the most frequent answer) to an emphatic "No! I could not ski better in women's boots. They are just tuned-down men's boots that rarely accommodate the differences." Most are suspicious. Says one woman (who works in the skiing industry), "My gut feeling is it's (women's equipment) a marketing gimmick."

Information about equipment is not getting through to women. Manufacturers advertise in ski magazines, but my survey shows few women read them. The SIA study shows more women skiers read *Self* magazine than those that focus on their sport. It's not surprising. With articles like "Courting the Demons of Death," (*Ski*, March/April, 1994), "Bad-ass Bumps," (*Skiing*, December 1994), "Two Men, Eight Summits and a Game of Poker," (*Ski*, November 1993), and those relentless photos of men hurling themselves off cliffs, who can blame them?

In defense of the media, however, the 1995/96 season reflected the industry's increased awareness of women skiers. *Ski's* December issue, with husband-and-wife team Eva Pfosi Merriam and Dave Merriam skiing in sync on the cover, featured an entire section on women. *Skiing* came out with its third *Skiing for Women*, and in March *Snow Country* asked "What Do Women Want?" in a questionnaire, the results to be published in late 1996.

With pressure from the Snow Sports Association for Women and women skiers themselves, I believe more of the same will surface in the next few years, making "Terminator" trivia and sexist advertising a thing of the past. Ski magazines are still excellent resources for teaching tips, resort reviews and other information about the sport — especially buyers' equipment guides published in season openers.

---

*Chapter Summary:*
With women making more decisions about ski equipment, manufacturers are beginning to pay attention to needs once largely ignored. Finally, for lighter weight skiers comes a variety of softer skis increasingly suitable for high-performance skiing. The new "shaped" ski could be the dream ski for women, or a single ski monoboard might be the answer for women who cannot get it together on two skis. Though women do not read them as often as men do, ski magazines continue to be one of the best sources of information on ski equipment.

*Product information:*
**World Ski Monoboard** — For more information or to order, call (800) SKI-WSKI. A limited number can be found in ski and rental shops throughout the United States. The board with bindings costs about $499.

**Information on women's skis** — Most ski manufacturers have a Web site where you can see pictures of their product lines and get brief information before you head to the ski shop. A good place to start is Ski Industries America's Web site (http:www.snowlink.com), which has links to many of the ski company Web sites.

## Chapter Seven

# *The buying game*

*"I don't know (about equipment). If I have a question, I ask my husband."*
— Melissa, age 23 from Texas

*"I don't like the ever-present sales 'dude' who thinks women aren't serious skiers. My ski ability goes beyond my gender and height."*
— Betsy, 20-something from Colorado

*"I would like to know how to buy equipment that enhances my ability to ski."*
— Annette, age 29 from Tennessee

Remember when one pair of sneakers covered a lot of ground? Not any more. We would not think of wearing tennis shoes for aerobics, or running shoes for volleyball, or boating shoes for hiking.

The same goes for ski equipment.

Store racks are filled with skis specialized for bumps, cruising and racing. Certain boards perform better in powder, others better on hard packed; some are designed to take you anywhere on the mountain, on- or off-piste. We can buy fat skis, short skis, long skis, hard skis, soft skis, torsionally stiff skis. And now, hourglass skis.

And boots! Have you ever seen such an assortment of high-tech hardware? After you check out what is there, it is a challenge to narrow the choice to the equipment that's right for you. But not to worry. After reading this chapter, you will know exactly how to disseminate the information overload.

Do not let someone decide for you. Only you can best assess your capabilities. You know in your heart how you look — and how you would *like* to look — coming down the mountain. One young woman told me, "I would like my body to face straight downhill, my legs [to] bend and give with the terrain with each turn. I ... want to look graceful, not like an abrupt, pole-planting skier who is trying really hard to get down the mountain. I want to look [as if] I weren't trying at all and it just came naturally."

Buy equipment with the idea you will improve each time you use it. Says *Snow Country* magazine's equipment editor, Jackson Hogen: "Buy for the skier you want to become, not the skier you are." This is excellent advice for women who tend to underrate themselves and take a reactive approach to skiing.

Do not be intimidated by men who make up 99 percent of the sales force in skiing hardgoods. Women normally are relegated to shades and suits instead of boots and boards. But you will find the occasional lone woman selling skis. Karen Hedger, has been selling equipment for nearly four years in Colorado.

"Men don't trust me at first," Hedger says.

"After one man bought clothes from me, he stepped over to the ski rack and said, 'Now, who can help me with skis?'

"When I said, 'I'd be glad to,' he looked at me and said, 'You? You're kidding?'

"I asked him, 'Why are you surprised? Is it because I'm a blonde or a woman?'

"He said, 'Both!'"

## Do your homework:

• Study buyers' guides in the fall issues of the major consumer ski magazines — *SKI, Skiing, Powder, Snow*

*Country.* Each uses a team of testers to try out the new crop of equipment and tell it like they ski it.

Recently, *SKI* magazine put more than 130 skis to the test. Women, usually racers and instructors (and now a few recreational skiers), participate in these test and review processes, and the magazines devote special sections to women's stock. (Some critics think the magazines enjoy a relationship with manufacturers far too cozy for objective testing.)

In addition, ski editors categorize every product, from poles to Power Bars, to make it easy. Some women's magazines, including *Women's Sports and Fitness* and *Skiing for Women*, publish reviews of women's equipment in the fall. Take advantage of these fingertip fountains of facts.

• Learn the terms. Know the difference between longitudinal and torsional flex. Find out how sidecut affects a ski's performance and why a ski turns. Learn about boot-cuff adjustments and forward-flex adjustments. Use the glossaries in this chapter to become an informed buyer.

• Spend a few hours in several *specialty* ski shops, where the staff sells ski-related products only, not guns and golf clubs. Different shops carry different brands, so do not limit yourself to one store. Talk with the most knowledgeable people you can find. Look for salespeople with experience, for those who routinely test equipment and attend product clinics, for those willing to give undivided attention.

## Find your skiing personality

Make sure the salesperson understands your "skiing personality," Dynastar's Charlie Adams emphasizes. "The critical thing is to gain confidence that this person understands you as a skier."

Once skiing needs are clear, you can easily pin down the model. "It's more important to understand that a woman is first an expert all-mountain skier, and then that she's a woman," Adams says. "Once he (the salesperson) understands that, he can go to the model. Then it is a matter of matching the right price tag, cosmetics and brand of technology."

If they know their trade, salespeople will begin the selling process by asking fairly standard questions to learn your skiing personality:

- Where do you usually ski?
- What kind of runs do you prefer?
- What conditions do you like/dislike?
- How would you *like* to ski?
- How many days a year do you ski, or anticipate skiing?
- What do you like/dislike about your present skis and boots?

If they recommend a ski or boot right off the bat before they know anything about your skiing, go to another store.

David Chutter sells ski and snowboard equipment at Princeton Ski Shop, a specialty chain known to skiers who live in the greater New York City area. He says most male customers come in with rudimentary information gleaned from skiers' guides in magazines.

Women skiers, except for the more advanced, still rely on the sales staff. "Beginner and intermediate women are totally in the hands of the salesman," Chutter says. "We do our best to inform them. But they must properly qualify themselves with us first."

How?

"Tell the truth!" Chutter says. "If a woman comes in and says she skis 15 days a year, but really skis five; or if she brags about going up to Killington and skiing Outer Limits [a black-diamond bump field] without stopping, but she's not telling the truth, I'm never going to be able to qualify her properly."

The Ski Industries America (SIA) survey shows an alarming statistic: Thirty-nine percent of women allow someone else to choose the brand of equipment they purchase. Those who choose? Fifty-eight percent are boyfriends or spouses!

In the end, the choices turn sour. Nearly half of women buying skis switch to another brand. Could be because they have switched boyfriends, too!

## Ski design trends

Ski trends for the second half of the '90s are cap skis, fat skis and a proliferation of super-sidecuts or shaped skis, according to SIA officials.

Cap skis (see Tech Talk) debuted in 1990 and now, thanks to customer demand, virtually every ski maker has caps in the market. Cap skis claim to enhance a ski's feel by transferring energy faster from the skier to the ski's edge, improving performance.

"Fat" skis continue to appear in manufac-turers' new lines. This ski, popular for deep powder and crud, has beefed up business for snowcat and heli-ski operators. The ski's wide body speeds up the learning curve for powder skiing and has brought more skiers to the steep and deep.

Critics of fat skis intially maintained those who used fat skis were cheating and would not be able to apply the technique to regular skis. But with increasing acceptance of weird shapes and sizes now found on the slopes, only a few still regard them as a crutch. Most credit them with the most fun they have ever had on skis!

Shaped skis have been called the most significant equipment breakthrough in the history of skiing. According to SIA representatives, the speed with which ski makers have jumped on this trend has set a record for product development. Virtually every manufacturer now offers shaped skis, and they exist in a category all their own.

## Shaped skis

As we learned in the previous chapter, the market is flooded with geometric skis. But how does a woman find the right shape?

First, know what kind of turn you would like to make. Buy the ski that will deliver that turn. For example, the rounder and tighter you want an arc, the deeper the sidecut should be. For more elongated turns and stability at higher speeds, you want less curve in the ski. For skiing powder and crud, a wider waist (the ski's, not yours) improves flotation. And for all-mountain versatility, a wide waist with flared tip and tail works best.

Some manufacturers engineer women-specific characteristics — softer flex, forward binding mount — into shaped skis. Ask your dealer about women's models.

Expect to pay anywhere from $350 to $840 for this new technology.

## Conventional skis

Though the industry holds high hopes for the shapes, conventional skis are not dead yet. I predict men, particularly younger ones, will find it hard to convert to the shorter lengths of the shapes, perceiving them to be a less macho "training ski." Can real men find happiness on a 173-cm ski? As Jackson Hogen said at SIA's trade show in 1996: "A lot of guys equate the length of their skis with a part of their anatomy."

Also, many women who can hold their own on any snow, any mountain, may have no desire to switch from the boards that got them there. As they say in tennis, "Don't change a winning game."

So with this in mind, here is the rundown on conventional skis:

• *Short-radius turns*
    For quick, squiggly turns or for skiing gates for fun, a *slalom ski* (often abbreviated SL in industry literature) packs the liveliness you need. It can be demanding, but good skiers like it for bumps, trees and hardpack; they hate it in powder and crud. Its carving ability comes from its stiff tail, fiberglass material and narrow waist.

• *Long-radius turns*
    If you like to cruise on blues with long, sweeping turns, look for a *cruiser* or *giant-slalom* ski (abbreviated GS). Its softer tail and straighter shape make it stable at higher speeds. It is perfect for gliding, especially on open, groomed runs.

• *All-terrain*
    Designed to go everywhere on the mountain, it is a cross between GS and SL. The versatile *all-mountain* ski brings you the best of both worlds, turning easily in varied snow conditions and terrain. *All-mountain extreme* skis are the "four-wheel-drive vehicles" you need for the gnarly stuff.

• *Bump bashing*
    If you are serious about refining your bump skiing, buy a *mogul* ski. This ski hops from edge to edge; its softer flex moves you over and around bumps like a snake; it is lightweight when airborne. Stay in the bumps, though. True bump boards ski squirrely everywhere else. If you've perfected the technique, stick with a slalom ski.

• *Powder prowling*
    Like your second car, a pair of fat skis should be your second pair. Twice the width of and softer than conventional skis, they are designed to float through deep snow and crud with a bazillion times greater ease in turning. Some models make the transition from powder to packed better than others. If you are going to play in powder all day, you will think you have died and gone to

heaven! Buy fat skis 10 centimeters shorter than normal skis.

## Ski categories

### • *Racing*

If you plan to buy racing skis, you do not need to read this section. You already know these skis are highly specialized for very strong skiers who want specific speed and turn shape. They come with GS and SL sidecuts and variations of both. Recreational racing skis suit skiers who want top performance in free skiing and occasional NASTAR-type racing. Average price: high, $625; low, $330.

### • *High performance*

This category fits advanced to expert skiers who might find a racing ski more than they can handle. High performance includes giant slalom, slalom, all-mountain, extreme and mogul skis and some women's or "light adult" models. Average price: high, $510; low, $275.

### • *Sport*

For overall enjoyment, intermediate to not-quite-advanced skiers buy in this category. Many women's skis are found here because they are more forgiving than high-performance skis and flex with less pressure. Names such as "Elle," or model numbers with "L," denote women's skis in all categories. If you want a balanced-flex ski that is easy to turn for a lightweight, less aggressive skier, look for these terms. Average price: high, $370; low, $190.

### • *Recreational*

A novice-to-intermediate ski, this should be *rented* when you are learning because you may outgrow it faster than your pocketbook will allow. *Snow Country's* Hogen advises against buying beginner skis, "They will only help you remain a beginner." Invest in warm ski clothes and good boots instead. Average price: high, $335; low, $160.

## Ski flex

The flex pattern determines a ski's ability to turn (longitudinal flex) and hold (torsional flex) under the pressure of your weight. (See the ski glossary at the end of this chapter.) Here is how you can check the flex of a ski before you buy it:

### Longitudinal flex
- To test the shovel, stand the ski on its tail, against the side of your foot.
- With one hand, hold it by its waist and angle it an arm's length out in front of you.
- With the other hand, grasp the tip (facing you) and pull it firmly toward you while you push into the waist with the first hand.
- For the tail, hold the ski in the same position.
- Bend down to press the tail of the ski about six to eight inches from the end.

Test several skis to compare their flex. If the tip and tail bend about the same, the ski has a *balanced* flex pattern. If the tip bends more easily than the tail, the ski has a stiff tail. Most women's skis have a balanced flex pattern or softer-flexing tip, making them easier to turn.

### Torsional flex
- Hold the ski's tail between your feet and steady the ski between your knees.
- Grab the right side just below the tip with your right hand.
- Place the left hand on the left side of the waist.
- Try to twist the ski by pushing with the right hand and pulling with the left.

If you cannot twist it, the skis will hold well in a turn. If you carve with your edges, make short, quick turns, or often ski on hardpack and ice a lot, you want torsional rigidity.

## Ski length

Now that you've defined your *skiing personality* and *ability level*, you need to factor in your *weight* and *strength* to determine proper length. At one time, the rule was that the ski tip had to hit the wrist of the arm held straight above your head. Now, the purpose and model dictate the length. Skis for long-radius turns should be longer than skis for short turns or bumps. Do not be afraid of ski length. Remember, the task is to pressure skis in reverse camber so they grab and edge an arc in the snow. The longer the ski, the more edge on the snow for stability and control.

So, a 130-pound woman in good physical condition who likes to make sweeping turns on groomed runs should ski on 190- or 195-centimeter GS or all-terrain conventional skis. If she's aggressive and likes to go really fast, she should buy the longer length; if she skis slowly and conservatively on the flats, subtract five centimeters. If she skis bumps and powder every chance she gets, she should be on a softer ski in the shorter length. Fat and shaped skis should be skied up to 20 cm shorter than conventional skis.

Experts suggest subtracting five centimeters across the board for skiers older than 50. They think that once you hit that age, your muscles and mind turn to mush.

I disagree. Skiing is like riding a bicycle — you do not forget. Skiers who maintain physical strength through conditioning should base ski length on their ability and the terrain they ski, not their age.

It might be more appropriate for older skiers to buy longer skis because many give up knee-jarring activities like bump skiing, preferring fast cruising. You know best. Do not let a salesperson talk you into a shorter ski because you have lived half a century. Find a salesperson with gray hair!

Once you decide on two or three models that fit your level of aggression, ability and weight, take them for a demo run. There is no better way to learn if you are compatible with a ski. (Refer to Chapter Nine for tips on testing demo skis.)

## Boots

When my mom took me to buy shoes when I was a little girl, the salesman put my feet in a big X-ray machine. Peering through the tiny window, I could see the bones of my feet filling the insides of the Buster Browns. The X-ray machine is long gone, but the desire for proper fit remains. Especially for ski boots.

For women, buying ski boots can be as scary as shopping for a bathing suit. (Or worse — if a bathing suit does not fit, you can always swim nude.) Your ski boots rank as the most important ski equipment you will ever buy. Proper fit is crucial to alignment and performance. Most upper-level skiers know this. Research shows performance as the No. 1 criterion that advanced skiers of both sexes use when buying boots.

The second and third reasons listed by men in making boot choices are comfort and color.

Women, however, rank color ahead of comfort.

Fran Woods, technical rep for Salomon ski boots, describes the bootmakers' point of view when it comes to choosing colors.

"Bootmakers go out of their way to see what colors are going to be predominant in clothes so they can coordinate with them," Woods says. Luscious jewel colors like pearl, amethyst and sapphire lure lower-level skiers, making color more important to them than function or performance.

Alpina's Steve Svinlaug believes women choose solely on color, not function or even price. "Women do not want ski boots to look like nurses' shoes anymore. They want beautiful colors," he says.

But skiing is not a fashion show, and boots should not be chosen as color-coordinated accessories. The best thing that could happen to women's skiing would be painting ski boots all the same color.

Jim Sczuka of Beaver Creek's Rightfit Sports says the way to choose boots is to look for fit, performance and comfort, and *in that order*. He calls boots the "transmitters."

"A boot should transfer whatever your leg does to the ski," Sczuka says. "If the boot's too soft, you can't feel it work for you; too stiff, you can't flex to control the ski; too loose, you can't steer."

In their desire to move their centers of mass forward, women should be careful not to overdo it, Sczuka says. "Too far forward locks you in a forward position, instead of solidly over the arch, and too much ramp angle puts you on the balls of your feet."

## Ski boot categories:

• *Rear-entry* boots are found mostly in rental shops and in beginner models because they're comfortable. Also, skiers, especially women, find them easier to put on and take off. This once-popular style is considered less performance oriented and not as laterally stiff as the other designs today. These boots virtually have disappeared from intermediate and advanced models. Average price: high, $337; low, $192

• *Front-entry,* or overlap, boots with four-buckle closures provide a better fit for women, with more support and performance, but can ruin a manicure! Average price: high, $498; low, $271.

• *Mid-entry,* or hybrids, combine the comfort and ease of rear-entry boots with some of the performance features of front-entry boots. Average price: high, $447; low, $280.

Higher-priced boots feature performance adjust-ments like cuff adjustments, forward flex, forward lean, micro-adjustable buckles and power straps.

# Boot sizing

Sizing a ski boot is like taking a math test. Three standards are used:

- *Mondopoint*, the international metric system
- *U.S.* sizes
- Salomon's *Heel Instep Perimeter (HIP)*.

Nearly all women's sizes come in U.S. sizes 4-10, which fall in the Mondopoint range of 23-27 and HIP 290-340. Sound confusing? It gets worse.

Jeff Rich, *SKI* magazine's technical editor, a pedorthist (person who makes and fits orthotics) and teacher of bootfitters, says there is no sure way to find the perfectly fitting boot. "Despite the presumed standardization of ski boot sizing, finding the right fit is still somewhat of a crap shoot," he said. Same-sized boots from different manufacturers vary widely, as much as four to five millimeters. Something as simple as innerboot padding density can radically change the perception of fit according to Rich.

"Ski-boot shells change only on the full size," Rich explains. "When you buy a half-size bigger, the shell's not longer. The extra volume of the inner boot's footbed tricks the foot into thinking the boot is longer!"

As sole length increases, so does overall inner volume. For each full size, length increases three-sixteenth to three-eighth of an inch, ball and instep girth by a quarter-inch, and ankle width by one-eighth to one-quarter of an inch.

So how do you find your size?

Rich advises working closely with a good bootfitter to find boots that wrap your foot snugly without pain — no matter the measurement.

## Bootfitters

Finding a ski boot that offers performance and comfort is like finding a bathing suit that fits *and* looks great. But, like skis, the variety of brands, models and sizes makes it difficult.

Where do you begin?

First, ask around for a store that employs a good bootfitter. Ask ski instructors who they use at the resorts. In urban areas, you will find bootfitters in specialty ski shops. Some bootfitters work independently in lab-type settings, fitting ski, skate and hiking boots as well as athletic shoes. Look for shops that advertise *guaranteed custom bootfitting, boot specialists,* or *board-certified pedorthists.*

Adopt a bootfitter as a friend. They will listen to you whine about pain, cold feet and bad skiing. They want to hear about heels that slip, shin bruises and aching knees. They will lend a sympathetic ear because your foot comfort and improved ski performance is their goal.

Some shops specialize only in ski boots, such as Rightfit Sports, a chain with stores at U.S. resorts in Colorado, Utah, Idaho, California and British Columbia in Canada. Buying ski boots at ski areas allows instant feedback. Fit-and-ski convenience lets you take care of buying and fitting during a single vacation, sometimes in a single day.

## Do-it-yourself sizing

Some skiers heed the advice of computerized foot- and boot-scanning systems, such as COMPU-FIT™ by Foot Image Technology based in Bend, Ore. The computer analyzes the dimensions of your feet, then compares them with all models of boots on the market and makes a non-biased recommendation of boots that best match your feet. Call F.I.T. with bootfitting questions or to find out which of 80 ski shops around the country use COMPU-FIT. Or order the bootfitting kit, which includes a skiing profile questionnaire, diagrams to show personal problem areas, and materials with instructions for measuring your feet, ankles and calves.

Within 24 hours of receiving your information, COMPU-FIT will send you a printout of your foot data, a Flex Index (resistance to flexing), and suggest three to seven boots. The mail-order package costs about the same as COMPU-FIT's service in ski shops. The personalized foot facts can be helpful when buying other types of boots and shoes as well.

And, if you want to know which companies are producing the best boots for women, call the hotline and ask for Jami, Mugsy or Jay. Tell them you've read about COMPU-FIT in this book. They will give you up-to-date findings on women's models, familiarize you with what to look for in women's boots, and help you narrow the selection by eliminating boots incompatible with your feet. You'll still need a bootfitter to tweak the boots you choose — few people, especially women, can fit into boots right out of the box.

## Bootfitting

When you visit your bootfitter, he or she first will measure your bare feet and study them for anything unusual. By studying your feet and asking about your skiing personality, an experienced bootfitter will learn which boot will fit you best.

"A bootfitter should suggest a boot for you," says Chris Cumsille of Denver-based Christy Sports. "We know what fits a wide foot, a narrow heel, narrow foot, low- or high-volume instep and big calf. I can look at feet without measuring and tell what boot will fit. Every company builds a good product, it is just a matter of finding one that fits." Sometimes, this means shopping in more than one store.

When choosing a model, the bootfitter will "shell-size" your feet — the most effective way to match shell shape to foot shape. "The shell is the most important thing," Cumsille says. "It is the only way to size. You can't go by measurements."

To shell-size, place your feet inside the plastic shells, liners removed.

- For a **comfort fit**, the space between your heel and the back of the shell should measure about 1 1/2 inches. Bootfitters feel the area with their fingers and call this a two-finger fit. Your toes should touch the front. Most recreational skiers like a comfort fit.
- A **performance fit** measures about an inch or 1 1/2 fingers. Aggressive skiers choose this fit.
- A **race fit** ranks as the tightest of fits, requiring a half of an inch or only one finger.

After adjusting the cuff alignment (if the boots have this device) so that the space between the lower leg and shell is even all the way around, the bootfitter inserts the liners back into the boots and asks you to stand in the boots. With the innerboot back in the shell, your foot should feel snug everywhere. Your toes should touch the front until you drive your knees forward. Then your toes should pull away, leaving a little wiggle room for a comfort fit. (A performance fit leaves less room; a race fit allows no toe movement.) You do not want any hot spots of intense pressure, nor do you want your foot to slip anywhere, especially in the heel pocket.

Bart Tuttle, Tecnica's bootfitter for World Cup racers, says women must be sure to size small enough so that the boot holds the foot securely with "no slop in there." A good bootfitter, he says, can configure a boot to reduce volume. "But," he adds, "most shops do not put in the time to fit correctly." This means if you do not speak up, you may end up with an ill-fitting boot.

Sue Booker, a 20-year veteran of ski and bootfitting at Loveland Ski Area in Colorado, holds the distinction of being one of only a few female bootfitters. Regarded in the skiing industry as tops in the field, she knows how the right fit feels.

"A proper boot fit feels like a firm handshake. It should feel like it is molded all around your foot and ankle,"

Booker explains. "And you need to be able to flex the cuff. A 120-pound woman can't flex a cuff made for a 220-pound man!"

Innerboots or liners use different densities of foam to achieve a balance of fit and comfort, explains pedorthist Rich. Expert boots (skill levels 9-10) use very stiff padding; performance boots (skill levels 6-8) use firm padding; recreational boots (skill levels 1-6) use more compressible foam. Generally, the firmer the foam, the tighter the hold; narrow feet do best in boots with firm padding, Rich says.

As we learned in Chapter Five, you'll find most of the difference in women's and men's ski boots in the liner.

## Bootfitting tips

• Do not forget to tell your bootfitter about chronic problems with your old boots, such as red spots on your feet or ankles, indentations, popping blood vessels or areas that cramp or go numb. Let him or her also know what you liked about the old pair.

• Wear or bring a pair of *thin* ski socks for trying on ski boots. (See Chapter Ten to learn why a thin pair is best.) If you borrow a pair from the store, make sure they're the same thickness and length as those you will wear.

• Wear a skirt, shorts or pants that can be rolled up past the boot tops. Nothing should wrap your lower leg other than a sock.

• Try on boots at the end of the day. Rich estimates feet swell five to seven percent standing or walking; eight to ten percent playing sports; 12 to 15 percent with excessive heat and friction. Altitude also makes them swell, so buy boots that will fit in skiing situations.

• Spend at least 15 minutes testing each pair to allow your feet to settle into the boot — walk, flex the cuffs, learn the buckle system.

• Remember, if you can barely flex a boot in the warm store, you will never bend it on a cold mountain.

• Do not freak out if new boots feel a little too snug — a few days of skiing will break them in.

• If you own custom footbeds and heel lifts, install them in every pair of boots you try on. (When you buy new boots, your footbed should be reshaped to perfectly fit in the new shell beds.)

• If you haven't had footbeds with heel lifts customized for your feet, consider it a necessary part of the expense of new boots.

## Custom insoles

We discussed the value of custom insoles, or footbeds, in Chapter Four and how they act as the foundation in the process of bootfitting and body alignment. Denver bootfitter Lee Kinney says it is like the old song about the knee bone connected to the leg bone, the leg bone connected to the ankle bone. "Any podiatrist will tell you what goes on in the foot affects the tibia," Kinney says. "When the arch collapses, the tibia rotates in ... the knee angles in, the femur rotates out, dropping the pelvis down. (the women's Q-angle, low center-of-mass syndrome)."

"When we bring the foot where it should be, we align not only the foot in the boot, but the knee *over* the boot, and help the hip line up correctly," Kinney explains. Custom insoles place the feet in a neutral position, distributing pressure evenly over the foot and balancing the stance.

Heel lifts, companions to insoles, help balance the foot fore-and-aft and side-to-side, fill the void in the heel pocket, move the center of mass forward, and raise calves to a better-fitting, more comfortable position in the boot shaft. As we discussed in Chapter Four, women find heel lifts extremely helpful for bootfitting problems and ski performance.

Allow about an hour for fitting custom insoles and heel lifts. Materials and labor cost $50-$95, depending on brand and work involved. Difficult feet require more labor and material.

Usually custom insoles cannot be interchanged from old to new boots without reshaping them. When a bootfitter molds the insole to a foot, he or she also contours the bottom of the insole to interface with the top of the footbed on which it rests. If the old boot's footbed is shaped differently than the new one, some modifications need to be made.

When getting your custom insoles made, make sure the bootfitter takes this interfacing into consideration.

## Canting

In Chapter Four, we touched on canting as a means of correcting the effects of the Q angle. You learned that wedges under the boots can redirect your knees over your feet for more effective steering, edging and carving.

Warren Witherell and David Evrard, who reintroduced canting in *The Athletic Skier,* explain the problems associated with canting: "The obstacles to working with canting have been greater than the ski industry's commitment to it. Boot and binding manufacturers have been focused on other issues, and ... concerns over liability have scared some shops from mounting cants under the bindings" they write.

With binding release and retention capabilities nearly perfected now, the ski equipment industry can be expected to pay attention to skier performance — and women's needs!

If you investigate, you are bound to find a technician — ski tuner or bootfitter — who will cant your skis. In Denver, Chris Cumsille says in one season out of 25 canting customers, only two were women. Not that women do not need it — on the contrary, it is the best way to align our Q-angled knees over our boots.

"Women either do not know about or do not think they need canting," Cumsille says. "Women come in and just want to get set up with equipment. "They don't want to hassle with it. Also, the money scares them away."

Cumsille charges $50 per ski to cant. He says men customers, on the other hand, will to do everything possible to ski better. "Men show off more," Cumsille says. "Their buddies are beating them up on the mountain and they *know* what will help them."

In my survey, I found a link between a woman's level of ability and how much she knows about bootfitting and canting:

• Beginners are clueless.

• A little more than half of intermediate skiers said they had heard about custom insoles, only 17 percent said they used them. Fewer than a quarter knew about canting; only six percent said they used it. (When asked if they meant cuff adjustments or under-the-boot canting, most said they used cuff adjustments only.)

• Advanced women skiers were a little more savvy about getting the most out of equipment. Though more than half knew about the techniques, fewer than a quarter said they used either.

• Women who ranked themselves as expert skiers knew the secrets to ski performance. All but one were aware of these methods; all but three said they took advantage of them.

## Determining canting needs

How do you know if canting will improve *your* skiing? This test is fun and simple: Grab a plumb bob, a pen and a partner. (A plumb bob measures vertical lines. Wallpaper and hardware stores carry them, or you can make your own by attaching a 2-foot-long string to the middle of a pointed weight.)

Follow these steps:

• Buckle into your ski boots.

• Stand on a hard, level surface like a wood floor.

• Have your partner mark the center of *knee mass* on the skin of each knee. Be sure your partner finds the middle of the *entire* knee area, not just the kneecap. (Do not be surprised if the mark does not land on the center of your kneecap.)

• Assume the normal skiing stance with feet parallel, about hip-width apart.

• Bend your knees as far forward as the end of the front of the boot. Do *not* force them to line up over your toes — just bend, then let them fall.

• Dangle the plumb bob from the mark on your knee until the weight settles in front of the boot sole.

• Mark the boot where the plumb bob points. Then, on the boot's toe, note a ridge or indentation in the plastic indicating the center.

• Measure the distance between the plumb-bob mark and the center line with a ruler.

If your pen line falls 2 1/2 degrees or more (about three-quarters of an inch) *inside* that center mark, you need canting under the inside edge of the boot sole.

If it falls outside the center mark or less than one degree (about one quarter of an inch) inside, the outside edge should be canted. (Your bootfitter can help you convert inches to degrees.)

If you are testing with old boots, be sure the soles aren't excessively worn or warped. Witherell and Evrard suggest checking this way: Set the boot on a flat surface, like a countertop, and tip it slightly on edge. Let it rock back to center. If the sole is smooth and even, the boot will quickly settle. If warped, it will continue to rock. Your bootfitter can plane the bottom so that it lies flat.

Also, if you're using old boots, leave in custom footbeds and other bootfitting aids before you measure. Remove any devices added for canting purposes, but adjust the cuff alignment if this feature comes with the boot. Do the same with new boots.

Canting also can be determined quickly and accurately in the shop by any number of measuring devices and a technician's trained eye. Shops charge $15-$25 for this, but usually roll the costs into the labor fee. Like the Princess and the Pea, the tiniest change under your feet can be felt in your entire alignment!

Once your bootfitter calculates the degree of canting for each foot, a thin plastic wedge is fitted under the binding plate. Special screws secure the material and the bindings to the skis. Done properly, the placement of cants does not interfere with binding-release mechanisms.

A wedge under the binding is the most common method of canting. Sanding or planing boot soles is another, enabling racers and those who use a variety of skis to switch without having to cant each pair. Interchangeable, cantable boot soles is a third method employed by DaleBoot, the only American-made ski boot.

### It's a snap

In 1996 DaleBoot introduced a do-it-yourself mail order kit for those in search of a perfect ski boot fit. When you order liners that can be molded to your foot, ankle and calf in a unique "Heat Fit Skin System" and appropriate shells (unisex), you can also order a plumb bob and directions for determining canting requirements. After you receive your boots and canting kit, send back the removable boot soles and your canting chart, and you will get a new pair of adjusted soles that easily snap onto your completely customized ski boots. Boots and canted soles purchased in this way cost about $450.

Additionally, the interchangeable sole combined with the revolutionary new material used for padding in the liner are expected to extend the life of a pair of DaleBoots, claims Mel Dalebout, who invented the boots 27 years ago. "If someone buys a pair, they can depend on the fit lasting 10 years," he says.

### To cant or not to cant

Is canting really necessary?

Let me answer that question with another: Why ski with a handicap? In Chapter Three you learned that perfect alignment is the overall principle in ski instruction. From beginners to World Cup racers, alignment makes skiing *easier* and *smoother*. Women, especially, should use every mechanical advantage in order to maximize ability. Bootfitting services, custom footbeds and canting, will give you the edge you need to become a more powerful, dynamic skier.

If you wanted to become a gourmet cook, you would not settle for flimsy pans or dull knives, would you? If you want to be a gourmet *skier*, look beyond the basics. These small additions to your ski-equipment cupboard will propel you to a higher level of harmony in skiing.

The Witherell-Evrard recipe:
- Awareness and assessment
- Custom insoles
- Fore/aft balance
- Cuff alignment
- Canting

Your bootfitter can do it all — usually for less than $200.

Participants of the 1994 Technique Weeks for Women at Beaver Creek learned the value of equipment enhancement. Following a bootfitting "chalk talk," those without custom footbeds (more than half) were fitted for them, nearly one third bought new boots, all had their boot cuffs adjusted, and all but one said they experienced a break-through in their skiing as a result!

## Poles

Buying ski poles used to hold as much excitement as buying car tires. Until recently, a pole was just a pole. The latest generation of poles use a composition of materials (carbon, Kevlar, graphite and fiberglass) lighter and stronger than aluminum, which allows for slimmer shafts. This adds another dimension to the selection process. Composites come in slender, almost pencil-thin diameters as well as traditional (16-18 mm) size. Goode Technologies, which makes composites exclusively, maintain they are to aluminum what aluminum was to bamboo. The company claims its newest generation of material, Vylon, makes its poles lighter and two times stronger than aluminum, and more durable. Skiers say composites provide better shock absorption for their wrists and arms because of the shaft's ability to bend.

In the store, compare the lighter, slender models with standard size aluminum ones. Notice the swing weight and springiness of the composites.

Expect to pay $40 to $155 for poles, aluminum to composite. The stronger and lighter the materials, the higher the price.

To determine pole size, turn the pole upside down with the handle resting on the floor. Grab the shaft so the basket is resting on top of your hand. If your lower arm is parallel with the floor, the pole is the right length. Poles that are too long will cause you to sit back. If yours need to be shorter, do not buy a new pair. Poles can easily be cut down to size by your technician.

### Grips 'n' tips

Poles with straps proved to be better than the strapless grip popular a few years ago. Many women are unsure about how to hold a pole while skiing. The correct way to hold a pole is as follows:

• Insert your hand *up* through the strap, letting it hang on your wrist.

• Wrap your palm around the handle and the top of the strap so the loop supports your wrist for a sturdy pole plant.

Some companies sell poles with special gloves that clip onto the grip, eliminating the strap. Others come with adjustable-height grips that screw up and down for skiing various terrain. Try out poles while wearing your gloves or mittens to be sure the grip feels comfortable.

Tips can be the rounded button kind or a spiked ice tip. Ice tips obviously are made for ice and rock hard snow. But they can be weapons and tear clothing. Unless you ski often on those conditions, you probably do not need them.

Painted surface finishes will scratch off of your poles; anodized graphics become part of the metal — like a tattoo — and will not fade or wear off.

Ski poles are the most abused piece of ski equipment. People toss them into the trunks of their cars, weigh them down with luggage and bang them with a vengeance across their ski boot as though they were smashing a poisonous snake. Then they wonder why their poles are bent. A crooked pole will make a crooked pole plant.

To remove snow from your boot, a gentle tap on the side of the boot with the hard rubber handle of the pole will usually do it. For snow packed under your boot, Skizone makes a pole basket that doubles as a boot scraper.

Sno-Terminator ski boot scrapers attach to the top of your skis just behind the binding. They provide a little door mat to wipe your boots clean before entering the bindings. Ask for these products in ski shops.

## Bindings

The original purpose of bindings was to secure the foot to the ski. Then foot-release mechanisms were installed for safety, followed by step-in, step-out convenience and ski brakes. Binding manufacturers have even invented ways to affect the way a ski performs. All six binding companies — ESS, Look, Marker, Rossignol, Salomon, Tyrolia — have developed specialized, mechanical, underfoot plates designed to enhance ski performance by affecting flex, increasing rebound, or dampening vibrations.

Racers know that riser plates (spacers about three-eighths of an inch thick) placed under the bindings lift them higher off the ski to create more leverage. Now women are finding them to be an uplifting experience. Ask your ski tech about adding them to your binding system, or check out bindings with this additional boost.

When purchasing bindings, ask about these features. If they do not interest you, do not pay extra money to get them.

Binding release systems have nearly wiped out boot-top injuries to the lower leg, such as the spiral fracture of the tibia I sustained in 1969. But a new type of injury — tears of the anterior cruciate ligament in the knee — have become epidemic. New data shows that bindings do not release in *80 percent* of all falls resulting in these injuries. Now Salomon addresses that critical issue with the Spheric, a new binding innovation that facilitates boot release on a new, third axis — down and outside — as needed for the type of falls associated with knee ligament tears and pulls in recreational skiers. Spheric technology made its debut in 1996 on 10 models.

ESS is the first fore and aft movable binding — ideal for women who want to experiment with moving their center of mass forward on the ski, as we talked about earlier. It can be adjusted in a few seconds, without tools, on the ski slope. Small adjustments allow you to find the "sweet spot" for binding location that provides the best ski performance in various snow conditions.

Marker's Selective Control system allows the binding to be flicked into three different positions for skiing soft snow and powder, packed and groomed surfaces, and hard snow and ice. Skiers I know who use this device love it, and sales of the SC system continue to flourish.

## Dis, dat and DIN

Your weight, height, age and skiing personality determine bindings best for you based on the DIN (Deutsch Industrial Norm) scale. DIN numbers correspond to the torque needed to jar the boot out of the toe piece of the binding. For example, racing bindings designed to release under racing stresses, may have a DIN range of 5 to 14. Beginner bindings and those for light-weight adults can have a DIN range from 2.5 to 9. A typical high performance binding ranges from 4 to 12. Standard is around 3 to 10. The higher the top DIN number, the more expensive the binding. Buy only what you need.

All binding companies make at least one model with a lower DIN-setting range for lighter weight adults and women. These cost from $150-$225.

NOTE: Shop for ski equipment early in the season when stores are well-stocked and sales staffs are enthused. If price is a consideration, shop the late-summer, early-fall or end-of-season sales. Choices will be limited, but you will find outstanding buys on the previous season's stuff, from socks to skis. Be careful not to compromise what you really need for less appropriate equipment at a cheap price.

## When to replace equipment

### Skis

Like all good things, the life of your skis must end. But look at the bright side. You are not losing your favorite boards, you are gaining a pair of rock skis.

You will know your skis are dead when:
- they lose their camber and spring.*
- they require more effort to turn.
- the bases show wear impossible to repair.
- the bases have been ground "to the bone."
- your technician tells you they're shot.

*If you can't tell loss of camber by skiing, stand the skis base to base as you would to carry them. Decambered skis fit together flat like books on a shelf with little room to insert a finger in the space between them at the center. New skis form a gap about an inch wide. (It varies from model to model.) Notice the size of the space when you buy your next pair. Watch for a decrease. This is especially important if you buy used skis. Make sure the camber has not been used too.

## Boots

After reading this far, you might be thinking about replacing your boots just to get a proper fit for better performance — a very good reason. Other reasons for buying new boots are the following:

• you find yourself saying, "I love my boots — they feel like bedroom slippers."

• your bootfitter can't help you regain that nice, tight fit everywhere.

• the shell breaks or stress cracks appear, usually on the front of the ankle.

• the bottoms of the soles are worn out or warped (from walking on hard surfaces).

• your technician tells you they're shot.

## Boot liners

If your shell is in good shape, but the liner has packed out, think about a replaceable liner. Most manufacturers keep some liners available for upper-end model boots. Check with any retailer that carries your brand of boot, or call the manufacturer's customer-service department. The liners wholesale for $75-$85; retail mark-up varies.

Better yet, *custom* replacement innerboots can be formed to *your* feet. They are the perfect solution for people with lumps and bumps and odd-shaped calves or feet.

Raichle's Thermoflex liner has won praise from both consumers and bootfitters because of its comfort, fit and warmth. The innovative liner can be custom molded and remolded from the top of the cuff to the toe, filling in all the little places and spaces of your foot, ankle and calf. A heat process similar to one used for forming custom insoles is used in fitting this liner, which can be installed in any front- or mid-entry boot. Alone, it retails for about $170. It also comes standard in several models of Raichle ski boots.

Rossignol makes a similar thermal molded liner, Comfor'Fit, which comes in a woman's model ($179), and an injected silicone liner, Sil'Foam ($349) for intermediate to expert recreational skiers.

Buying a new liner might be an interim solution while you are waiting for manufacturers to make that magic boot for women. Call distributors to find a store near you that carries them. (Numbers are listed at the end of Chapter Five.)

Also, such things as buckle parts and power straps can be replaced on ski boots.

## Bindings

Long before the first run of each season, make sure your bindings work. Bring your skis and boots to your ski shop for a preseason boot/binding inspection. The technician will test the release and retention mechanisms and check all components. If they fail the test, you will need to buy.

# TECH TALK
## A SKI PRIMER

If you do not want to get buried in an avalanche of ski technology, these terms, courtesy of *Ski Tech* magazine, will help you become an informed skier.

**ABS:** A tough, resilient plastic used for the sidewalls, topskins and caps of some skis.

**Cap:** The latest ski construction genre in which the top and sides of the ski are covered by a seamless cap running from one edge to the other, tip to tail. Caps play different roles in different skis, from a simple way to finish and seal the ski to an essential structural element.

**Camber:** The "arch" under the middle of a ski between the tip and tail that distributes a skier's weight evenly over the ski. Reverse camber allows the ski to rebound after being pressured into contact with the snow.

**Carbon fiber:** Used for strength in skis as an additive in fiberglass cloth. Lighter and stiffer than fiberglass or metal but very expensive. Very strong in both tension and compression.

**Core:** Usually made of wood or foam, the core is the raw element around which the rest of the ski is built and in most skis the core's shape affects flex and weight. In skis that use a structural, load-bearing cap, the core plays a less significant role. While wood is the most common core, foam is increasingly being used either as the first basic building block or injected into the ski later in the construction process.

**Dampening:** The tendency of a ski to absorb vibration. Today most high-end skis (as well as boots and bindings) include some element designed to reduce vibration that fatigues skiers and hinders performance on hard snow. Some companies include a rubbery layer running the length of a ski in or below the core. Others use rubber or metal pieces in different spots along the ski, like the tip and tail.

**Extruded base:** One of two different ways to produce polyethylene bases. More dense with smaller molecules, extruded bases are easier to repair but wear faster and hold less wax.

**Foam:** Usually polyurethane, the foam in cores of high end skis is durable, lighter than wood and does not compress. In lower-end skis, foam is usually injected into a molded cap-type ski or mixed with other materials to form a light, inexpensive core.

**Kevlar:** An aramid fiber with very high strength and low weight. Excellent dampening qualities and toughness.

**Laminate:** A ski constructed of multiple layers of one or more materials glued to a core of wood or foam. Also called "sandwich construction."

**Longitudinal flex:** The lengthwise bend of a ski which creates the shape of the turn when pressure is applied. Usually a soft-flexing shovel will initiate quicker, slalom-type turns; a stiffer flex is better for longer-radius giant slalom-type turns.

**Shovel:** The curved up part of the front of a ski.

**Sidecut:** The hourglass shape of a ski from tip to tail. The more pronounced the sidecut, the greater the ski's short turn capability. A lesser sidecut will make a longer turning arc.

**Sintered base:** A high grade polyethylene base with longer, tougher molecules that hold more wax, usually found on high performance skis.

**Titanal/Titanium alloy:** Has the same stiffness as aluminum but is considerably more resistant to permanent bending.

**Torsion Box:** A ski construction method entailing wrapping a stiff material around the core. Some companies use wet, resin-soaked fiberglass cloth as a wrap; others use cloth impregnated with partially cured resin. The method results in very strong, flexible and durable construction.

**Torsional Flex:** The sideways twist of a ski. A torsionally stiff ski has a greater tendency to hold and turn on hard snow as the tip and tail grab more than a torsionally soft ski, which tends to be more forgiving.

**Waist:** The narrowest part of the ski just behind the mid-line and under the foot.

# TECH TALK
## A BOOT PRIMER

Do not buy ski boots without knowing their ins and outs. Read this glossary, courtesy of Jeff Rich and *SKI* maga-zine. Rich is a board-certified pedorthist, president of Custom Sports Lab in New York and chief faculty for the STN/SKI Master Boot Fit University for professional bootfitters.

## Shell Designs —

**External Tongue:** A three-piece shell similar to an overlap boot but with easier entry and exit. Buckles close over a plastic tongue hinged at the toe to reduce interior boot volume.

**Mid-Entry:** A hybrid of front-entry and rear-entry, combining overlap closure with mechanical fit adjustment devices. Many employ a release lever or button on the rear spine, allowing the cuff to splay open for easy entry, exit and walking.

**Monoshell:** A two-piece overlap shell in which the walls of the lower shell rise almost as high as the upper cuff. The shell parts are virtually locked together, creating a stiff, responsive flex.

**Overlap:** Also called a *traditional* shell, this is usually a two-piece boot in which the cuff section wraps over itself and the top part of the lower shell; the lower shell closes down over the instep and forefoot, reducing volume within the boot between the shell, innerboot and foot.

**Rear-Entry:** These shells can fit a wide variety of feet because they generally have more interior space than traditional boots. To duplicate the retention achieved by buckles in front-entry designs, rear entries employ various fit adjustments. A series of cables attached to plates push or pull the innerboot down and back from the interior wall of the shell to hug the foot. Rear-entry boots are usually more comfortable and easier to put on and take off.

## Innerboot Designs —

Innerboots or liners use a combination of materials and densities of foam padding to balance each skill level's need for response with comfort. Softer foam is used in sensitive areas near the forefoot, around ankle protrusions and the instep. More responsive, high-density foams, stiffeners or support pads are used in critical areas, such as behind the ankle, front of the shin, and under the heel where a snug fit is necessary. Novice and recreational boots often use softer foam to make the boot more comfortable and less responsive to foot movements.

## Innerboot Features —

**Flex Gussets:** Channels or grooves embedded into inner-boots around the ankles and over the instep to allow the innerboot to flex without creasing or bunching.

**Injection Molding:** Innerboots constructed by stretching a lining material and sometimes foam pieces over a last inside a mold. A soft polyurethane is then injected and left to cure. The construction yields a warm, virtually leak-proof innerboot.

**Lasted:** Innerboots made by stretching high-density foam padding and quality component parts by hand over a last (mold) and sewing them together. Seams are sealed with a waterproof material. The longer an innerboot is left on a last, the better it conforms to its shape.

**Preformed:** These innerboots are usually found in less expensive boots. They use precut foam padding and less expensive component parts. They are sewn together by machine inside out and then flipped back to obtain the shape. Seams on preformed innerboots are sometimes left unsealed and are prone to leaks and cold.

## Fit/Performance Adjustments and Features —

**Achilles tendon volume reducer:** A device that hugs the heel pocket to reduce heel lift during forward flexion.

**Adjustable Arch:** A foot support system that raises or lowers an arch pad built into the shellbed. Eliminates voids beneath the arch for better foot-to-ski response.

**Cantable Soles:** A removable sole that tilts the sole to align and support the foot and lower leg in the correct position for edging the ski.

**Cuff Cant:** Used to correct a bowlegged or knock-kneed condition. Mechanical device adjusts the boot's cuff angle, pushing or pulling the outside of the shell from the ankle area to follow the contour of the lower leg. A *dual cant* adjusts from both the inside and outside of the shell. Since the lower leg shape never changes, the cant need be set only once and should be done by a professional fitter.

**Footbed:** Not to be confused with shellbed, this is a soft, flexible prefabricated bed upon which the foot sits inside the innerboot. Also called *insole.*

**Forefoot Volume Adjuster:** Usually found in rear-entry boots, it secures the forefoot for more responsive control. Some devices merely lower a plate onto the forefoot to restrict movement. More sophisticated systems wrap the foot while drawing it to the inside of the shell to concentrate turning forces over the ski's edges.

**Forward Flex Adjuster:** A device that changes a boot's flex resistance. Numerous methods are used including springs in rear housings, block-in-channel devices located over the instep and cam-type regulators on top of front cuffs. When buying a boot, determine how important adjustable forward flex is to you and how often you think you will want to change it. Also note that some systems offer infinitely adjustable flex while others, like the cant system, offer only a few choices.

**Heel Height Adjuster:** A mechanical device that raises or lowers the height of the shellbed to reduce volume between foot and shell. It can also increase the shellbed angle, increasing forward lean.

**Instep Fit or Volume:** Refers to the space between the shell and foot above the instep. Volume in rear-entry boots is usually controlled by tensioning a cable or strap attached to a flexible, molded plastic plate between the shell and innerboot from the top of the instep to just before the toe box. The plate is designed to evenly distribute the pressure created during closure and draw the foot down and back into the innerboot heel pocket.

**Instep Flap:** In overlap boots, a plastic flap riveted to the lower shell above a cutout on the instep of the shell. Provides increased lateral stiffness and power transmission while permitting easy entry and exit.

**Shellbed:** A sloping, rigid foam insert that rests between the innerboot and bottom of the shell and runs from heel to toe. Serves as insulation and provides forward lean.

**Rear Spoiler:** A wedge between the shell's rear cuff and innerboot. Used to create additional forward lean and reduce excess cuff volume for thin lower legs.

**Power Strap:** A strap that wraps around the top of the innerboot or shell cuff to keep it snug to the leg and increase boot-to-ski sensitivity.

---

# TECH TALK
## HOW A SKI WORKS

I believe one factor inhibiting women's skiing is simply lack of knowledge of how skis work. Many of us aren't interested in physics, and few salespeople take time to offer an explanation. Consider the shape of the ski. It has an hourglass figure: narrow at the waist, widest at the shovel and wide again at the tail, sort of like a spoon. When a spoon sits on a table, only the bowl and the end of the handle touch the surface, while the middle arches above it. In a ski, this arc is called *camber*. If you press on the spoon just below the bowl, you can flatten the arc so the entire length of the spoon is touching the table. In a ski, this is called *decambering* or *reverse camber*. Now if you put the ski with its wide-narrow-wide sidecut on edge and bend it into reverse camber, the entire edge will follow a curved trajectory led by the tip of the ski. It has to. The harder you press, the more of an arc you make in the snow. This how you vary turn shape and get control.

Quite simple, really.

It is easy to understand why women, if they do not have the body weight and flexibility in their boot cuffs to pressure the ski into reverse camber, can't get results.

With improved materials and technology, skis practically ski themselves. Skiing can be more relaxed and natural. Pat Campbell, assistant director of the Jackson Hole Ski School, says today's style of skiing evolved in part because of the advance in technology of boots and skis. "The basic skills have been same throughout the years," she says. "Balance is the overriding skill. Then you've got steering, edging, and pressure. With changes in equipment, the emphasis of skills has changed. Now there's a *blend* of the steering, edging, and pressure." She explains in the past we needed more steering in turn initiation because we could not edge as early. "The skis were stiffer and didn't bend like they do now," she recalls. "The leather boots with a low cuff didn't offer as much support in the lower leg, so we had to use more pressure and edge at the bottom of a turn. Now boots are a lot stiffer, so we can edge and pressure earlier and with more support throughout the turn."

*Chapter Summary:*
With hundreds of skis, boots, poles and bindings on the market, choosing the right ski equipment without being prepared can be nearly impossible. To be an informed buyer, study the buyer's guides of ski magazines, learn the terms, talk to knowledgeable salespeople in specialty ski shops. Then, determine your skiing personality and match it with the appropriate models.

The mystery in buying boots can be solved with the help of a good bootfitter. In this chapter, you learned how to find one and what to expect when selecting boots. You learned more about custom insoles, cuff alignment and canting, and how to assess canting needs.

---

*Product information:*
**COMPU-FIT** — To order a F.I.T. Ski-Boot Analysis Kit, send $29.95 or a Visa or MasterCard number and expiration date, with your name, address and phone number to: Foot Image Technology, P.O. Box 5475, Bend OR 97708-5475; or call (541) 389-8844; FAX (541) 389-1707.

**DaleBoot USA** — 2150 So. 3rd West, Salt Lake City, UT 84115; (801) 487-3649; FAX (801) 487-3880.

**Skizone** pole-basket boot scraper — 45 North Phyllis St., Suite 213, Mesa, AZ 85201; (602) 461-1936; FAX (602) 461-1907.

**Sno-Terminator** — distributed by Bolle America, Inc., 3890 Elm St., Denver, CO 80207; (303) 321-4300; FAX (303) 321-6952.

## Chapter Eight

# Whistle a happy tune

---

*"I've never felt I was a good enough skier to buy and take care of my own skis."*
— *Gloria, age 47 from Colorado*

*"I don't think it's anything special to have your own stuff."*
— *Marina, age 43 from Holland*

*"Equipment doesn't really matter. To me, equipment is equipment."*
— *Anonymous, age 21 from Texas*

---

In Chapter Seven you learned the importance of finding a good specialty ski shop, one that deals primarily in ski goods and has a full-time, knowledgeable, dedicated staff. You are in luck if a full-time, knowledgeable, dedicated ski technician works in the same shop.

A good ski tech is like your auto mechanic. You visit on a regular basis, pop in when you need a quick fix, get the inside story about new products and advice on upgrading. And, yes, occasionally you can blame your technician when you are not skiing well. Get close. After all, you are trusting this person with your life!

A good ski tech will keep your skis as smooth as a baby's bottom, the edges as sharp as a good kitchen knife, and the bindings as clean and as finely tuned as your car's engine.

"A well-tuned ski is a safe ski," says Rick Roberts, a veteran ski tuner.

---

Some people find their technicians close to home. Others take their equipment to a shop at the resort where they ski most of the time. How do you find the good ones? Ask around. You will probably end up with more names of shops *not* to go to, but keep asking.

Ask men. The reality is that men are more into the mechanics of skiing than women. Ask a good male skier who skis 30 times or more a year. Ask a man or woman who races — someone who loves competition and is serious about skiing. A racer's skill and a technician's knowledge are important elements of a winning team.

## Ski tuning is a guy thing

Right now there just are not many woman ski technicians. (If there were, would backshops take down those revealing Lange Women posters?)

Nonetheless, Olga Jones, 29, who lives in Telluride, has been tuning skis since her high school racing days in New Hampshire, even though she found shops put her to the test to see if she knew what she claimed.

"They were very discriminating," Jones recalls. "But I've always been able to prove myself. I've had to work harder than the guys to get into the industry."

Jones is confident she is as good as the next man. "I know what I am doing. I can do this job and be willing to learn what's new on the market and learn the mechanical end of it."

Here is advice to other women looking for backshop jobs: Be dedicated and determined. Find a shop that is open-minded, and that has invested in good equipment.

"They're out there. They're hard to find, but they're there," Jones says.

This is good advice for female consumers as well. A shop employing a woman ski tuner, a hard-goods saleswoman and "bootfitter*ess*" may be more supportive of women who want to take responsibility for their own skiing, rather than hand over equipment maintenance to husbands and boyfriends.

But if you find a male tuner tuned in to your needs, bake him cookies and follow him anywhere!

## What to look for in the backshop

• *Experience and certification*

When shopping for your personal ski tech, find someone who demonstrates *experience* and provides *certification.*

Binding manufacturers require technicians to attend clinics and pass a certification exam in order to work on their products. Procedures must be followed and paperwork completed for each job so that manufacturers can protect the ski shops from liability claims.

Some shops, particularly those in large sporting goods chains, hire part-time schoolkids to work under a certified manager. I am all for teenagers having jobs, but on busy days it is doubtful the manager can be looking over every shoulder.

And, when holes are drilled into the wrong place on your favorite skis, the mistake is permanent. Three holes and you are out: Safety standards allow only three pairs of holes in skis, whether it is intentional for three pairs of bindings, or whether it is carelessness.

If a tech does make a mistake drilling your skis, the shop might replace the skis, but you will wonder about other blunders you cannot see.

Holes for new bindings were once drilled in my skis so close to the old ones that on one ski they ran together when I was skiing. A screw popped out — and so did my foot. I was not hurt when I fell, but I was furious. When I went back to the shop, the tech just drilled another set of holes. I trashed the skis because I did not know enough then to demand a new pair.

• *Up-to-date machinery and tools*

You pay serious money for skis, boots, bindings and poles ($1,000 and up), so you want a serious ski tech to work on them. A tuner uses machines for stone-grinding, and files, stones and sandpaper for hand finishing. Dull tools and poorly maintained machines can ruin your investment. Montana and Winterstieger make the top-of-the-line stone grinders, but the machinery is only as good as its operator. When you watch a ski pass through the grinder like dough through a pasta machine, you realize the importance of the hands that guide it.

• *Good working environment*

A sloppy work area with poor lighting and bad ventilation can also indicate a slipshod operation. Check it out when you are at the counter. Sometimes it is not possible to see the backshop at all, so you must rely on what others tell you about the service.

## What to expect from your tech

Times you should visit your technician are the following:
  • Installation of a boot/binding system
  • Preseason binding and boot inspection
  • Repairs and tunes
  • Rentals and demos

When installing new bindings to new or old skis, checking bindings or releasing rental and demo equipment the shop should take these steps:

• *Check to make sure boots are compatible with the bindings.*

All boots and bindings are compatible; however, when fitting old boots to new or rental/demo bindings, the technician may find a warped or worn out sole, which inhibits binding function and prevents the brake from engaging. On the flip side, new boots may not work with old bindings.

At the bottom of the toe piece of the binding is a Teflon or metal pad called the anti-friction device. Its surface should be clean and smooth. If it is torn or pitted, this could interfere with the release of the binding. These pads are easily replaced. Ask your ski tech.

• **Install the bindings on the skis and adjust the boots to the bindings.** If you want your new bindings placed forward on the skis to compensate for your lower center of mass, or if you want a riser plate installed, this is the time to tell the technician.

• **Determine binding-release settings.** This is important! Your *honest* input about height, weight, skiing ability and age helps your ski tech calculate the binding setting so that it can release in a fall and free your foot from the ski.

The comment I hear most from the rental and repair guys is that they suspect women "fudge" about their weight. This is no time to lie — nobody in the rental shop cares!

If you have gained or lost significantly over the summer, or if you are pregnant, your DIN setting needs changing. If it is a new binding, be truthful! An error in the setting will increase risk of injury.

You must also *accurately* assess your skiing ability. The International Standard Organization uses the following guide for skier types:

TYPE I SKIERS
• ski conservatively.
• prefer slower speeds.
• prefer easy, moderate slopes.
• favor lower than average release/retention settings.
• Type I settings apply to entry-level skiers uncertain of classification.

## TYPE II SKIERS
- ski moderately.
- prefer a variety of speeds.
- ski on varied terrain, including most difficult trails.
- do not meet descriptions of either Type I or III.

## TYPE III SKIERS
- ski aggressively.
- usually ski fast.
- prefer steeper, more challenging terrain.
- favor higher-than-average release/retention settings.

Once you decide which type fits your skiing style, the technician applies it along with your height, weight, age and boot-sole length, to the binding-adjustment chart to assign a recommended DIN setting.

If you prefer a DIN setting different from the one prescribed, you can change it yourself by turning the screws on the front of the toe piece and on the back of the heel piece.

Depending on shop policy, some technicians will adjust it for you, if you sign a release waiving liability. Others will provide a workbench and screwdriver but refuse to do it, rightly so. The last person to touch the setting is responsible if you crash and burn, injuring yourself because the binding failed to release.

If a skier is 50 or older, the tech is required to move up the chart one skier code, lessening the tension of the binding. But this may be too loose for a very aggressive, all-terrain skier older than 50.

This happened to my friend who nearly killed himself on a steep run at Snow King in Wyoming. Someone changed the DIN setting when his skis were tuned at a shop in Denver, apparently trying to match it to chart requirements. He is a big man, older than 50, and he keeps his DIN setting a notch or two high.

When he set a hard edge at the top of a steep section of trail, both bindings released, sending him on a slide that left him tangled in plastic fencing, which stopped him from slamming into a tree. His face was badly cut. Miscommunication was the culprit in this instance. Now, he never skis without first checking the DIN window!

• *Inspect each component of the ski/boot/binding system.* There is a safety check list for boots, skis, binding toe piece, binding heel piece and ski brakes. A good technician should not sign off on equipment without components in optimum working order.

## Tuning

Tuning prepares and repairs skis. As a rule, shops *do not* check binding and brake function with a tune, but you can ask if you are nervous about it. These terms will help you communicate with your ski technician:

• *Stone grinding* — a machine method of smoothing and buffing ski bottoms.

• *P-tex* — a polyethylene material that coats the base and fills gouges.

• *Bevel* — edges ground at an angle.

• *Edge geometry* — angles at which the bottom and side of the metal edge are ground to each other.

• *De-tune* — when the edge of the ski at its tip and tail is dulled rather than sharpened, to prevent skis from catching in the turn.*

• *Convex* — a base higher than the edges.

• *Concave* — a base lower than the edges.

• *Railed* — edges raised completely above the base.

The last three conditions are *not* what you want on your ski bottoms.

A *full tune,* which costs between $25 and $40, includes stone grinding, P-tex application, sharpening the metal edges, de-tuning tips and tails* and coating the bottoms with fresh wax.

A *quick tune,* or mini tune, costs from $10 to $20, and usually means sharpening and waxing. Some shops will do everything in a quick tune that is included in a full tune except P-tex the base.

Sometimes, burrs or rough spots will form on the edges of skis. You can feel them if you run your finger along the metal. (You also can rub a wadded tissue along the edge. The tissue will catch on the burrs.) Instead of paying for a full sharpening, which you may not need, buy a small tuning stone at a specialty ski shop and remove the burrs yourself. I carry a stone in my ski bag with all my other junk and buff my ski edges just as I file my nails when they get scraggly.

Depending on snow conditions, skis should be fully tuned every 10-12 times you ski and quick tuned every five. Skis need more tunes and sharper edges for hard packed, icy conditions. Softer snow is easier on skis.

If you gouge the bottom of only one ski, bring the other one with it to the shop. Skis should be repaired and tuned as a pair, never separately.

Check your tune when you pick up your skis. Scrape a fingernail across the metal edge next to the binding. If it does not skim off a little nail powder or polish, it is not going to hold well on hard-packed snow. Ask for more sharpening. Run a fingernail up the base. If you do not scrape off a little wax, ask for more. Don't be intimidated. You are paying for a service. Treat it like a dry cleaner.

Occasionally, you run into ski-shop guys with an attitude. One year, while staying at a well-known resort, I sent my skis to the shop for a mini-tune as part of guest services at the lodge. The tune was lousy.

When I called to tell them the edges needed more sharpening, the young man shot back, "I think I am a better judge of that than you."

I am sure if it had been a man's voice on my end he would have offered to re-sharpen the skis, no questions asked. When I spoke to the manager, he apologized, sent the skis back to the technician, and offered me a complimentary tune the day I left.

To protect your freshly tuned ski bottoms, hook them back-to-back with Velcro holders that slip between the skis to keep them from scraping together and make them more sturdy to carry. Ask for them in ski shops or call Reliable Racing at 800-223-4448.

*NOTE: Warren Witherell believes skiers who are properly canted and whose ski bases are flat should *not* de-tune the tips and tails. "De-tuned skis do not make good, carved turns," he says. Shops routinely de-tune skis and bevel edges because customers ask for it. Witherell says 90 percent of skiers are over-canted (on the inside edges) and have trouble with skis "grabbing" the snow. So they blame it on sharp edges. De-tuning serves as a band-aid to the problem. The real solution is fix the alignment and leave the skis sharp. "Virtually all skis are made to perform best with the edges sharp all the way to both ends," Witherell says.

## Preventative maintenance

Doc Tully, a long-time ski technician, says if you are good to your skis, they'll be good to you. As with your car, a few common-sense practices on your part will help you keep your equipment and your turns in good shape.

### Skis

*Rust* can accumulate on the edges of your skis and *dirt* will build up in the base.

Skis can rust when they are stored in a damp place like a basement. Dirt of the plain household variety can be absorbed into an *uncovered* ski.

The best place for summer storage is in a ski bag kept in a room or garage with moderate temperature and minimum dust. (And do not hang skis by the tips; it can affect their camber.)

Before covering skis for storage, run a bar of paraffin down the edges or have your ski tech apply a coat of wax on the bottoms without scraping them. This will seal the bases from the elements during the off season.

Another problem is *de-lamination* of the ski base, which is caused by water seeping into gouges and unfilled holes. This can be serious, especially if the holes are near the metal edge, which can expand from freezing water and then separate from the base. You can prevent this if you glance at the bottoms of your skis after every ski day and, if you notice any deep scrapes, get them filled with P-tex right away.

Waxing your skis does more than make you go fast. A properly waxed ski will not stick to snow and will turn with improved control. The base will glide better and last longer. Oxidation from abrasion, air and sunlight can cause a white discoloration on the bottoms of skis. This means the bases are drying out and need wax. Water your plants ... wax your skis, advises tuner Rick Roberts.

You will not have skis to keep healthy if they get stolen. Always split your skis when storing them on racks or in the snow at lunch break. A single ski will not be as likely to be taken as a pair. A ski lock really keeps them safe. A cable combo lock costs about $15. To order, call Tognar Toolworks at (916) 926-2600 or FAX (800) 926-9904.

## Bindings

The heel piece of the binding attracts dirt, especially if you carry your skis in a car ski rack. Keeping the bindings closed, or better yet, covering them with a waterproof nylon binding cover will prevent road grime and salt from getting inside the binding mechanisms. Always transport skis inside your car if there is room. Snap bindings shut when not in use.

For air travel, I stuff clothes in the ski bag to keep my skis from banging around inside and wrap towels around the bindings to protect the brakes during handling. The last thing you want on your first morning out is ski repairs.

At the end of the season, you should release the pressure of the binding by unscrewing the DIN setting.

This will prevent the spring from becoming fatigued over months of non-use. Do not forget to reset it in the fall!

## Boots

*Shells* — Plastic has memory. Keeping your boots buckled while not in use will help them retain their shape. As it is, women break enough nails spreading the hard plastic shell open. Do not make it worse by letting the plastic have a mind of its own.

The sun can dry and eventually crack the shells. To prevent this kind of damage, clean shells with warm, soapy water applied with a soft cloth. Then spray with silicone. This also helps with snow sticking to boot soles. If you find a crack, a technician might be able to stop it from spreading temporarily, but be prepared to invest in a new pair.

Periodically check all metal components like buckles, rivets and hinges. These small but crucial parts can loosen and/or rust. You can replace them, but tightening and cleaning them is cheaper. Apply a little WD40 to get them working smoothly.

Just as you avoid puddles when you are wearing your best evening shoes, avoid walking in your ski boots on hard surfaces like gravel or concrete. The wear and tear, plus dirt and gravel contamination of the soles, can cause the bindings to malfunction when they interface with the boots.

If you must walk on a surface other than packed snow, buy rubber walking soles. I use Cat Tracks, which clip onto the boots and protect the soles from deterioration and prevent slipping. (I've seen some nasty falls in icy parking lots.) Save the plastic wrapper so you can store them in your pocket or pack without getting road muck on your ski clothes. Cat Tracks become a necessity if you've had your boot soles shaved for canting. Scuffing the bottoms can skew the precise measurements.

*Liners* — Never buckle up boots for storage without allowing the liners to dry completely. This ensures warm, comfortable boots next time you put them on, and helps prolong their life by preventing bacteria build-up.

To dry, take the liners out of the shells at night. If you have trouble removing or putting them back in, Air Dry Systems makes two models of nifty portable dryers that dry boots and gloves simutaneously with circulating air. (Do not dry boots with a hair dryer. Hot air can melt insoles and break down materials.) The Air Puck ($45) and Turbo Air + ($65) are small enough to travel inserted in the boots. Home dryer units are also available for slightly more.

Sew loose seams and minor tears with heavy upholstery needles. Major rips and badly worn spots need repair from a boot technician.

Taking responsibility for your equipment puts *you* in charge of your skiing. The more knowledge you have about your skis, boots, bindings and poles translates into more control on the mountain. Try it ... you'll see!

## America's best ski shops

The following ski shops consistently have landed in the "top 50" list of *Snow Country* magazine for all three years of its existence. The stores were rated by readers in customer service, friendliness, bootfitting, imaginative merchandising and other categories. (Reprinted with permission from *Snow Country.*)

*Far West*
>  *Granite Chief*, Olympic Valley, Calif.
>  *Footloose Ski Shop*, Mammoth Lakes, Calif.
>  *Newport Ski Company*, Newport Beach, Calif.
>  *Sturtevant's Sports*, Bellevue, Wash.

*East*
>  *Cury's Sport Shop*, Ramsey, N.J.
>  *Langhorne Ski Shop*, Langhorne, Penn.
>  *Nestor's Warming Hut*, Whitehall, Penn.
>  *Ski Chalet*, Arlington, Va.
>  *Ski Center*, Washington D.C.
>  *Snow Country*, Rochester, N.Y.

*Midwest*
   ***Bill & Paul's Sporthaus***, Grand Rapids, Mich.
   ***Hoigaard's***, St. Louis Park, Minn.
   ***Ski Hut***, Duluth, Minn.
   ***Viking Ski Shop***, Chicago, Ill.

*New England*
   ***Aspen East***, Killington, Vt.
   ***Buchika's Ski & Sport***, Salem, N.H.
   ***Competitive Edge Ski & Bike***, Holyoke, Mass.

*Rocky Mountains*
   ***Boulder Ski Deals***, Boulder, Colo.
   ***Greenwood's Ski Haus***, Boise, Idaho
   ***Kenny's Double Diamond Ski Shop***, Vail, Colo.
   ***Jan's Mountain Outfitters***, Park City, Utah

*Chapter Summary:*
In this chapter you learned the value of a good ski
technician, where to find one and what to expect. We
covered how safety standards protect you, how to
determine your DIN setting, terms and times for ski
tuning and repair, and maintenance and storage of
equipment. You also learned where to find the best ski
shops in America.

*Recommended reading:*
***World Class Ski Tuning*** by Michael Howden (World Class Ski,
$12.95)
***Alpine Ski Maintenance*** by Seth Masia (Contemporary Books,
$9.95)

*Product Information:*
**Air Dry Systems** — P.O. Box 88, Broomfield, CO 80038-0088; 800-
237-6779; FAX 303-466-6260.

**Cat Tracks** — distributed by Seirus; Rocky Mountains: 2200 West Alexander, SLC, UT 84119; (801) 972-8849; Pacific: 9076 Carroll Way, San Diego, CA 92121; (619) 271-9797.

**Tognar Toolworks** catalog — the company carries mostly tuning tools, but also sells great little inventions for skiers, many of which I mention in this book. To order the catalog, which is chock full of useful information, call (916) 926-2600 or FAX (800) 926-9904.

**Reliable Racing** catalog — ditto for this company, which carries hard-to-find items for racers and recreational skiers. They also sell gift certificates. To order, call 800-223-4448 or FAX 800-585-4443.

Chapter Nine

# *The rental maze*

---

*"My boots were not only uncomfortable but really a misfit the first time I rented."*
— *Becky, age 42 from Colorado*

*"I'm so confused about equipment. I've gone to what I thought were reliable ski shops and I get a different story every time."* — *Judy, age 42 from California*

*"Women are numb. They assume others will mae decisions for them, so they've never had ro think about equipment."*
— *Betsy, 20-something from Colorado*

---

Most women know as much about renting ski equipment as they know about repairing their cars. Do not let rental shops fool you. From shop to shop and resort to resort, you will find great variances. Cost, quality and variety of rental packages are determined by the store's owner.

"There are no industry standards for renting," according to Mike Weber, of Mogul Mike's ski shops in Summit County, Colorado. "You just have to *trust* the shop."

"Trust me." Are these not the two most dreaded words a woman hears from a man? Yet women walk into rental shops and give themselves over to the mercy of the young men behind the counter.

Most rental staffs take the position, "What you do not know won't hurt you." Skiers, who do not bother to learn about equipment, can end up with ill-fitting boots and trashed-out skis. It is up to you to determine what you need and know what you are getting.

Jay Gump at Blue River Sports, a rental shop in Breckenridge, says fitting someone in rentals is not difficult. Before recommending equipment, he says, the rental tech should ask the customer about experience and skiing preferences, the same procedure as when the customer buys new products.

"After I talk to someone for only a few minutes I can tell what kind of skier they are," Gump says. "Sometimes it is just their tone of voice, sometimes it is their attitude."

Telling the truth about how and where you like to ski, and boot problems you have experienced, will help the rental clerk make a more accurate decision. If he or she shows an unwillingness to chat with you about your skiing, go to another shop.

Let us discuss what you need to know.

## Quality and variety

A rental package includes skis, boots and poles. If you are a never-ever, rent all three until you decide whether you are going to stick with skiing. Then buy intermediate-level equipment you can grow into as skills improve.

Traveling skiers often rent skis to avoid the hassle of baggage, and carry their own boots on the plane. Some people who ski only one week a year prefer to rent rather than invest in gear. Then there are skiers who want to sample new skis for fun or for serious comparative shopping.

Ski shops try to cover all the bases by carrying several classes of equipment. Categories can include *budget, standard, sport, high performance* and *demo,* or some variation of these.

What one shop calls standard, another might call budget, which can mean anything from two- to eight-year-old skis. Some shops use budget stock of old, untuned skis to sell upgrades to a standard category "for a few dollars more." Beware of how crummy the crummiest gear is! Do not request the standard or basic package. Find out what the range is and ask to see the equipment. Performance class is a good bet.

Dave's Ski Shops in Tahoe City and Truckee, California, carry a standard package of low-end equipment and a demo package. The demo class includes performance, high performance and exotic (no kidding!). Mogul Mike's keeps it simple: standard and high performance. Blue River Sports stocks recreation, deluxe, performance and competition.

(Refer to Chapter Seven about matching your skiing personality with ski and boot categories.)

## Boots

Skiing in rental boots is like walking in someone else's shoes — they may be your *size*, but they just do not fit right. Avoid it if you can.

If you must rent boots, everything you learned about buying boots and bootfitting should be applied. You will find fewer choices of models in rental boots and, in some cases, less quality. Shop owners carry easy-to-fit boots they know will offer the most comfort, but not necessarily the best performance. Boots on the low end of the rental scale are usually rear-entry models lacking any adjustments. Avoid these.

Even if you are a beginner, try to find boots with alignment features. It may be hard. Manufac-turers think lower-level skiers do not need boot adjustments. But starting off with proper align-ment, fit and comfort is as important for a skier as learning how to grip a racquet is for a tennis player.

Do not accept a boot that hurts or a cuff you can't bend. If you have to clamp down on the buckles to the point of pain to make the boots snug, go to another shop. An ill-fitting boot can ruin your day!

Wear or bring your own ski socks. The socks used for fitting boots in the rental shop may not be the same thickness as yours.

Ask lots of questions about fitting and alignment. I observed one woman step into a basic boot and say, "It is too big in the heel." The rental tech diverted her attention to her toes and never did address the heel problem. Worse, the woman neglected to bring it up again! She paid him, and went to try skiing in those improperly fitting boots. She has probably taken up golf.

Some shops that specialize only in rentals, such as Blue River Sports, offer excellent boot-fitting. They use pronation pads, arch supports and heel lifts to get it right, and they rent only new boots in all but their lowest packages.

If you find most rental boots too stiff, ask for women's boots. A specialty shop with a large inventory may carry them. Chances are they will flex easier and fit better too. Make sure the boots are new.

Some shops try to pass off older models as women's boots because the shell is a pastel color. Call them on it! Let them know *you* know the difference. Ask about woman-lasted liners, flexibility and cuff height. The reason most shops do not carry women's boots is because they claim there isn't enough demand. Let's create it!

## Skis

After you go through the initial Q&A drill, the rental tech will ask what length of ski you want. Women seem to be intimidated with anything longer than 170 cm. But remember, length is determined by weight, ability and type of ski, not your height.

Be honest about your weight and ability when it comes to filling out the form for your DIN setting. Every rental binding must be reset for each renter's requirements. (See Chapter Eight.)

You also should check the skis for a good tune. The bottoms of rental skis usually show plenty of wear and tear underneath the P-tex. But if they feel smooth and waxed, and the edges feel sharp, they'll do.

Managers and owners of most rental shops want their customers happy. A skier's comfort and enjoyment is at the mercy of their employees. But consumers must be reasonable, too.

Weber recalls a teenage girl at the start of a ski vacation asking for purple boots to match her skis. It happened that the purple boots were a terrible fit and, despite Weber's recommendations, she insisted the boots were for her.

"I know she must have been uncomfortable the whole vacation," Weber says. "We can recommend all day, but if the customer won't listen...."

## Poles

Rental poles are usually of one variety and your choices are limited. Refer to Chapter Seven for selecting the right length.

## Cost

Ski-area rental shops are more expensive than shops in ski towns, or cities removed from skiing. You pay for the convenience of not having to lug skis, boots and poles farther than, say, 20 yards. And you pay for the accessibility during the day that allows you to switch boots that are uncomfortable or skis that need sharper edges. But keep in mind ski-area rental shops maintain an assembly-line approach to fitting customers, due to sheer numbers. You might not get the personal attention you want and need.

The best time to line up equipment is the evening before you ski, when you are more likely to find someone who can help you through the process. Late morning, 10:30 or 11 a.m., and mid-afternoon, before the end of the ski day, are good times, too. Avoid Saturday and Sunday mornings.

Prices for rentals vary greatly. Where the lift ticket costs a lot, you can bet the rentals are high, too. Multi-day and multi-person rates are lower than single-day/one-person rates, and prices take a hike in high season. Sales tax is charged on rentals in states where applicable.

Damage deposits are covered with a credit-card imprint that the shop destroys when you return equipment intact. If you do not have a card, a driver's license normally will do.

## One call does it all

Arranging equipment needs by telephone is helpful, especially for families and large groups. Some resorts' central reservations will reserve rentals, and some shops provide 800 numbers. If you know exactly what you want, requesting in advance saves time and ensures you will get what you need.

You can also call National Sports Rental, "Your Winter Sports Concierge," at 800-765-2SKI. As the "FTD florist of ski rentals," NSR makes reservations for customers in major destination resorts throughout the U.S. and Canada. After spending three years setting up the system, owner George Koutsakis possesses a local's knowledge of the best shops.

Depending on the resort and the shop, Koutsakis charges an average of $10, $15 and $20 a day for three classes of equipment. A bulk rate is available for more people and days.

Each customer receives a confirmation of the order and a map showing the location of the shop. NSR asks questions to eliminate most chances of ill-fitting boots. If that does happen, the shop and NSR will find a replacement pair.

## Demo programs

Most retail shops offer the option of testing skis before buying, and then applying the cost of demos to the cost of new skis. This is an opportunity to match your skills with the right skis, but taking skis for a test drive can be tricky. Women say they have a hard time determining what makes a good run: Is it the skis, the snow, or the driver? Here are some rules to follow for the ideal demo:

• Watch for Demo Days at ski areas when the public can test skis from manufacturers' vans of inventory at the base. Same-day testing can also be done from ski-area rental or retail shops.

• Ski one long run on the same trail, the same day, on several pairs of skis. This way you can compare based on similar surface conditions.

• Pick a run with varied terrain to test how the skis perform on the flats vs. steeper pitches and mogul fields. Or take several trails with this kind of terrain.

• Test mogul skis on moguls, powder skis in powder, and cruisers on wide, open fields. Use the ski for the purpose for which it is designed. If it is an all-mountain ski, take it everywhere.

• Give your full attention to the task at hand. Do not let the exhilaration of skiing take away your concentration on how the ski *feels* and *reacts* to your commands. Try to be consistent with each pair of skis.

Here are a list of things to loof for:
• How easily do the skis turn?
• Do they feel stable in the turn?
• Can I carve and hold the edges?
• Are they stable when riding flat?
• Do they ski well in different situations?
• How do they ski at slow and high speeds?
• How do they perform in soft and hard snow?

**Test centers**

More and more manufacturers are working with ski areas, their ski schools and shops to set up test centers where consumers can take their products out for a spin. One such place is Vail and Beaver Creek's New Technology Center. Focusing solely on the latest innovations, the ski-in, ski-out NTC pavilions hold a huge cache of specialty skis — powder, shaped, mogul, and women's (conventional and shaped) — and CADS (a revolutionary leg-saving, ski-enhancing device, which I will discuss in Chapter Twelve). You might even find a future market ski not yet available to the public.

For an hourly fee, skiers check out products as if they were library books, exchanging one for another to experiment with the newest designs. If you are unsure how to adapt technique to the strange equipment, instructors ski with you for the first couple of runs. You do not have to be a prospective buyer to demo; however, if you find something that changes your life, you can probably get a deal purchasing at one of the local ski shops.

"We want to bring fun back into skiing," says Terry Nolan, general manager of Vail rental operations. "The new technology products truly make skiing easier."

Aspen runs similar on-mountain performance centers at three of its four mountains — Aspen, Buttermilk and Snowmass — with the added benefit of alignment services for skiers in ski school. Technicians work with ski pros to evaluate students' needs and make necessary adjustments in their equipment right there on the mountain.

**Boots**

Some upscale shops, such as Pepi's in Vail, are moving toward allowing buyers to demo boots. This beats any other way to ensure comfort, fit and performance before buying.

Most retail stores offer a guaranteed-fit policy with the purchase of boots, which leaves the door open for returns. They allow three tries to work on a perfect fit before they take boots back.

To demo boots take the following steps:

• Follow bootfitting procedures outlined in Chapter Seven.

• Wear your custom footbeds and any other boot aids when testing.

• Get familiar with adjustment features and buckle systems.

• As with skis, establish a pattern of testing.

• Test for comfort, fit and performance. Pay attention to pressure points, whether your foot slides or slips anywhere in the boot (especially in the heel) and whether you can flex the cuff to control your skis. Notice lateral stiffness.

• *Always* demo boots with your own skis.

---

***Chapter Summary:***

In this chapter you learned about variances in price, quality and variety of rental packages, how, when and where to rent boots, skis and poles, and how to demo skis and boots. Test centers, such as those in the Vail and Aspen areas, offer opportunities for increased skiing enjoyment through specialized equipment.

---

***For Information:***
**Ski Schools of Aspen** — (800) 525-6200.
**Vail/Beaver Creek Rentals** — (800) 595-0525.

Chapter Ten

# Lady, it's cold outside

---

*"I'm definitely a fair-weather athlete. I'm always looking for ways to stay warm."*
— Polly, age 34 from Minnesota

*"I'd like cooler clothes like men can buy, warm and technical, not just fashionable."*
— Amy, age 30 from Colorado

*"Larger sizes are needed. Fat people like to ski too!"*
— Pilar, age 33 from Colorado

---

Do you know what ceramics, soda pop bottles, zirconium carbide and insects have in common? They're all sources of materials that go into your ski clothes.

The list of state-of-the-art fabrics and fibers that make up ski clothes reads like a chemistry book. Today's technical threads move moisture, block wind, shed water, wick vapor, trap air, transport perspiration, heat up, cool down and breathe. They do everything but carve turns.

Warmth, comfort and a pocket where you need it are the hallmarks of ski clothing of the '90s. Think of it as equipment.

Although department-store jackets may look and feel like those you see on ski slopes, look closer. Read hangtags. If you want real warmth, you want the latest technology from companies that make clothing specifically for cold-weather sports.

---

Taking a cue from equipment makers, ski clothing designers listened to women who said they want function with their fashion. Hard Corps Sports reflects the clothing side of skiing's gender revolution. When Hard Corps started in 1984, its male-only line was designed to keep the serious skier comfortable, warm and dry, says Skip Rapp, founder and owner.

Do I detect an implication here that women were not serious skiers in 1984?

"The perception most manufacturers and retailers had is that women preferred to do their skiing in the lodge," Rapp says. "But now they are more receptive to the rising voice of young professional women demanding equality in all areas of their lives."

Women speak. Hard Corps listens.

In the 1993/94 ski season, Hard Corps intro-duced its first women's technical line made like the men's. It includes weather-protective features and fabrics such as sturdy hoods, high collars, lots of Gore-Tex, ballistic nylon shoulder protection for carrying skis (it is less bulky in the women's suits), and pockets for avalanche beepers.

"They are not de-tuned garments for women," Rapp says. "The big-shoulder, narrow-waist look is for freedom of movement for the attractive athlete. Our clothes have become a political statement for female skiers."

Interestingly, Hard Corps' research shows that skiers indicate strong interest in technical ski clothes in the West, the Rocky Mountain region and New England. The research shows some interest in the Midwest and not much in the South or Southern California.

"The percentage of hard-core female skiers out there you could put in your ear," argues Linda Klein, the outspoken co-owner of Willi's Ski Shop in Pittsburgh, Pennsylvania.

Klein began a career in ski retailing nearly 30 years ago, "since the days of lace-up boots," as she puts it. The family-owned store, nationally recognized for its excellence, was named "Eastern Retailer of the Year" for 1994 by Ski Industries America.

"The extreme-ski look is not up my alley," Klein says, "and the majority of women are like me." She is right. High-tech features captured only 12 percent of the vote in SIA's women's survey.

When women ask for technical lines, Klein believes they're asking for durable fabric and construction that will keep them warm and dry, but also looking good. Women in the National Skier Opinion Survey rank warmth, style and color on top of the list of considerations when buying ski apparel.

But what technical means to skiwear design-ers is the mountaineering look or the uniform look of the ski team, instructors and ski patrol, Klein says.

"We wanted technical fabrics; we got men's suits in women's sizes," she laments. "Women do not need pit zips; the last thing we worry about is sweating. I counted 11 zippers on one jacket. We do not want armor; we want style!"

Klein applauds The North Face for its designs that include a softer technical look for its women's line. Other technical lines with women's styling include Gerry, Nevica, Killy, Degre 7, Marker Ltd., Marmot, and Spyder.

If you are into making a style statement on the slopes, rather than a political one, there are plenty of companies to fulfill your high-fashion fancy, including Nils and its signature empire-waisted stretch suit, elegant Skea, Silvy Tricot and fur-trimmed M. Miller. There's also Bogner, whose classic skiwear designs have become status symbols, and Sport Obermeyer, whose clothing for women has wide appeal. Klein says Obermeyer's success is a result of listening to consumers. Its clothes are consistently comfortable, warm, good-looking and affordable.

Whichever look you are after, you cannot go wrong if you stick with major skiwear brands made with weatherproof fabrics and well-planned features.

## Just for women

The line that best combines fashion with practicality is Lundstrom, the work of the innovative Canadian designer Linda Lundstrom. Designed for women skiers by a woman skier, her collection is feminine and romantic in feeling but engineered with the latest technologies for warmth. More than any other designer, her clothing addresses special needs of women, such as drop-seat pants, a multi-convertible jacket with a built-in "backpacker" for hanging the jacket on your back, a safety whistle on the front zipper, and reflective tape on pockets and back. Her mix-and-match ski components coordinate with apres-ski sportswear, footwear and accessories.

For a bit of *femme fatale* fun on the slopes, Vi-Ski makes the Ultimate Lady ski *skirt*. The ankle-length, flared skirt connects to empire-waisted two-way stretch wool leggings, making it a unique one-piece skirt-pant outfit with matching jacket of insulated, weather-proof nylon. If you think the long skirt might get in your way, there's a smashing mini-ski-skirt, certainly a conversation piece in the lift line.

## Long tall Sally

Women who do not ski, or quit because they couldn't find warm clothing in their size, need look no further. Terry Lamé specializes in fitting the horizontally and vertically challenged. If you wear an 8, 10 or 12 you won't find your size in her unique store, T. Lamé, in Vail. But if you are used to shopping in children's or menswear departments in order to find ski clothes that (almost) fit, you'll encounter no problem selecting stylish, high-quality ski clothes and winter outdoor wear that fit your hard-to-fit frame.

Eight years ago Lamé decided to fill a void left by ski-store buyers who think all women are shaped like beach volleyball players. By offering only extreme sizes, she carved out a niche in the market and now carries such clout that Nils and Roffe produce styles exclusively for T. Lamé.

Other skiwear companies, such as Obermeyer, Killy, Columbia, Kaelin, Canyon, Fila, and Beauti-ful S-K-I-E-R, supply her with women's and men's styles in their lines that are most flattering in the special sizes, from 3 to 30, tall and small.

Each season Lamé publishes a catalog with an 800 number but no mail-order form. That's because she wants her consultants to personally speak to every person who calls in to ensure a custom fit.

## Warmth is not wimpy

Whatever your preference — high fashion or high tech — warmth is always in. My survey shows that being cold puts a freeze on a woman's ability to enjoy skiing, and it is one of the reasons women quit skiing.

When buying ski clothes, the first consideration should be your body chemistry: Are you warm-blooded or cold-blooded? Combine that answer with the terrain you usually ski and the amount of energy you put out to determine how much warmth you need.

Layering continues to be the smartest way to foil foul weather. Warm air trapped between layers of clothing creates insulation that keeps you warmer than a single piece of heavier clothing.

## Underwear

The clothing layer closest to your body should be made of a fiber that wicks away perspiration, keeping your skin warm and dry. Look for long underwear with moisture-moving fibers and fabrics such as Thermax, Thermastat, Capilene and Dryline. Cotton and cotton blends absorb and retain water, leaving your skin cold and damp. Silk feels warm, soft and luxurious next to your skin, but when it is wet, it doesn't work as well as other fibers. Look for good ski underwear at ski and outdoor-sports shops, not department stores.

In your t-shirt and unisex long johns, do you ever feel like a lumberjack? Give them to your husband.

Now, you can wear Wintimates, feminine, fashionable and functional thermal bodywear from Jackson Jill, a company based in Jackson, Wyo. Jill is lingerie designer Jill Woodard.

Wintimates' sleek, sexy, shapely bodysuits are constructed for a woman's curves and fit like a second skin. They're available in two styles: snap-crotch bodysuits with matching leggings and full-length, one-piece union suits featuring drop seats or fanny flaps.

Wintimates are made of *Thermastat* and *Lycra Spandex* for a four-way stretch. Some feature built-in bust support; others are accented with lace; all are fitted, flattering and feminine. Think about it: one less shirttail bunching up under your ski pants!

## Middle layer

On top of thermalwear, the next layer should be a turtleneck (polyester is better than cotton) topped by a fleece pullover or jacket. With its new weather-resistant treatments, fleece holds as much warmth as a traditional ski sweater, plus it resists moisture and wicks away perspiration.

If you choose a sweater, make it wool or wool-blend. Wool wicks moisture from the skin and retains heat well; sweatshirts absorb perspiration, become damp and stay damp. You'll get cold very quickly in cotton.

## Outer layer

The final layer should be the insulated or non-insulated parka and pant, or one-piece ski suit. Insulated clothing traps air, creating a barrier that keeps warmth in and cold out. It stays warmer than non-insulated clothing, but for some people can be too warm.

According to Sport Obermeyer's Barbara Owen, "Insulation requirements for an outerwear garment that will be worn with other layers will vary depending on the user's needs. For example, someone skiing on a damp, cold day will require more insulation than a person skiing where conditions are warmer and drier.

"In general, lightweight insulations are more versatile because they are less bulky and easy to layer over or under. This translates into a greater level of comfort and freedom of movement."

## One-piece suits

Once you wear a one-piece suit, you will never want to go back to pants and parkas. One-piece outfits are comfortable, convenient, figure-flattering and, I think, warmer. It is just your body and lots of trapped warm air in there!

Of the three types — insulated, non-insulated and stretch pants attached to an insulated top — you will find insulated the warmest.

I love my one-piece ski suits, especially now that I've found a solution to going to the bathroom! You know the problem: You get in the stall, take off your goggles, hat and gloves and find there's no place to put them except between your knees.

You unzip and drop your top, trying like hell to keep the sleeves from dragging on the dirty, wet floor. Still clutching your hat, goggles and gloves with your knees (the one time your Q angle proves beneficial!), you attempt to pull your long underwear bottoms down around your bum. Then you remember what your mother told you: do not ever sit on the seat!

The price of expensive resorts is justified in my mind by bathroom stalls with racks or wire baskets for loose stuff. And I've solved the problem of dragging one-piece suit sleeves by sewing small clips on the insides of the sleeve cuffs and hooking them to my belt loop when I sit. This way, the sleeves fold up close to my hips and out of reach of the floor. Velcro works also: one strip inside the suit, the other inside the cuff.

## Stretch pants

The two- and four-way stretch materials made of wool, lycra, cotton and nylon blends make fabulous unitards and pants. But they're not as warm as warm-air layered insulated pants or one-piece suits.

In-the-boot pants invite snow and wind to creep into your boot tops. Skiing powder? Out of the question. Also, stretch pants can hinder leg contact with your ski boots (your bootfitter will have a fit!), and the stirrups can cut off circulation in your feet.

Roffe always has made over-the-boot stretch pants, now called "on-the-boot." Unlike the bell-bottoms of the '70s, cuffs zip tight over the boots. You still must deal with a pant liner taking up boot space, however.

## Little things mean a lot

Real-estate agents say the key is location, location, location. In ski duds it is details, details, details. You do not realize their importance until you need them.

One beautiful spring morning in Vail, I boarded Chair 3 en route to a St. Patrick's Day picnic. Half-way up, a fierce wind kicked in, swirling snowflakes around us like feathers shaken from a pillow. Wouldn't you know, the lift stopped! There we sat, dangling like wind chimes in this surprise spring storm (Colorado is famous for them.) Naturally, I wasn't wearing a hat. Then, I remembered the hood tucked in the back of my Obermeyer ski suit. I pulled it around my head and was snug as a pea in a pod waiting it out.

Barbara Alley, former fashion editor for *Snow Country* magazine, emphasizes that skiers should not be fooled by skiwear in discount or department stores. Though a parka might resemble a brand carried in specialty ski shops, she cautions, its cheaper price tells you the fabric, construction and features are not the same quality and won't protect you from the elements like the real thing.

Look for these features:

• Wind flaps over zippers for wind and snow protection.

• Pull-tabs on zippers for easy grabbing with mittens or gloves

• Strategically-placed pockets for outside ac-cess, such as a trail map pocket on a pantleg.

• No hip pockets on tight-fitting pants — they make the garment too bulky.

• Sealed seams — wind can rip through seams of poorly made clothes.

• Snug or adjustable cuffs at wrists and ankles.

• Collars and inside closures that can be zipped or buckled to the chin.

• Elasticized drawstrings at waists and hems of jackets that can be tightened for protection from the elements.

## Buying tips

• Bring long underwear, turtleneck and sweater to ensure a good fit when trying on ski clothes.

• Sit and squat in pants or suits to make sure they do not ride up. For all-day, active wear, they must be roomy.

• If leg length looks too long, it is probably OK. Remember, ski boots add about an inch.

• Too loose is more flattering than too tight.

• Black and dark navy create a more slimming silhouette than any other color, particularly in pants.

• A jacket with a long peplum looks better on big hips than a short one. This belted style emphasizes big shoulders, narrow waist and legs.

• Do not be afraid of white. Water-repellent coatings also contain stain repellent tough enough to be scrubbed. Most fabrics can be machine-washed, but always follow instructions. (DuPont makes a waterstain-repeller laundry additive under its Second Wind label.)

• One-piece suits cost less than two-piece outfits, but you can wear a long jacket over leggings or slacks, doubling its use.

## Repair the tear

With ski gear fabric so tough and tight, tears seldom appear. But when they do, who ya gonna call?

Rainy Pass Repair has been sewing seams in outdoor clothing and equipment since 1986. The Montana-based company stitches for more than 350 retailers and manufacturers like Eddie Bauer, Columbia and REI, to name a few. It can sew for you, too. Send your items to be repaired with instructions. Rainy Pass, one of few facilities authorized to repair Gore-Tex, will make garments like new, drawing upon a huge inventory of fabrics, snaps, zippers, and buckles. Turn-around time is four to 10 days, and the work is guaranteed.

Call the Rainy Pass people for free estimates and advice on everything from ski suits to sleeping bags. Alteration and laundry services are specialties.

## Accessories

Matching accessories can make a nice outfit really great. Alley suggests buying two T-necks or sweaters for the same outfit for a change in color. Many manufacturers make color-coordinated hats, headbands, neck warmers and sweaters. It is a good idea to buy them at the time you make your major purchase because other stores may not carry the same brand. Three years ago, I bought a gorgeous mauve Head suit and I am still trying to find a hat!

### Hats and headbands

Headwear sections of ski shops are looking more and more like costume departments. With the snowboarders' influence, hats express more freedom and fun. If dredlocks, cone heads, the Scrunch, the Octopus, Jughead, Robin Hood or the Annie Hall style aren't your type, plenty of traditional styles remain.

Several companies make hats, headbands or ear muffs featuring pockets over the ears for inserting disposable heat packs.

Alley says she likes the look of a long neck warmer pulled up over the head and crossed with a matching headband. She reminds us that half our body heat escapes through our head. Keeping your torso warm and covering your head will help hold heat in fingers and toes.

When my children were little and trying to be responsible for their ski gear, I taught them to think in threes: hat, goggles and gloves; skis, boots and poles. To this day, I use this rule — except I've added neck to the list. When my neck is bundled in fleece, my whole body stays warm!

### Gloves and mittens

Keeping hands dry ranks as important as keeping them warm, because hands lose heat 30 times faster when they are wet. Look for gloves or mittens made with high-tech insulations and materials for heat retention and water resistance. Mittens keep hands warmer than gloves and mittens with liners are warmer yet.

Many gloves and mittens feature pockets for heat packs for those bitterly cold days. Expect to spend from $40 to $100 for good hand protection.

Here's the scoop on disposable heat packs:

• Heat Factory makes them for hands and feet, but do not substitute one for the other — they can burn your palms. If you have held on to unopened packs from last year, you can use them this season; they are good for two to three years. Small-size packs for kids are available, too.

• The Heat Flow glove, featuring a heated- liquid system, works like this: Insert an activated heat pack in the glove's wrist pocket, which adjoins a liner containing a non-toxic fluid. Normal hand movements circulate the heated fluid in the liner, warming the entire hand. On less cold days, omit the heat pack and the liner will capture natural body heat and distribute it. Zero makes the gloves and mittens. Swany and Grandoe make similar products.

Thin glove liners made with moisture-moving materials work well inside gloves or mittens for added warmth and dryness. I like mine when I need to use my fingers outside my gloves for taking notes or opening trail maps.

## Cold feet, warm socks

If cold feet are a chronic problem, or if you cannot feel your toes while skiing, your boots could be cutting off circulation. Next time you take them off, check your feet and lower legs immediately. If you see any bulging blood vessels, this means they are pumping blood to get it back to the toes. It is an indication your boots are too tight in that spot. A bootfitter can correct this.

Nothing makes you more miserable than wet, clammy feet. Pedorthist Jeff Rich says the average skier's foot sheds half a pint of perspiration a day on the slopes. Wearing the right kind of socks and taking simple precautions can prevent perspiration and circulation problems that cause cold feet.

• Socks should be made of the same moisture-wicking materials that is used for long underwear. ProperSox uses a material called Transpor, a new fiber that transfers vapor and perspiration from the skin without soaking the sock. One way to determine a fiber's resistance to saturation is by observing how fast it dries. When I take my socks from the washer, they are hardly wet and line dry in a flash. Cotton socks, on the other hand, take forever in a dryer. Thorlo and Wigwam brands also are good ski socks.

• Layering does not apply to socks. Wear one thin sock (about the weight of men's dress sock). Heavier socks or layering will create more perspiration and circulation problems. Remember, boot liners are designed to be warm.

• Pantyhose and nylon workout tights do *not* make good substitutes for ski socks. They contribute to cold feet in women more than anything. Nylon doesn't allow feet to breathe, making them wet and clammy. Nylon also makes feet slide in the boots, causing loss of steering and edging control.

• Wear clean socks every day. Dirt and perspiration interfere with wicking, causing loss of thermal quality.

• Wipe your feet dry before putting on socks and never put on boots when socks still are damp.

• Do not put on wet or cold boots. Your feet will stay wet and cold all day, making them susceptible to blisters and frostbite. When you drive to a ski area, keep your boots on the heated floor of the front seat. (See Chapter Eight on drying out boot liners.)

## Boot heaters

More and more women are discovering boot heaters as a great way to keep their tootsies toasty. The heating system consists of a small, rechargeable battery pack that attaches to the back of your boots by screws or a removable strap. It plugs into wires that flow to a heating element on the footbed, which warms your foot.

- Hotronics is favored by ski instructors in the Northeast, where cold can be brutal. It has four heat settings for durations of 55 minutes to eight hours. Suggested retail price is $149.
- Winter Heat lasts from one to three hours and is the smallest unit. It costs about $130.
- Extreme Comfort costs the least (about $80) and runs from one-and-a-half to six hours.

If you use any of these heaters, make sure the battery pack is secure. Packs that clip on the back of boots can be knocked off when you are riding the chair lift or going down stairs.

*Note:* Before spending big bucks on a sport you are trying out, borrow ski clothes from your skiing friends. Or you can rent skiwear at a few ski rental shops. You may not create a fashion sensation, but at least you will be warm. Do not wear blue jeans — they soak up snow and stay wet all day. Besides, that '70s look went out with bell-bottoms.

---

*Chapter Summary:*
This chapter serves as a handy reference guide for fibers, fabrics and fillings of winter wear. You learned tips that, hopefully, will keep you warm, dry and comfortable from head to toe, where to find hard-to-fit sizes and where to go for repairs.

---

*Product information:*
Ski clothing and accessory brands mentioned in this chapter can be found in most U.S. retail ski shops. The following can also be ordered by mail:
**Lundstrom** — U.S. sales representative: Leslie Trudeau, Trudeau & Co., P.O. Box 701, Oconomowoc, WI, 53066; (312) 467-9118; (800) 66LINDA; (800) 665-4632.
**Rainy Pass Repair** — (800) 733-4340.

**T. Lamé** — 100 E. Meadow Dr., Vail, CO 81657. To order a catalog, call (800) 294-4636.

**Ultimate Lady Ski Skirt** — Vi-Ski, Vickie Hodges, 2514 Johnston St., Pearland, TX 77581; (713) 489-0055; FAX (713) 997-8885.

**Wintimates** — Jackson Jill, P.O. Box 8849, Jackson, WY 83001; (307) 739-0866.

Chapter  Eleven

# *Mountain Mamas*

---

*"I love just about everything in skiing — the outdoors, the challenge, the people giving a bit of myself and getting a lot in return."*
— *Deborah, age 41 from New Mexico*

*"When I am skiing I gain strength, energy, spirit and a true sense of being alive in a vibrant way."*
— *Dianne, age 45 from California*

*"I love the balance and power I feel in motion when I'm skiing."* — *Barclay, age 28 from Vermont*

---

You don't have to be an expert to appreciate the aesthetics of skiing. The winter outdoors, the natural beauty of the mountains, glorious views, fresh air, and closeness to nature are the most frequent answers to my survey question, "What do you love about skiing?" Others mentioned the sound of skis on the snow, the warm sun and the solitude. Marcela from Mexico likes just "seeing the snow!"

Exercise and the challenge of skiing are listed second. Again, all ability groups agree on this. Vicki, 37, from Colorado, sums it up: "I like doing something hard and good with my body!"

Exhilaration, feeling free and the rush of flying down the mountain rank a close third. Many women say they are happy with the feeling of well-being after a day on the slopes and the satisfaction of "getting it."

---

Twenty-eight-year-old Sue from Massachusetts says she likes "Feeling good about myself when I perform well." Catherine, 24, from Wyoming, skis 70 days a year and "loves the floating, airy feeling I get when I make good turns." Melissa, 29, an instructor at Telluride, is completely in tune with her sport: She loves "the glide, the cuts through gravity, the feeling of controlled falling, the power of the ski."

Nothing comes close to being on top of the world under a blue canopy of sky. People who do not ski never get the opportunity to experience the mountains as we do.

## Rare mountain air

But the best of days can be marred by high-altitude sickness, also called acute mountain sickness, Anyone who ascends from sea level or the lowlands to the thin atmosphere of higher altitudes can be affected. Studies show that 25 percent of all persons visiting moderate elevations (6,300 to 9,700 feet above sea level) will experience unpleasant symptoms due to altitude.

A sudden change in environment can bring on headache, sleeplessness, fatigue, shortness of breath, lack of appetite, dizziness, nausea and vomiting. These symptoms can appear within the first six to 12 hours, and usually begin to dissipate within 72 hours. If symptoms persist and become severe, get medical help immediately. The doctor may administer supplemental oxygen and send you temporarily to a lower altitude.

Acute mountain sickness is not something you can condition yourself for, and you will not know if you're susceptible until it happens. Equally as perplexing is the fact that if you suffer a singular incidence of AMS, you may never have a reoccurrence. However, if you have had it once, be aware you could get it again.

## Take simple high-altitude precautions

Julie Ann Lickteig, a registered dietitian and professor of nutrition, specializes in high-altitude field research. Her studies conducted at mountain base camps on six of the seven continents show that symptoms can be minimized by awareness and the ways in which individuals adapt to higher altitudes.

"The transition period or acclimatization requires an alert mind that listens to body messages," Julie Ann says. Acclimatization involves four elements, which compose the acronym SEAT:

• *Speed* — At each successively higher altitude, a progressive adaptation needs to take place. Do not jump off the plane and onto the slopes. Plan your vacation accordingly. Research shows that people who stay one or two nights at an intermediate altitude, such as Denver at 5,280 feet, before heading to the high country above 8,000 feet are less likely to develop acute mountain sickness.

• *Exercise* — The intensity of exercise can contribute to symptoms. Pace yourself. Begin with a half day of cruiser runs and gradually work up to more physically demanding slopes.

• *Altitude* — Know the altitudes of your final destination for sleeping and skiing. For example, Sun Valley's base is 5,750 feet. The top is 9,140 feet. Breckenridge's base is 9,603 feet; the highest skiing point reaches nearly 13,000. Do as the climbers say, "climb high, sleep low."

• *Time* — The more time you spend at altitude, the more acclimated you get. There are advantages to two-week ski vacations!

## Eat, drink and ski merry

An important part of the acclimatization process involves diet, a relentless concern for women wherever they are. Julie Ann recommends the following:

• Push fluids to prevent dehydration. A minimum of three quarts a day is suggested. Liquid foods such as gelatin, soup, sherbet, etc. can be included. Stop frequently and drink small amounts. This should be easy — you are thirsty anyway from loss of moisture caused by the low humidity.

• Alcohol is not one of the fluids you should push, at least not the first two or three days, and you should lighten up on it the rest of the times. Alcohol contributes to dehydration and affects breathing. Remember, one drink at altitude equals two at sea level. Substitute water or fruit juice for your second après-ski drink.

• Cut back on caffeine, which is also dehydrating. Adding a little milk or cream to coffee or tea will dilute caffeine effects.

• Eat lightly. Make high-carbohydrate foods like whole-grain breads, cereals, pasta, rice, fruits and vegetables 55–65 percent of your total calories. Fats should make up no more than 25–30 percent of calories, and proteins about 10–15 percent. Eat several small meals a day instead of three large ones. You will feel better because this pattern utilizes available oxygen more effectively.

• Decrease salt, which causes fluid retention.

Thankfully, the trend at ski areas to upgrade mountain restaurants helps our efforts to eat well. Food choices no longer are limited to high-fat hot dogs and greasy hamburgers. They now offer gourmet salad bars with baked potatoes, grilled chicken breasts and healthful pizzas. Didi Lawrence, an instructor at Beaver Creek, introduced me to a lunch of baked potato with cottage cheese and a dollop of low-fat honey-mustard dressing, sprinkled with black olives and pepper. Yum!

*Julie Ann's Healthy Pocket Foods*
  *Milk products:* Cheese wedges, string cheese, yogurt.
  *Meats, etc.:* Beef sticks and jerky, peanut butter sandwiches, nuts, hard-boiled eggs.

*Fruits:* Fresh or dried fruits, fruit leather, date and fig bars, trail mix.

*Grains:* Granola, bread sticks, crackers, popcorn, bagels, muffins, soft pretzels, tortillas, cookies, corn nuts, breakfast and energy bars, dry cereal.

*Beverage Mixes:* Cocoa, instant breakfast, cider, eggnog, instant soups, sport drinks.

## Rx if you need it

Recent experience shows that some people find relief from acute mountain sickness by taking a small dose of a prescription drug called Diamox. When taken 24 hours before arriving at altitude, and for two days afterward, it may lessen or prevent symptoms and speed acclimation. Ask your doctor about it.

## High and dry skin care

Winter can be devastating on your skin. In high altitude, air contains less humidity, thus disturbing the skin's natural moisture barrier and resulting in dry skin. Indoor heating further intensifies the damage. Moisturizers with ingredients that reproduce skin's lipids, which recreate the moisture barrier, can help. These include Vaseline's Intensive Care line, Clinique's Moisture On-Call, Chanel's Total Defense Moisture Lotion, and Estée Lauder's Day Wear.

We all know we're exposed to even more dangerous levels of ultraviolet radiation now with the depletion of the ozone layer. Skiers risk even more damage from the sun at mountain elevations. Reflections off the snow intensify the sun's effect as well.

With most skiers hitting the slopes from around 10 a.m. to 3 p.m., precisely the hours when the sun's rays are strongest, they need to be vigilant about protecting their skin.

Barbara Reed, a Denver dermatologist, warns that ultraviolet rays increase two percent with every 1,000 feet of elevation above sea level. In the Colorado mountains, for example, where skiers ride lifts to about 12,000 feet, they are exposed to 24 percent more ultraviolet rays than on a Hawaiian beach!

Because 80 percent of ultraviolet rays are *reflected* off of snow, a sun visor or a hat with a brim does not help much. The best defense is sunscreen slathered on face, lips, and especially nose and ears, which are more susceptible to malignancies. You can also make like a bandit when it is sunny *and* cold by wearing a ski mask. Do not be fooled by gray days: 80 percent of ultraviolet rays penetrate clouds.

## UVA and UVB

Remember that sun affects skin two ways. The burning ray, UVB, causes skin cancer; the aging ray, UVA, causes skin damage. UVA, which can pass through glass and penetrate deeper into the skin, usually does not burn; however, it causes wrinkles, liver spots and sagging tissue.

## Sunscreens

While all sunscreens protect from UVB rays, Dr. Reed says only one brand offers *more extensive* protection against UVA. Shade UVA Guard contains Parsol 1789, an ingredient found to battle the full spectrum of UVA rays. Other brands contain a less inclusive UVA shield. Shade UVA Guard is sold over the counter in drug, grocery and discount stores.

Rocky Mountain Sunscreen, developed in the mile-high city of Denver, is formulated especially for dry, high-altitude environments. It contains moisturizing ingredients like aloe vera, and vitamins A, D, and E. Use it by the gallon, literally. This size container can be ordered directly from the manufacturer for refilling the two-ounce and eight-ounce bottles sold in stores and at ski areas and national parks throughout North America.

If your skin is sensitive or allergic, use products made for children which are less harsh, will not sting your eyes and contain no PABA. PABA causes allergic reactions in many people. (It also can permanently stain clothing.)

If you have fair skin or have undergone a facelift, chemical peel or dermabrasion, or if you regularly use Retin-A, cortisone creams, or alpha hydroxy acids on your face, you must be extra careful. Your skin is thinner and more sun-sensitive. Ditto for expectant mothers and women taking birth control pills or hormones. Hormonal states can cause a discoloration on the face and neck that the sun can intensify. Use sunscreen liberally if any of these exceptions apply to you.

Do not wait until you get to the mountains to pull out your sunscreen and lip balm. Dr. Reed suggests wearing sunscreen during the drive up. "We see more skin cancers and pre-cancers on the left side of the face (of skiers who drive west)," Reed says. Sun can be intense when it beats through a car window.

Smear on sunscreen 30 minutes before going into the sun. Throughout your ski day, reapply every 90 minutes if the sun is bright, if perspiration causes you to wipe your face, or if a runny nose has you wiping it often. Areas that have sunburned before are delicate and require heavier sun block. "This is really, really important," Dr. Reed says.

### SPF rating

When sunscreen testers try out a product, they heavily apply the cream, then give it an SPF number, a multiple of the number of minutes you can remain in the sun without burning. If you usually burn in 15 minutes without sunblock, a sunblock of SPF 2 would allow you to be in the sun 30 minutes without burning.

Dr. Reed reminds us the ratings are derived from heavily applied sunscreen in test laboratories — not the lighter coating most people use — and usually pertain to sun at sea-level intensity. Experts recommend an SPF of at least 15 for most people. At higher altitudes, use products with a rating even higher than 15.

Hats, especially baseball caps, will not make you sun-safe. If you can see the sun through your hat, burning rays can get through. Hair sprays with sunscreen, such as Topcoat by Dermatone, are recommended for people with thin hair who want to ski hatless or with a head band. Give the part in your hair a shot, too. Choose a pump spray — it penetrates more directly than an aerosol. This product also works great in preventing scalp-burn on the balding men in your life.

### Frostbite

Sunburn's effects are more long-term than frostbite's, but frostbite can be dangerous if untreated. Caused by extreme cold when blood vessels constrict so that blood cells cannot pass through them, frostbite turns affected skin unnaturally white and numb. Most susceptible to frostbite are ears, noses, hands and feet.

Treat frostbite immediately. Cover the affected skin and ski to a shelter or mountain lodge. Restore circulation gradually, warming the affected skin under blankets, clothing, or warm — not hot — water. Never rub frostbitten skin because you could further damage tissue. Once flesh is frostbitten, it may remain especially sensitive to cold. Special care should be taken to keep affected areas warm and dry.

Some skin-protector products guard against frostbite by allowing you to stay in the cold longer, as well as lessening the severity of damage. Ask about them at your drugstore's pharmacy.

Penny Moore, an instructor at Smugglers' Notch in northern Vermont, offers this tip: for an emergency shield against frostbite, grab a few napkins at lunch. Tuck a thick strip of one under your goggles, covering your face and nose completely. Replace it with another after it gets wet. Those die-hard women in the Northeast will do anything to keep skiing!

Though she has never treated a case like this, Dr. Reed says it is conceivable that the telltale whitening of a frostbitten spot on the face could go unnoticed under heavy makeup. So, save your model look for night life. Sunscreen and the natural, healthy glow from crisp, clean air are the only makeup you need on the slopes. Frequent applications of SPF 15 lip gloss will keep your lips shiny and the cold will give your cheeks a rosy hue.

### Frost nip

Some women are affected by Raynaud's Disease, a disorder of the small blood vessels of the hands and feet. In cold weather — not necessarily just severe cold — vessels constrict, blocking blood flow and turning the skin white, then blue. If you suffer from chronically cold hands and feet, take extra care to keep them warm. Immediately treat cold hands by vigorously moving your arms in big circles to get blood circulating to the fingers.

### Hot tubs

There is nothing like a moonlight soak in a hot tub after a day of cold skiing. It feels soooo good! But if your skin is sensitive, the extreme heat and harsh chemicals can cause a prickly rash and burning sensation. If you can't resist the hot tub, take a *brief* dip, then follow immediately with a shower to wash off the chemicals. Then, smooth non-perfumed lotion liberally over your entire body. (Perfumes can irritate sensitive skin or cause an allergic reaction.)

Winter environment also contributes to stuffy noses and dry mouths. Sometimes, increased activity in low humidity can cause nosebleeds. Be prepared with a jar of Vaseline for a few dabs in the nose every morning and night. Some lodge rooms come equipped with portable humidifiers. Look for one in the closet, or ask the bellman.

Chewing gum or sucking on hard candies will help alleviate cotton mouth, as will drinking lots of fluids.

## Eye care

Meticulous care should be taken to protect your eyes from sun when you're skiing. Ophthal-mologist Joel Goldstein says he has treated hundreds of cases of sunburned eyes in his practices in Denver and Vail.

"People get fooled when it is overcast or cloudy, and ski without eye protection," Goldstein explains. "After skiing, they feel OK. Their eyes may be a little red but they go to dinner and out partying. Then, about 3 or 4 in the morning, they wake up in pain." Eye sunburn requires immediate medical attention.

People from areas of high humidity and low altitude find their eyes dry out at high altitude resorts with low humidity. Because *dry eyes are more susceptible to burning*, Dr. Goldstein recommends carrying a tube of over-the-counter artificial tears while you ski. Apply five or six times a day. The non-preserved solution is less likely to cause an allergic reaction than preserved. People who wear contact lenses find dry eyes a nuisance and should follow this advice.

### *Eyeware*

Goggles, wrap-around shields, or sunglasses with side covers protect eyes and the delicate skin around them from damaging sun.

Eyewear should be considered part of your basic ski equipment, not an accessory. Women often shun goggles for more flattering sunglasses, but when light turns flat or weather becomes stormy, dark-lens sunglasses are worthless as eye protection.

A good pair of yellow-lens goggles acts like a glass house for your eyes. It protects them from the elements and vastly improves vision by increasing contrasts in snow. Do not go skiing without them.

Goggles cost from $20 to $200. Goggles are useless if they fog up, so make sure they are anti-fog — usually made with double lenses. If applied frequently, de-fogging solutions and cloths will work. Never wipe goggles with tissue or paper towels because their abrasive surfaces will damage anti-fog coatings. Either use a soft cloth or let your goggles air dry.

Try on goggles before you buy them. I have rejected several pairs with wavy lenses that distorted my vision. Women's models, designed for smaller faces, might fit better than unisex styles. Goggles that are too big look geeky and also allow cold air to leak through the gaps.

Goggles that fit over eyeglasses are available — ask for OTG models. Bolle makes a nifty adapter frame for people who wear prescription eyewear. An optical shop inserts prescription lenses into the frame, which then snaps into certain models of Bolle glasses and goggles. Carrera makes goggles for contact lens wearers (OTC) that have special air venting.

Shields are an alternative to goggles. They fit over the ears like sunglasses but wrap around the face, providing protection similar to goggles.

Sunglasses are categorized in three types by the U.S. Food and Drug Administration: cosmetic, general-purpose and special-purpose. The optical clarity and color treatment best for high-altitude glare are in special-purpose lenses. You will find them in ski shops, optical stores and some opticians' offices, but not at grocery, drug, or discount department stores. Prices begin at $30 for plastic lenses and can go up to $250 for quality glass lenses. Do not buy lenses offering anything less than 100-percent protection from ultraviolet rays. If you're wondering about the glasses you already own, most optical shops will read the UV level of your sunglasses at no charge.

For maximum protection, wear glasses with gray or green lenses for bright sun. You will do better with yellow lenses on overcast days. Leave the mirrored lenses to the movie stars: they scratch and act like a magnet for UV rays to your face.

Protect your eyewear: Store frames and goggles in hard-cover cases. (Glass case, under $10; goggles case, about $8. To order, call Tognar Toolworks at (916) 926-2600; FAX (800) 926-9904.) During your lunch break, do not toss goggles in the pile of gloves and hats that builds up on the table. I've seen expensive goggles ruined from food spills. Instead, wear them backward around your neck, on top of your head, or around your arm — you will protect them from scratching and breaking this way, too.

On warm, sunny days when you're wearing sunglasses, carry your goggles on your shoulder inside your ski jacket. Place them so they snugly fit the curve of your shoulder like a shoulder pad. For balance, stuff your knit hat or neck warmer in the other shoulder. You will be styling! And you will have everything you need if the weather turns bad.

## Hair care

Hat hair, matte hair ... every ski day is a bad-hair day for women! Not all of us have long, thick tresses we can pull away from our faces and weave into luxurious braids. But your hair can stay healthy and shiny even after long hours of fun in the sun.

"The best thing you can do for your hair when skiing is to cover it," says Denver hairdresser Mary Ann McGreggor. As with skin, sun reflecting off snow and beating down overhead can damage hair, especially if it is chemically treated.

Here is McGreggor's prescription for high-altitude hair-care:

• Shampoo in the shower.

• Use an inexpensive, generic baby shampoo that is *not* pH-balanced. If the product lathers well the first time, do not shampoo again. Rinse completely.

• Apply a moisturizer — not a conditioner — according to directions. Moisturizers penetrate the hair and keep it flexible; conditioners coat it, leaving it dull and lifeless. Unless you're in the sun a lot, you do not need to moisturize all of your hair with every shampoo; just work in a little on the ends, which tend to get dry and brittle.

• While rinsing out moisturizer, run a wide-toothed comb through your hair with the rinse water. Do not pull too hard. Let the water and the moisturizer untangle your hair.

• Pour an acidic rinse over your head made with one part vinegar or lemon juice diluted with 20 parts water. This step is essential.

• Rinse lightly with warm water.

• Blot, do not rub, your hair with a towel. With long hair, wrap the ends in a towel and wring out moisture.

As for hat hair, First Lady of Ski Fashion Barbara Alley wears a *balaclava*, a silk hood for the head and neck, under her knit hat. Her red mane does not get as mashed as when she wears the hat directly on her hair. (Balaclavas are found in catalogs that sell silk underwear.)

For a quick touchup for après-ski, try a curling iron that runs on propane or batteries. It can be used anywhere and is light enough to carry in a backpack or fanny pack. Pack a travel-size hair spray or gel with it. You will find the curling iron wherever hair appliances are sold.

NOTE: If you do not find sunscreen or hair-care products in health and beauty sections of drug and grocery stores, ask your pharmacist. Or look in catalogs of network sales marketing companies such as Avon or Amway.

## Skiing for two

To ski pregnant is a choice mothers-to-be should make with their physician based on level of fitness as well as comfort threshold. If you're not relaxed, you may fall more easily. Although the fetus is fairly well protected in the amniotic fluid, any injury suffered by a woman during pregnancy can become complicated because doctors are more hesitant to prescribe medication.

In addition, a hormone in pregnant women called relaxin causes ligaments to loosen, making them more prone to tearing in a fall.

I skied through five healthy pregnancies and found that my protective instincts took over, making it easy for me to proceed slowly and in control. I shunned difficult slopes and skied on the sides of crowded runs. I rested a lot. During my daughter's pregnancy, her doctor advised her not to let her heart rate go higher than 140 beats a minute and to avoid extremes in temperature.

Clothes are definitely a problem, but pregnant skiers learn to improvise during the early months. Most do not ski when their tummies are really large. One garment everyone agrees on is a good support bra!

Telluride ski instructor Cindy Smith, who skied during two pregnancies, found that her stance and balance improved. She felt more grounded and moved more effectively with her skis. "Skiing during pregnancy," she says, "is a great way to feel light again — letting gravity do most of the work."

You might notice that your boots fit differently during pregnancy and after you have given birth because most women's feet grow wider during pregnancy. Your bootfitter can make necessary adjustments. Also, the DIN setting of your bindings will need to be reset as you gain weight, and then later when you regain your pre-baby figure.

## The mid-life skier

There is no better time for skiing than in mid-life. The children are raised, time and money are more available, lift-ticket prices are lower for seniors, and at many resorts, after 70, skiing is *free!*

Skiers 50 and older can even belong to their own ski club — Over the Hill Gang, International. More than 4,500 members in 50 states and 13 countries enjoy skiing and schmoozing with other outdoor enthusiasts "in the prime of life."

Membership includes: Discounts on lift tickets meals, lodging, transportation, and equipment rentals (detailed in a benefit directory), frequent ski and summer adventure trips in this country and abroad; and learn-to-ski programs tailored to older skiers. The most requested trip? Technique Clinic for Women at Winter Park.

You can join this international club through chapter membership ($62 annual dues for a single; $100 a couple). Local groups host social events and ski trips of their own. If there's no Gang in your area, you can join as an at-large member for $37 or $60.

Five bucks and a copy of a legal document proving you're 70 or older buys a lifetime membership into the 70+ Ski Club. Newsletters inform members about discounts, world-wide trips and races.

Founded and still run by Lloyd T. Lambert, the group provides inspiration and companionship to those who might be thinking of giving up the sport. The encouragement has paid off: the organization has swelled from 35 members in 1977 to 12,600 in 1996. Like its founder, "It is one of those things that just keeps going," says Lambert, 95 years young!

## The "changing" woman skier

Menopausal women may want to consider:

• Because of the overall "drying out" in this hormonal state, some women will experience more eye dryness. Relieve this condition with frequent applications of artificial tears.

• Loss of muscle mass can be detrimental. But older women who maintain a regular routine of strength training can build muscle power to match that of younger women, physiologists say.

• The greatest health concern for post-menopausal skiers are fractures to bones weakened by osteoporosis, the disease that thins bone tissue. Ironically, weight-bearing exercises, like skiing, can help maintain and even increase bone density, if it is done often and combined with a calcium-rich diet.

• As women get older, their risk for coronary heart disease increases. Those who lead sedentary lives have a 30–50 percent greater risk of developing high blood pressure. It is no wonder the American Heart Association has long touted the benefits of physical activity, which also increases HDL, the good cholesterol, and can reduce the risk of coronary heart disease.

Clearly, rather than shunning skiing as we age, we should embrace it as an important part of the prescription for an active, healthy lifestyle.

## Bare necessities

If you are flying to a resort, carry on a bag containing items you deem essential in case your luggage goes astray. Some of the most important items are: your ski boots (once you get them to fit right, you do not even want to think about not skiing in them!), medication, knee brace, contact lenses and cleaning solutions or glasses (whichever you're not wearing), and tampons.

Once in Jackson Hole, where three men are available for every woman, a hotel clerk told me she did not know of a place in Teton Village that sold feminine hygiene products. I finally discovered a convenience store where Tampax was tucked behind the motor oil and chewing tobacco.

Playtex Portables or Tampax Compak are half the size of regular tampons and fit neatly in a ski jacket or fanny pack.

One of my skiing necessities is Advil, which I rely on to relieve swelling and pain from a bulging disc in my lower back. I have always taken my pills on the sly, not wanting to be known as a pill popper. One ski trip changed that. I was on a bus traveling on the Icefields Parkway to Lake Louise in Alberta, Canada. When we approached the ski area, I was wondering where I was going to find water to take my Advil. All of a sudden I heard Velcro ripping, buckles snapping and zippers zipping. I looked around to find almost everyone strapping on knee braces, back braces and supports of all kinds, and ingesting every brand of ibuprofen on the market. One young photographer from Utah with a bad back carried a veritable medicine chest in his backpack. It was comforting to know I wasn't the only one who needed more than sunscreen to prepare for my day on the mountain!

---

*Chapter Summary:*
The best of ski days can be marred for women by high-altitude sickness, sunburn, frostbite, Raynaud's Disease, and eye burn. Even hair needs special attention in high, dry climates. In this chapter you learned tips for protection and prevention. We talked about nutrition, skiing pregnant and skiing in mid-life and reviewed the bare necessities to carry with you on the plane.

---

*Product information:*
For brands of sunscreen that contain the best protection against high-altitude sun, send a stamped, self-addressed business-size envelope to: **The Skin Cancer Foundation**, Box 561, Dept. SR, New York, NY 10156.
**Dermatone** — sunscreen frostbite protection and hair-care products are distributed by **Swix Sport USA**, (800) 343-8335.
**Rocky Mountain Sunscreen** — (800) 442-1442.
**Bolle America** — 3890 Elm St., Denver, CO 80207; (303) 321-4300; FAX (303) 321-6952.

**Carrera International Corp.** — 35 Maple St., Norwood, NJ 07648; (201) 767-3820; FAX (201) 767-8984

**Julie Ann Lickteig, MS, RD,** is available for lectures, workshops and slide shows in high altitude nutrition. She can be reached at (970) 468-0831 in Frisco, Colo.

**Over the Hill Gang** — 3310 Cedar Heights Drive, Colorado Springs, CO 80904; (719) 685-4656; FAX (719) 685-4162.

**70+ Ski Club** — 104 Eastside Dr., Ballston Lake, NY 12019; (518) 399-5458.

## Chapter Twelve

# Eyes on the thighs

---

*"I have stopped skiing until I get in better condition,
which will improve my confidence, technique and
form."* — Anonymous, age 52 from Colorado

*"No, I don't do any regular exercising for skiing. Yes,
I know I should."* — Jane, age 48 from Texas

*"Skiing is exhausting. Being physically conditioned
would help tremendously."*
— Anonymous, age 47 from Colorado

---

Skiing is a sport you must be fit to do, not a sport you do to get fit. More and more, however, the ski industry glosses over the physical aspect of the sport by promoting it as "a total winter experience." Ski resorts refer to their ski mountains as products and market themselves to families as winter vacation destinations complete with sleigh rides, shopping and snowmobiling.

A ski vacation includes all of this, but we must not forget that the sport of skiing is, first and foremost, demanding physical exercise. People unprepared and ill-equipped, along with "couch potatoes" looking for fresh air, need to understand that they subject themselves to serious injury when they try to ski. It is a real bummer to fly home from a ski trip with X-rays of your bones instead of Kodak moments of your skiing. I've done it, and I can tell you crutches and stiff knee braces do not fit in commercial airliner seats.

---

Injury remains the No. 1 fear experienced in skiing by men and women. Yet, in my survey, fewer than one-fourth of the women said they regularly perform any exercises to prevent injury. Many of the women in my survey said they do engage in physical activity, from walking to once-a-week tennis to aerobics, but most said they do not maintain a program for ski conditioning.

Pat Barbier, owner and director of the Vail Center for Physical Therapy, witnesses the results of failing to prepare. "The women we see in therapy [following injury] definitely lack physical conditioning for skiing," Barbier says. "We ask them what they did to get ready for skiing and they might say, 'I went biking last summer.'"

Many women do not realize that the right exercise can help them avoid ski injuries and improve performance. They simply did not grow up understanding, as men did, the link between fitness, mental toughness and enjoyment. If they knew, I am convinced more women skiers would be huffing and puffing, stretching and flexing, crunching and curling.

Orthopedic surgeon Laura Flawn, who also advises The University of Texas Lady Longhorns basketball team, believes physical fitness can prevent injury in every sport. As a skier, she also knows that sore muscles and tired legs can take the fun out of skiing. "When you are not fit you cannot do the skills and skiing is not any fun," Flawn says. Her own fitness regime includes aerobics, weight training and running.

Many private fitness clubs offer ski-conditioning classes. But Herb Wetzel, who teaches these classes at the Athletic Club at Monaco, in Denver, estimates that women comprise only one-fourth of his students.

I am not surprised. When I took the class a few years ago, the male teacher (not Wetzel) also happened to be a competition racquetball player. He geared the workout to match the strength and vigor of the majority of students in the class — strapping, *young*, male jocks. The gym oozed testosterone.

The pace wiped me out. After a few sessions, I opted for an exercise class taught by a woman. Although I found it more suited to women's sta-mina and strength, it was not targeted to skiers.

It is the same dilemma found in the aerobics industry by former heavyweight housewife-turned-fitness-maven Susan Powter: Overweight, unfit women looking for a beginning exercise program become turned off by aerobics classes filled with energetic, trim bodies bouncing around at a pace impossible for them to keep up.

No wonder when I talk to fitness instructors about teaching ski-conditioning classes for wo-men, they contend that the demand is not there.

One physical fitness teacher, Patty Wade, did find success in Aspen. Her classes are predominately women because her work-at-your-own-pace format allows gradual building of ski fitness levels. Wade's ski conditioning circuit has been captured on a video, *In Shape to Ski* (The Aspen Workout, $19.95).

There is more than one way for women to flex their skiing muscles. But before we get into a down-to-basics discussion on exercise, I am going to tell you a story about one woman who learned in a single frightening encounter the power of training body and mind.

## Empowerment

A man assaulted a tennis pal of mine from behind in the stairwell of a busy downtown parking garage when she was on her way to a luncheon. The attractive, slender woman, who stands 5 feet, 6 inches tall, was wearing a silk dress and 3-inch heels. Whirling around when the assailant grabbed her, she slammed her elbow into his chest. Face-to-face with the stranger — who she felt wanted more than her purse — she fought with such force that he finally gave up and ran.

Normally, this genteel woman admits, she could not have mustered the courage or strength to fight with a bigger, stronger man. But just before she drove downtown, she had worked out strenuously in an hour-long, individual tennis lesson, leaving her with an adrenaline high. By the time she encountered the stranger, it was a case of Wonder Woman meeting Peter Rabbit.

"My first instinct was *this guy is not going to get my jewelry!*" she recalls. "Then, with the mental image of hitting a big forehand still in my head, I pivoted and swung my arm back, thinking I would knock his head off with my racquet." My friend, by the way, has never taken a course in self-defense. "The ferociousness of my actions and the words out of my mouth were totally unlike me," she says. "I just felt invincible at that moment."

The woman police officer who responded told my friend that most women freeze in similar situations. The officer even admonished her for struggling, not knowing whether the attacker carried a weapon. Even though my friend explained her high energy level from the workout, the police officer didn't get it.

It is this kind of mental preparedness and empowerment derived from physical fitness that women need in order to be motivated in skiing. Authors John Naisbitt and Patricia Aburdene, in their best-selling book, "*Megatrends for Women*," define empowerment as "feeling confident to act on your own authority." In the case of my friend in the parking-garage stairwell, she fought off an attacker because she believed she could. Feeling fit and strong gave her confidence and authority.

## Cross training

Cultivating strong bones and muscles and maintaining a sound cardiovascular system should be goals in every woman's fitness program. How these goals are attained is a matter of preference. Women in my survey said they enjoy participating in other sports rather than taking regimented classes.

Dane Thomas, a Vail physical therapist and certified strength and conditioning specialist, believes in the power of motivation. "People are more easily motivated to do something that is beneficial and fun rather than something that is merely beneficial," he says. Thomas believes participating in other sports can be good ski training for recreational skiers who have neither the time nor interest for fitness exercising. It is the anything-is-better-than-nothing theory. Be sure to seek qualified assistance whenever you learn a new sport, he emphasizes.

Training should be frequent and consistent. He recommends a minimum of 20 minutes of sustained, elevated heart rate for aerobic activities at least three times a week. This means you do not start timing until you have reached your elevated heart-rate range. To achieve maximum benefit from your workout, go for the minimum 20 minutes, or longer, within this range.

To calculate your target heart rate
• Subtract your age from 220.
• Multiply that number by .65 and then .85 to get the low and high parameters of your target heart-rate range.
• When you take your pulse immediately after exercising, you want the beats-per-minute reading to be between this range.
• Before beginning a new aerobic exercise as part of the same workout, rest a few minutes until your pulse drops to a recovery rate of 120.

Risk factors should be figured into this formula. Primary risk factors include the following:
• being 45 years of age or older.
• blood pressure higher than 145/95.
• cigarette smoking.
• electrocardiogram abnormalities.
• diabetes.

- family history of heart disease occurring in people younger than 50 years old.

If you fall into any of these categories, check with your doctor to determine your safe maximum heart rate. Tops in cross training for skiing is in-line skating. Techniques and muscles used for in-line skating mimic those used in alpine skiing. Other good ski-training sports include mountain biking, running and road cycling.

These sports develop and maintain the physiological requirements for skiing: endurance, muscle strength, quickness, agility, flexibility, coordination and balance. They also develop mental fitness for skiing, including one's learning ability, confidence, visualization skills, the desire to succeed, and the motivation to overcome challenge. Last but certainly not least — they are *fun!*

Other sports activities good for skiers include water skiing, windsurfing, kayaking, rock and ice climbing, snowboarding, soccer, volleyball, racquet sports (tennis, racquetball, squash), basketball and motocross.

Yes, motocross. Racing dirt bikes is the cross- training sport Norwegian skier Stine Lise Hattestad took up to break through barriers she believed prevented her from edging out long-time rival Donna Weinbrecht in World Cup mogul competitions. She also added parachuting, rock climbing and barefoot water skiing to her training program. Her cross-training paid off: Hattestad conquered her foe and her fear by winning the gold medal for mogul skiing in the 1994 Winter Olympic Games. TV viewers around the world shared her victory when, after winning, she relayed her secret. "I skied on the limit today," she said.

What about more feminine activities for ski conditioning, like aerobics and dance?

"Excellent exercise for skiing," says Lisa Feinberg Densmore, a ski racer on the Women's Pro Tour from 1984 to 1990 and a nationally recognized expert in fitness and skiing.

"I have used and taught aerobic workouts extensively for ski training because they incorporate all five areas of fitness," Densmore says. She believes the best aerobic exercise for skiers is a step workout. "I have been using step exercises and drills since the mid-1970s as a junior racer. Music keeps my tempo up and I have fun doing the choreography," she said.

Densmore also believes ballet provides beneficial exercise routines for women skiers, increasing flexibility, toning and balance. "Balance is the most critical skill for skiing," she says. "Ballet teaches you to have a strong center, while working your limbs independently." (Sound familiar?)

And when she learned that the entire Dartmouth College football team had enrolled in a ballet class, Densmore knew she was on the right track. "Although a few men take aerobics or dance, it is really a woman's domain," she says. "The guys don't know what they're missing. It could really help their skiing."

A varied fitness program incorporating cross-training sports, aerobics and dance will help you avoid mental and physical burnout. The best thing any woman can do for her skiing is to make physical activity a *lifestyle*. I don't know any women who ski well who do not also excel in other sports. Ski instructors who live near resorts bike, hike and kayak in summer months. Accomplished women skiers living in urban areas play tennis, ride bikes, run and do aerobics. To become a skier means to live an active, healthy life.

### Bend zee knees, ouch!

Because knee injuries represent the most predominant ski injury in both men and women, let's focus on knees.

In Chapter Three, we learned that the Q angle can cause women's knees to be dangerously out of alignment for skiing. While doctors know a woman's ligaments loosen during pregnancy (then recover following childbirth), some people believe women's ligaments naturally are looser than men's, although no scientific evidence supports this. It could be women's ligaments are just more fragile because muscles supporting them are less developed.

Physical therapist Thomas believes "the general density and size of the female ligament system leads them to be more susceptible to ligament injury." Combined with the Q angle, which puts more stress and higher forces on a woman's knees, it is as plain as your kneecap: Women — and women *skiers* in particular — are predisposed to knee injuries.

## After the fall

At the Steadman-Hawkins Sports Medicine Foundation in Vail, an on-going study based on knee exams of employees of Vail Associates has been successful in identifying risk of injury involving the knee. So far the study shows that skiers with prior knee injuries are 50 percent more likely to be injured again. However, it also concludes that wearing a knee brace (specifically the C.Ti.2 from Innovation Sports) lowers the anterior cruciate ligament (ACL) injury rate in those with previous injuries.

Karen Briggs, director of clinical research at the Foundation, states, "Our goal is to keep people out of the operating room and on the ski hill." To do that she recommends that skiers be aware of their knee status, wear a brace if a knee condition or prior injury exists, and be *ready* to ski, both mentally and physically.

What kind of fall actually causes ACL injuries? Many different mechanisms contribute, says Briggs, and though the Foundation continues to explore the data, it has not issued a definitive statement yet. "Just keep in balance," she warns.

Meanwhile, in Vermont a man named Carl Ettlinger, a mechanical engineer who has spent more time than anyone — some 25 years — researching ski injuries, has identified six elements that make up what he calls the Phantom Foot Syndrome. This kind of ACL injury is so named because the tail of the weighted ski acts as a lever, or another foot, which twists the knee in a fall. It accounts for about 60 percent of all ACL tears, according to Ettlinger.

When all six of the following elements are present, the skier is at extreme risk of injury to the downhill leg, Ettlinger says:

- Uphill arm back.
- Skier off-balance to the rear.
- Hips below the knees.
- Uphill ski unweighted.
- Weight on inside edge of downhill ski tail.
- Upper body generally facing downhill ski.

His suggestion for avoiding these situations is to develop good skiing habits by routinely correcting technique. Ski with arms forward and hands in view, hips above the knees, and maintain balance and control.

Many injuries might be prevented by learning a few simple rules, he says, and eliminating altogether certain types of high-risk behavior:

- Do not fully straighten your legs when you fall. Keep your knees flexed.
- Do not try to get up until you have stopped sliding. When you're down, stay down.
- Do not land on your hands. Keep your arms up and forward.*

(*From "Training Tips for Knee-Friendly Skiing," reprinted with permission of Vermont Safety Research. Look for "Training Tips" at trail map displays at many ski areas and at ski shops with the purchase of most new bindings. )

While the Phantom Foot Syndrome (based on analysis of more than 14,000 skiing accidents and more than a score of videotapes of actual ACL injuries) is probably the most common cause of ACL injuries, it is not the only cause. But a skier would be foolish not to heed the warnings coming out of Ettlinger's Vermont Safety Research lab: "Avoiding high risk behavior, routinely correcting poor technique, and recognizing and responding effectively to potentially dangerous situations are as important to injury reduction in alpine skiing as having your bindings checked, keeping your equipment in good shape, and following the Skier Responsibility Code."

That code, established in 1966 by the National Ski Areas Association, now is called "Your Responsibility Code" to apply to skiers, snowboarders and anyone else who rides lifts and slides down slopes at mountain resorts. It states:

• Always stay in control, and be able to stop or avoid other people or objects.

• People ahead of you have the right of way. It is your responsibility to avoid them.

• You must not stop where you obstruct a trail, or are not visible from above.

• Whenever starting downhill or merging into a trail, look uphill and yield to others.

• Always use devices to help prevent runaway equipment.

• Observe all posted signs and warnings. Keep off closed trails and out of closed areas.

• Prior to using any lift, you must have the knowledge and ability to load, ride and unload safely.

To help skiers gain a better understanding of how their technique may be putting them at risk of knee injury, Vermont Safety Research has developed a video and accompanying pamphlet for home viewing. Proceeds go toward the lab's on-going studies of ski injuries. (See the end of this chapter for information on ordering.)

## Strengthen muscles supporting the knees

A psychological boost comes from knowing that you also reduce risk of injury by building a strong, flexible body.

Experts say it is important for all skiers, perhaps more so for women, to strengthen *quadriceps and hamstrings*, which support the knees and maintain an appropriate strength ratio between the two muscle groups.

Quadriceps are four muscles extending down the front of the thigh and joining in a single tendon at the kneecap. These muscles straighten the knee and extend the lower leg. Hamstrings, a group of three muscles, run from the back of the hip bone to back of the knee, where they connect with the bones of the lower leg. Hamstrings flex the knees. These two groups of muscles balance each other. Hamstrings reinforce the restraining function of the anterior cruciate ligament. Similarly, the quads support the posterior cruciate ligament and both reinforce functions of medial and lateral collateral ligaments.

"When the knee joint is subjected to a force," physical therapist Kacey Conway explains, "the muscles are the first line of defense. If the muscles are weak or fatigued, the next line of defense in an attack [injury] is the ligament." Clearly, muscle strength ranks as one of the most important factors in preventing knee ligament injury.

To compensate for the knock-knee tendency related to the Q angle, women need to develop their abductors and adductors — fancy names for the inner and outer thigh muscles. These muscles move the knees out and in. You use them to ride a horse and to keep your knees from turning in while skiing. (Remember our dry-land drill in Chapter Three?)

# Ski conditioning exercises

## *Quadriceps*

**Health club workout:**

(Fig. 2): The best machine for developing quads is the leg extension. Sitting comfortably in an upright position, place your feet under the round pads and slowly, five seconds each way, extend your legs to a locked or parallel position and then let them down.

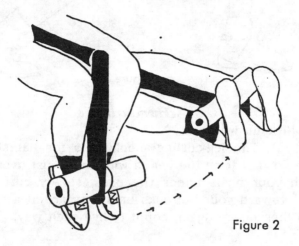

Figure 2

**Home workout:**

(Fig. 3): Lunges are excellent for quads and buttocks. Holding hand weights at your sides for balance, take a "giant step" forward with your right leg and bend the knee until your thigh is parallel to the floor. Concentrate on lining up your knee over your second toe, and do not extend the knee beyond the toes. Hold for five seconds. Repeat with the left leg.

You can also use the bottom step of a stairway, or a chair. From a standing position, place the toes of your right foot behind you on the step. With your left foot in front in the lunge position, knee lined up over toes as above, raise and lower your hips in a set of five. Repeat with the other leg.

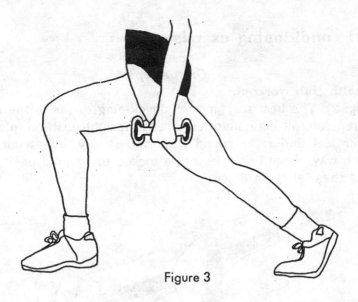

Figure 3

## *Hamstrings*

**Health club workout:**

(Fig. 4): The leg-curling machine is for hamstrings. Lie face down, flat on the bench with knees just over the edge. With your heels under the pads, slowly curl your legs back toward your buttocks until they are at a right angle, and then down. Again, count to five each way.

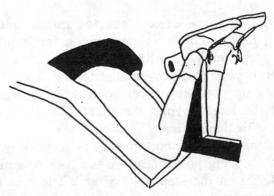

Figure 4

**Home workout:**
(Fig. 5): Lie flat on your back. Slide your knees up to about 45 degrees. Push on your heels to lift your hips as far off the ground as you can, pulling the abdominals down. Hold for as long as you can, then rest and repeat. This works both hamstrings at the same time.

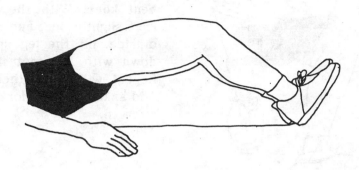

Figure 5
*Inner-thigh muscles*

**Health club workout:**
(Fig. 6): Using the low pulley, stand with your back to the weights, strap attached to the left ankle, slightly bending the right leg. Bring the left leg behind the right; then, keeping it straight, bring it around in an arc, ending in front of the standing leg. Repeat. Use light weights and lots of repetitions with each set.

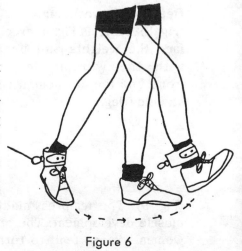

Figure 6

**Home workout:**

(Fig. 7): Sit up with your back straight, hands around one bent knee. With the other knee slightly bent and to the outside, lift the leg up and down with the foot flexed. Repeat with the other leg. Add ankle weights for more strength.

### Outer-thigh muscles

**Health club workout:**
(Fig. 8): Same as Fig. 6, except face the weights and begin with the working leg in front. End the arc behind the standing leg.

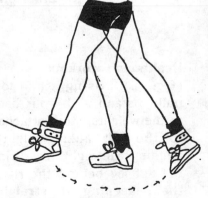

Figure 8

(Fig. 9): The leg-press machine is good for overall thigh muscle development. The athletic director at my club says women's knees tend to turn in when pushing on the foot rest. (Have you heard *that* before?) So, when extending your legs to press, strengthen your outer quads by maintaining alignment of knees over toes.

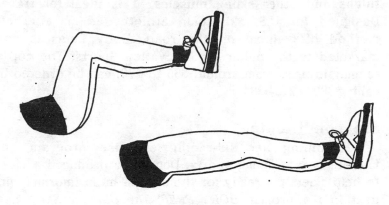

Figure 9

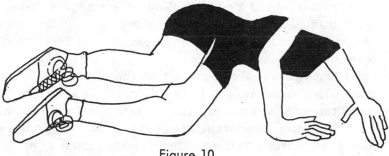

Figure 10

**Home workout:**
(Fig. 10): Lie on your left hip, propping up your side with your left elbow. Bend your knees to form a right angle with your torso. Lift the right leg about six inches parallel with the left, then lower. Without touching the bottom leg, lift again. Do a set, then repeat on the other side. You can also do this lying on your side with your hands between your knees, straight legs at a right angle to hips. Lift the upper leg with flexed foot as above, being careful not to turn your knee in. Ankle weights can be added here also.

***When you're on the road***

A self-contained, portable exercise system, called Body Lines, uses resistance cords and is perfect for working the thighs and other skiing muscles. It is ideal for travel. Designed for U.S. Ski Team athletes as an alternate method of training on the road, Body Lines is now marketed to the public by Innovation Sports. The cords, ranging in price from around $55 to $70, can be ordered by calling (800) 222-4284.

## Ski conditioning

Combining her ski-racing exercise program and favorite cross-training sports, Densmore produced a video to help skiers get ready for the slopes. In an informal, girl-next-door approach, *BODY PREP! The Ultimate Ski Fitness Video* (Driscoll Communi-cations, $29.95) features Densmore and fellow pro-racers Leslie Baker-Brown and Laurie Baker-Wertz demonstrating how easy exercising in your own backyard can be. The video also shows how to intensify your training with the seasons and build toward winter.

I like the way the first part of the tape demonstrates how the exercises apply directly to skiing. In simultaneous sequences, the women perform dry-land exercises and cross-training sports; a smaller frame on the same screen features them skiing, illustrating how the exercises relate. The second segment shows a follow-along workout of aerobics, strength training and stretching.

Borrowing from *BODY PREP!* and the *U.S. Ski Team Training Manual*, here are suggestions for a ski-conditioning program to combine with the knee-strengthening exercises detailed earlier.

# Five areas of fitness

## *Endurance*

The ability to contract muscles against resistance over a long period of time is important. In skiing, good endurance will reduce fatigue and build energy. The following activities should be sustained at least 20 minutes to receive maximum endurance benefit:

- Hiking
- Running
- Biking
- Stationary biking
- Aerobics
- Treadmill or stair stepper
- Rowing machine

## *Strength*

Strengthening the muscles by progressively adding resistance is the most effective way to improve overall athletic ability. Without strong muscles in the legs, abdomen and arms, skiing is not as safe or enjoyable. Remember to breathe properly during strength exercising. These two Xs work together: eXhale on eXertion. Heavy weights and fewer repetitions increase muscle; lighter weights and more repetitions will tone muscles without increasing mass. Do strength exercises every other day to allow muscles to recover.

Strength exercises include:

- Floor exercises for abdominals, arms and legs (detailed later in this chapter)
- Body Lines or other resistance bands
- Weight machine/hand or free weights
- Rowing machine
- Water skiing
- Wind surfing

## *Quickness and Agility*

The ability to change directions rapidly in a smooth, fluid manner is essential for skiing bumps and gates.

Good agility exercises include:
- Tennis
- Soccer
- Squash

### Coordination and Balance

These are associated with agility and quick-ness, all excellent indicators of athletic ability. Balance is the overall skill required for skiing.

Good conditionig and balance exercises include:
- Jumping rope
- Kayaking
- In-line skating
- All other sports

### Flexibility

Before starting any activity, proper warm-up and stretching is most helpful for reducing the risk of injury. Physical therapist Thomas has seen it firsthand. "Flexibility cannot be stressed enough," Thomas says. "Without it, every activity will be compromised."

A skier whose muscles are flexible is less likely to tear or pull a muscle in a fall. Pre-stretched muscles allow greater strength and power for the workout. The *U.S. Ski Team Training Manual* suggests stretching after skiing to guard against muscle soreness and tightness.

Here are good exercises to enhance flexibility:
- Stretching exercises (detailed later in this chapter)
- Dance

## Floor exercises

Perform each exercise one to three times, depending on your fitness level. Do each for 15 to 30 seconds, rest for the same amount of time, then repeat. Rest two to five minutes between each exercise.

• **Lateral thrust** (Fig. 11): Explosively jump from side to side from one foot to the other. Develops quads and simulates side-to-side motion of the legs in skiing.

Figure 11

• **Stomach cramp** (Fig. 12): Lie on your back, knees bent and feet crossed in the air. With hands behind the head, slowly curl up and touch elbows to knees; then do a set crossing right elbow to left knee and alternate. Works the abdominal muscles, one of the most neglected muscle groups in fitness and one of the most important for skiing. A strong stomach helps you recover when you sit back and helps maintain upper body control while the feet work independently.

• **Push-up** (Fig. 13): With your back straight, lower chest to the floor and raise back up. To make this exercise a little easier, drop knees to the ground. Increases arm strength needed for carrying ski equipment and getting up after falls.

Figure 13

• **Bouncing tuck** (Fig. 14): In a tuck position like downhill racers, bounce by lifting feet off the floor. Start high and drop to a lower tuck. Develops quadriceps and hamstrings in the legs. These muscle groups should maintain equal strength and are important in all levels of skiing.

Figure 14

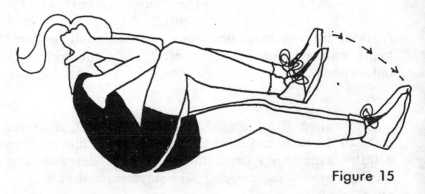

Figure 15

- **Stomach crunch** (Fig. 15): Lie on your back, hands behind the head, curl upper body as you raise your knees; then extend legs and lower upper body, not letting feet or head touch the floor. More work on the all-important midsection of the body. A strong stomach means a stable back.

- **Arm dip** (Fig. 16): Supporting yourself be-tween two chairs, firmly grip the chair backs and raise your body un-til your feet leave the floor. Then, slowly lower your-self until your feet contact the floor again. Strong arms help with race starts and poling on catwalks.

Figure 16

- **One-leg knee bend** (Fig. 17): Stand on one leg with the other extended out and knee bent; slowly lower the standing leg, making sure not to go below 90 degrees. If you have knee problems, do not go as low. For easier balancing, use a chair for

Figure 17

support. Uses the same leg-muscle control as weighting and releasing a ski.

• **Sit-up** (Fig. 18): With knees bent and your lower back on the floor, slowly curl torso up, elbows to knees. A strong stomach means a strong back and helps prevent lower back pain after skiing.

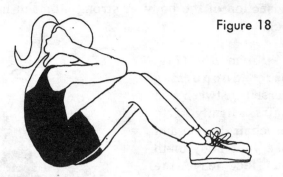

Figure 18

• **Side push-up** (Fig. 19): Lie on your right side, right hand on left side of waist, left hand on floor in front of right shoulder; extend left arm, raising torso off floor and then lower. A sturdy upper body will help direct the hands forward and up, creating a solid pole plant.

Figure 19

• **Squat thrust** (Fig. 20): Start with hands on the floor slightly ahead of your feet; kick feet back to push-up position, then return to squat; make an explosive jump up and land in the next squat. Creates the muscle power needed to ski dynamically and aggressively and to handle faster speeds.

Figure 20

## Agility exercises

The goal of these exercises is to gain the ability to move quickly under any circumstances.

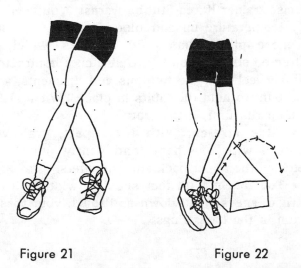

Figure 21                           Figure 22

• **Carioca** (Fig. 21): Lateral running, crossing left leg in front of right, right in front of left, in a line. Develops quick feet.

• **Bench hops** (Fig. 22): Hop quickly from side to side over a low bench or pillow with feet together, hands forward. Start with 10, build to 20. Helps you feel quicker from ski to ski, especially when making jump turns on steeps.

• **Step-ups:** Using a variety of patterns, step up and down the bottom step of a stairway as fast as you can. Helps with making snappy, short turns down the fall line.

• **Backward run:** Stay low, pumping shoulders and arms while backpedaling in different directions. Keep the upper torso quiet — no hip mobility. Develops independent footwork.

## Flexibility exercises

Each of these positions should be held for 20 seconds, creating the sensation of mild stretching in the muscles. Do not bounce through the stretch; breathe normally. *Do not stretch until you have done a thorough warm-up.* Exercise trainer Karen Stubbs warns: "You need to get the body temperature up and blood pumping. Warm muscles are more pliant than cold muscles, which are in a contracted state. If you try to stretch a contracted muscle, you may feel it in the tendons and ligaments, which need to be tight to hold the joints in place." When skiing, take a warm-up run first, then stretch.

• **Side stretch:** With legs apart, grab your wrist overhead with one hand and gently pull to the side, stretching the upper back and shoulders.

• **Toe touch:** With feet shoulder-width apart and soft, not rigid, knees, bend down and touch your toes, feeling a stretch in the hamstrings.

• **Standing quad stretch** (Fig. 23): Balance on one foot, grab the other by the top of the foot behind you and bend forward at the waist, stretching the quad to balance the stretch of the hamstring.

Figure 23

• **Lunge stretch** (Fig 24): With both hands on the floor in front of you parallel to your left foot, extend your right leg back, bending the left leg at a right angle, taking care to keep the knee at a right angle over the foot. Repeat on the other side. This stretches the groin, hamstrings, quads and hips.

Figure 24

• **Leg crossover** (Fig. 25): Sitting on the floor, cross your right leg over your left knee. Place your left elbow to the outside of your right knee and look over your left shoulder. Repeat on the other side. Feel a stretch in your lower back and hips.

Figure 25

Figure 26

- **Calf stretch** (Fig. 26): Lean hands against a wall. With toes pointed straight ahead, extend one leg behind you and feel a stretch in the calf and Achilles' tendon. Repeat on the other leg. Make sure your heels stay flat.

## Move it on the mountain

After your first run of the day, when your blood is flowing fast and your muscles are warm, do these stretching exercises:

- **Torso twist**: Keeping your hips quiet, swing your arms from side to side, giving your upper body, shoulders and arms a good stretch.

- **T-stretch:** Bracing yourself with ski poles, lift your leg so the tail of the ski is perpendicular to the ground in front of you and your extended leg is parallel to the ground. Feel a stretch in your hamstrings.
- **Tip-drop stretch:** Do the reverse, placing the tip of the ski on the snow behind you, stretching the quads.
- **Side Lunges:** Bend the left leg as you slide the right leg as far as you can to the side and back. This stretches quads, hamstrings and groin.
- **Calf Stretch:** Leaning on your ski poles, slide one leg back until you feel a stretch in the calf.

Do neck rolls, side stretches and toe touches in your skis. If you have lower-back pain when you ski, tuck your ski poles in the small of your back and lean on them, gently stretching through the mid-section when you are standing in the lift line.

Whatever you choose for your ski conditioning regime, make sure you include plenty of aerobics for your heart and lungs and exercises for the specific muscles used in skiing.

Make home exercises a part of your day. I do mine while catching up on the TV morning news. I also do leg lifts, knee bends and stretching while I am on the phone. Focus on keeping your knees over your toes throughout the day while climbing stairs, sitting, even standing. Contract your inner thigh muscles while you "squeeze a dime" with your butt muscles. You will create new muscle memory that you will notice on the slopes!

## What if ...?

If you are injured while skiing, play it safe and visit the medical clinic. Jack Mason, director of the ski patrol at Winter Park, has observed many injured women over the years. He believes women tolerate more pain than men. "If you don't believe that, you have never had a baby," Mason jokes.

Do not ignore pain. Women who have given birth and post-menopausal women (because of osteoporosis), in particular, can sustain pelvis fractures from falling hard on their butts. Because the pelvis houses the bladder and other vital organs, the danger of not being treated lies in bone fragments piercing your innards. So save the toughness for childbirth. On the slopes, be sensible when it hurts: Reach out and tell somebody.

Carry a credit card when you ski. Most ski-area clinics are not set up for billing health insurers. If you are younger than 18, you will also need a parental permission slip for treatment.

On being sensible, Mason shared an interesting statistic: He says 87 percent of people killed by lightning are men. Does this tell us that more men play golf, or that more men do not know enough to come in out of the rain?

## Born-again skiers

Women who have given up skiing or are thinking of giving it up because of chronic knee pain, knee or leg injuries, or weak legs due to illness or age should know about CADS. I am including this remarkable piece of equipment in this book because I wholeheartedly believe in it.

CADS stands for *Constant-force Lift Articulated Dynamic Struts.* The name may be technical, but the results are straightforward: CADS dramatically reduces strain on knees, thighs, hips and lower back, consequently lowering the chance of knee injury in a fall and diminishing fatigue.

Even more exciting, CADS enhances ski performance and control because of the increased snow contact and edging power.

My friend Adele, who suffers from chrondro-malicia, a knee condition related to the Q angle, was forced to bring an end to 40 years of skiing because of pain, even on bunny slopes. I convinced her to try CADS with me. We noticed the effect immediately. For me, it felt as though a giant pair of hands was lifting my butt, taking weight off my legs while at the same time pushing my skis onto the snow, making it easier to carve. I cruised faster with more stability and felt more in control of my skis than ever before.

As for Adele, she kept waiting for the old pain to set in. It never did. We skied four hours straight, on bumps and groomed, and neither of us experienced tiredness in our legs. Adele was thrilled. I was amazed.

The system consists of a harness worn inside your ski pants, attached by strings and rods to pulleys screwed into the backs of your ski boots. (The strings come out of two small grommets poked into the seat of your pants.) It may look funny, but for those who otherwise could not ski, it is worth the hassle. Plus, it is a great conversation piece in the lift line!

Inventor Walter Dandy, who moved to Vail from Baltimore to market his product, has an inch-thick book of testimonials from born-again skiers. Their message — CADS allows skiers to pile up vertical miles without pain or fatigue.

"The idea is brilliant," writes a 51-year-old woman who teaches physical education. "It counterbalances unnatural constant forward weighting of ski boots ... extending years of skiing by avoiding abusive muscle strain."

Says Dandy, "We think we have the highest customer satisfaction of any consumer product in the world." And a remarkable rate of purchase: 90 percent of those who demo the device buy it.

The CADS package costs $388, and all parts are replaceable at no charge.

*Chapter Summary:*
We emphasized that skiing is a sport you must be fit to do, not do to get fit. You risk injury and enjoyment when you are not physically and mentally prepared.

A good fitness program includes cross-training sports as well as exercises for specific muscle groups used in skiing. For women, strengthening the muscles that support the knees is most important because of the Q angle.

You learned to calculate your target heart rate and how to exercise in order to develop and maintain the physiological requirements for skiing: endurance, muscle strength, quickness and agility, flexibility, coordination and balance.

Knee injuries are the predominant injury in skiing. On-going research shows us that being aware of susceptibility and avoiding certain situations can help defend against ACL injury.

A device called CADS allows people with knee problems or leg fatigue to ski comfortably for a longer time.

---

*Recommended viewing:*
**ACL Awareness video** — To order, write to Vermont Safety Research, P.O. Box 85, Underhill Ctr. VT 05490; or call (802) 899-2126; FAX (802) 899–3677.

*BODY PREP! The Ultimate Ski Fitness Video* — To order, write to Driscoll Communications and Densmore Associates, 45 Lyme Road, Suite 206-A, Hanover, NH 03755, or call (800) 424-0033.

*In Shape to Ski* — To order, write to The Aspen Workout, P.O. Box 1305, Aspen, CO 81612, or call (800) 925-9754.

*Product information:*
**CADS** — For more information, call Walter Dandy in Vail at (800) 364-3148.

**C.Ti.2 knee brace** — Innovation Sports, Inc., 7 Chrysler, Irvine, CA 92718; (800) 222-4284 or (714) 859-4407; FAX (800) 453-4567.

Chapter  Thirteen

# *Fear less*

---

*"I'm terrified of getting on a slope I can't ski and not being able to get down."*
— LeAnn, age 35 from Texas

*"Fear of injury and speed keep me from skiing as well as I'd like ... Skiing more and getting over some simple fears would greatly improve my skiing. I would like to ski down moguls, knees together, with a smile on my face."*
— Anonymous, age 40 from Oklahoma

*"I don't know if an inner fear holds me back or if I just don't care enough. I guess it will take the right person, not only to teach me to ski, but to help me overcome the fear (or whatever it is)."*
— Maureen, age 53 from Colorado

---

Mary Jo has skied off and on for 34 of her 54 years. She
loves everything about the sport and enjoys ski vacations with family, even though they long ago surpassed her in ability. Mary Jo's biggest drawback is a paralyzing fear of getting hurt.

Sometime she finds herself on terrain beyond her capabilities. "I am in *agony*," she says. "I try to avoid being in these spots because I know I am not going to feel good about myself. Consequently, I haven't fallen in 20 years. But I haven't gotten off the green slopes, either!"

Still, Mary Jo has had fun on the slopes over the years. She remembers three occasions when she even skied without fear. Each time immediately followed a traumatic episode in her life: the Cesarean birth of her daughter, her open-heart surgery, and the removal of her wisdom teeth.

"In my mind, I said, 'If I can go through this, I can do anything,'" Mary Jo recalls. "And I skied better than I've ever skied."

But the little positive voice turned negative again and the petrifying fear returned.

Now, however, Mary Jo is putting into practice two new tricks to manage fear. "I indulge in a Bloody Mary before I go out, and then I ski to Placido Domingo and John Denver on tape when I want to get through the rough parts," she says, laughing.

## Two types of fear

The feeling of being paralyzed with fear atop a ski run is familiar to anyone in a high-risk sport like skiing, especially anyone still learning. Your stomach agitates like the rinse cycle of a washing machine, your knees and hands shake, your heart pounds. You lose whatever motivation got you there in the first place.

I remember a time in 1963 when I froze atop Bradley's Bash at Winter Park. My late husband, a ski racer when he was in high school and college, was encouraging me to ski more difficult runs. Looking down that steep, wavy trail blanketed with fresh snow (this was in the days before grooming), I was terror-stricken. The longer I stood there, the steeper and bumpier the run became. I could not get my legs to turn. I could not move forward in a traverse, let alone go down. A kick-turn in my shaky state was out of the question.

Finally, after much coaxing and cajoling, I took my skis off and slid down, embarrassed to tears. The next day, I signed up for a lesson.

In their book, *"Inner Skiing"* (Random House, $4.99 for revised paperback), learning expert Timothy Gallwey and psychologist Bob Kriegel describe two types of fear:

• Fear I is the paralyzing fear that interferes with our ability to perform at our best.

• Fear II is the body's natural response to challenge, the fight-or-flight response. In emergencies, mothers react instinctively to protect children from harm. This good fear heightens perception and provides energy to move beyond normal capabilities.

Fear I, the type we mostly feel in skiing, has three essential components:

• The sense of *danger*.

• The sense of *vulnerability* – you can get hurt by this danger.

• The sense of *inability to overcome* the danger.

If any one of these ingredients is missing, Gallway and Kriegel maintain, no real fear exists.

They explain: In skiing, the slope usually is perceived as the danger and the skier as vulnerable. But if the skier feels competent to ski the trail, no fear exists. Likewise, if the skier is incompetent but the hill is too flat to be perceived as a danger, no fear exists. Lastly, if the skier feels no vulnerability to being hurt (hard to imagine) no fear exists.

The solution to coping with fear is to increase awareness of the realities of a given situation — that is, learning to perceive *real* danger, to know one's competence and one's *actual* vulnerability. By allowing realistic fear to guide us, inappropriate fear may diminish, even disappear.

Though some people feel less fear, no one is immune to it. A beginning skier may be afraid of going too fast. A more advanced skier may feel the same degree of fear in the bumps. Following her gold-medal-winning Super G run in the 1994 Olympic Winter Games, U.S. Olympic Team member Diann Roffe-Steinrotter said she was "so nervous at the start I almost lost my stomach."

Teammate Picabo Street, who won a silver medal in those Games, said the memory of Austrian downhiller

Ulrike Maier's death on the race course two weeks earlier was "all over the faces of the women here [at Lillehammer]. It is right on the surface. I look at it as God's way of looking down at all of us and saying, 'Watch out; be careful.'"

## Dealing with fear

In skiing, learning to recognize, understand and manage fear will go a long way toward en-hancing performance and enjoyment. Realize that every skier, regardless of ability, deals with fear. Said Roffe-Steinrotter of her winning run: "I just let my instincts go. I said, 'I can do this.' Then I relaxed and had fun."

Another Olympic competitor tries to think about task-specific things in her skiing to take her mind off the bigger picture, which is "scared to death!" she says.

Asked about the danger of fast skiing, Olympic skier Street says she uses her head to manage fear. "I try not to think about it," Street says. "When it hits me, I am able to pull back a little bit."

Pulling back is the No. 1 tactic cited by most of the women who participated in my survey. They admitted to skiing cautiously, skiing slower and skiing more in control when they find themselves on terrain that freaks them out. Others said they work on improving their skills with lessons.

Women are less fearful when skiing with instructors or people they trust — an important aspect of exploring new or more challenging terrain. One woman who participated in my survey said when she does not feel safe, "Sometimes I cry and swear I'll never go back. But somehow I 'get it' and get down. It is not pretty!"

Still, many others completely avoid anything that sends shivers down their spines. In some cases, this is smart — like the woman afraid of being hit by a reckless or out-of-control skier. She skis only weekdays and on uncrowded runs.

But sometimes avoidance can become self-defeating. For anyone wanting to improve skiing technique, small risks on more difficult runs are necessary. An example is the woman who says skiing in the trees scares her. She still skis in them, but slowly rather than not at all. Drawing the line at skiing certain types of threatening trails comes easy for some women. After all, skiing is supposed to be enjoyable and rewarding. Not everyone thinks challenge is fun. "I am happy skiing with my family for recreation and fun," says Jean, another survey participant, who skis five times a year or so. Those skiers who are not willing to risk a little prefer to save anxious moments for the inevitable poor conditions like flat light, blizzards and ice.

A few women in the survey said they feel no fear at all about skiing. An intermediate skier from Tennessee swore that if she had any fear, she would not ski!

Fear of injury is the overriding concern for women (and men) in skiing. Situations women in my survey said they fear most include losing control, hitting an object, such as a tree, careening over "the edge," and getting stuck on a trail beyond their abilities.

It is finding themselves on a too-difficult trail that intermediate-level women said they fear most. Though mentioned a few times by my survey respondents, fear of failure and not keeping up ranked low on the list.

The most dreaded snow condition among women is ice. The most terrifying terrain is a mogul field. And steep or icy moguls really blows them away. Consequently, what most women in my survey said they wanted to improve was bump technique.

Others worry about other things. "My greatest fear is not having fun," says 24-year-old Christie, who skis nine times a year. Her solution is to, "Dress warm, go with cool people, and do not ski on holiday weekends (especially in California!)."

Annette, 29, said she worries about someone running into her. "It happens a lot in the East at small ski resorts that are overpacked," she said. To overcome it, she fights for her space. "I ski aggressively, and when it happens, I preach to them and turn them in."

The best way to avoid being hit is to ski in your "corridor." I like to pretend I am in an alley about as wide as a highway lane. If you learn to make short, quick turns down the alley's fall line, you can stay on the side of the slope, away from the maddening crowd. The snow is usually better there, too.

I was surprised that most of the beginner and expert woman skiers in my survey said they dealt with fear in the same way — improving technique. Advanced skiers, meanwhile, said they were more likely to use caution and ski within their abilities than to take lessons or practice skills to get through intimidating situations. Skiing slow and in control ranked first with intermediates. The second-rated choice, intermediates said, was that they would just as soon avoid harder terrain than figure out how to tackle it.

For me, practicing skills and focusing on technique prove best for coping with fear in skiing.

## New skills for conquering fear

*Ashley Fischer, team leader of Women's Turn at Vermont's Sugarbush Resort, sees every kind of fear imaginable expressed by hundreds of women who participate in the clinic each season. Here is an example of how her staff helps alleviate fear in women skiers. (With help from Nancy Luke, psychiatrist Patricia Simmons, and psychologists Barbara Kester and Peggy Sax.)*

Women seem to experience fear more often and more intensely than men. It occurs at all levels and for many reasons.

It is important to understand the difference between appropriate fear and inappropriate fear. Fear can be appropriate when it gives us proper respect for the task at hand and protects us from doing something dangerous. Fear can also be disproportionate and interfere with performance. It can paralyze us or drive us away from a situation that might have been quite safe, even fun.

A novice skier may be afraid of speed. An advanced skier may be just as afraid of bumps. Adverse conditions scare some. Terrain may scare others. Some are afraid of wind, some of heights, some of powder. Almost everyone is afraid of being hurt. We have yet to meet a woman who is unafraid of losing control.

We do not have control over weather or conditions, and the terrain is laid out for us. However, we do have the skill to gain or regain control. Through skill development and positive psychological training, we can learn to look at each threatening situation that presents itself and, rather than panic or respond in an inappropriate manner, say to ourselves, "I can do this. What skills and attitude do I need to accomplish the task?" Through repetition and continued success, our responses will become more and more automatic. We can learn to trust our skills and ourselves. We can allow realistic fear to guide us while inappropriate fear lessens, even disappears.

### Skill development

First and foremost, everyone from the never-ever to the advanced skier needs the appropriate skills. Everybody benefits from proper coaching. The broader our repertoire of technical skills, the greater number of challenges we can meet with confidence. While other chapters in *"WomenSki"* deal more specifically with the technical aspects of skiing, in this section we will focus on helping women choose the skills they might want to use in fear-producing situations and framing our teaching in a way that develops confidence and minimizes anxiety.

### Language

Traditional ski teaching often teaches skills in a way that isn't comforting to most women. How many of us have been told to "launch ourselves down the hill" when initiating a turn? How many of us have had our lack of aggressiveness thrown in our faces? Even the term "fall line" contains negative connotations.

We teach skiers to become more masterful, not necessarily aggressive. Instead of fall line, we say *flow line*, a more accurate term describing what we want to do. You would rather *flow* down the hill than *fall* down it? Our skiers are not told to *launch* their bodies down the hill. Instead, one of our participants imagines Mel Gibson is standing downhill from her and she rises across her skis to embrace him. Which do you find more appealing?

### Imagery

Women's Ski Discovery also uses imagery to enhance learning and control fear. When you are skiing on a crowded slope, imagine a white light emanating from your center and enveloping you. Nobody can penetrate that light, so you can keep skiing down the hill in its protection. In the moguls, think of your ski tips as playful dolphins. Imagine how dolphins ride the swells. They plunge, they jump, they cavort. Most important, their flexible bodies undulate up and around, in and out of the waves, just as skis do in the bumps.

Relaxation combined with visual imagery is an even more powerful tool for dealing with fear. In a relaxed state, you can learn to introduce vivid images of yourself skiing. You can create your own drama as rich and as detailed as your imagination will allow. Sports psychologists and professional athletes most often use imagery to enhance performance. We have found it helps women gripped by fear or apprehension to create alternate scripts. Imagine yourself gliding freely down a favorite trail rather than careening out of control. Some women picture themselves skiing confidently down the same trail where they once experienced a frightening fall or an injury. What you see is what you get. A positive inner image and expectation will lead to a positive slope experience.

### Non-threatening terrain

Not only do we use less threatening language and imagery, we also introduce new skills and concepts on less threatening terrain. It is important to remember you will be less likely to experiment with something new if you are concerned about the terrain. We only need one challenge at a time. An important component of learning to ski is trust — trust in the instructor, trust in the new skill, and most of all, trust in ourselves and our abilities. Trusting is difficult if we're afraid before we begin. There is plenty of time to practice new skills in the real world after we have begun to understand and feel them in our skiing.

### Massage the comfort zone

Another way to create a more positive learning environment is to retain your old skills. You have been getting down the hill in a way that works for you. We may modify your movement pattern and enhance certain skills or de-emphasize others, but we want you to keep everything else (unless it is completely counterproductive). The bigger your bag of tricks, the more versatile you can be and the better you can cope in an uncomfortable situation. Everyone has occasions to be happy they know how to snowplow. And the side-slip can be incredibly useful in difficult sections. We do not want to lose these skills just because we now know how to make a parallel turn. These skills can keep us out of trouble. (*Survival skills* are discussed later in this section.)

It is important to keep challenging yourself by moving in and out of your comfort zone. If you do not, your zone will get smaller and smaller until you have regressed and feel anxious about everything. You will never improve or learn to use your new skills if you do not keep moving, physically and emotionally. We do not advocate throwing yourself out of your comfort zone. This can promote anxiety and fear. We like to think of massaging its barriers. Ease yourself in and out. When you leave it, return to it on the next run.

### Psychological techniques

As important as technical-skill development is, we also need to learn to manage our fear. The most skilled skier can forget everything in a moment of fear.

Unfortunately, that is usually when we most need to tap into the technical survival skills that are going to get us out of the dilemma. We need to empower ourselves to accomplish the task.

### Make good choices

First and foremost, it is important to make appropriate choices, to know what you can and can't handle. It is also important to learn to say no when peers (often males) ask you to ski something you know is beyond your ability. Learn to choose an alternate route, meet them later and continue to feel good about yourself. When you do make the choice to follow them, which may mean leaving your comfort zone, learn to listen to yourself. You might prefer the challenge early in the day when you feel fresh, not late in the afternoon when you are exhausted. Challenge yourself if and when you want, not because you — or someone else — feel you have to. The choice should be yours.

There are times when you find yourself in a state of fear. The weather conditions may have changed. You misread the trail map. Someone told you a trail was groomed and it was all bumps. A well-meaning friend took you to a run you can't handle. By training yourself to take control, you can trust your own ability and ski to safety.

### Relax

One of the first techniques we teach is *Progressive Relaxation*. First we establish a general state of relaxation before we go out on the hill. This is done by systematically tensing specific muscle groups, holding that tension and then relaxing those muscles as we feel the tension flow out through the extremities. Tension and contraction alternate with release.

"Letting go" is extremely important in maintaining flow and rhythm in our skiing. Try one right now. Make a fist and tighten the arm muscles throughout the forearm right up through the biceps. Now, hold that tension for 30 seconds. Take a deep breath and allow everything to relax. Feel the tension flow right out through your fingertips? Repeat with the other arm.

You can then move through the whole body, shoulders, trunk, legs and feet. For maximum effect, try it with relaxing music. You should feel much more relaxed and open. As you get more practiced, you can start associating a word or sound with the state of relaxation. Ideally, you will learn to invoke this relaxed state by calling up your word whenever you find yourself in a fear-producing situation.

You can also do a mini relaxation on the chair lift, or right on the hill, whenever you start to feel anxious. As you get more adept at recognizing where you carry your tension, you can isolate that part of the body and relax only it.

How often do you scrunch up your toes when you hit ice? It is as though you are trying to hold on to the surface with your toes, right through your ski boots! All you gain is pain. You probably never developed skills for skiing on ice because you wasted energy holding on for dear life. Next time you find yourself on an icy slope, try stopping and squeezing your toes. Hold that tension and feel it. Take a deep breath and allow the tension to flow out the bottom of your feet, relaxing them in your boots. Start again and see if you and your feet aren't more relaxed for the rest of the run.

### Positive alternate response

Finally, when confronted by a fear-producing situation, we need to replace a useless panic response with a *positive alternate response*. The more we rely on the appropriate positive alternate response, the more automatic its use will become. Eventually the fear will disappear.

If you are on a trail with trees, try looking between and around the trees, not at them. How many times have you focused on an ice patch and then found yourself on top of it? Next time, try looking for the good snow instead. Confronted by a steep section of the trail, look at the flats beyond. It is a much more comforting focus and you will find, in a few turns, that you have reached those flats.

Look at the bumps as a series of opportunities to turn, rather than a minefield. You know you can make turns, so look for the paths and go at your own pace. It may not always be a pretty sight, but you will get down!

### Survival skills

Our survival skills provide excellent positive alternate responses. In Women's Ski Discovery, we teach key words to help us tap into those survival skills in times of stress.

For example, as many of us approach ice, our mind screams, "Ice!" Our downhill arm flies up in the air and our skis slide out from under us. Instead, try this. As you are sliding over the ice looking for good snow, fully extend your downhill arm in front of you and lower it to the ground. This will help you balance over your more stable downhill ski. It also helps you keep your center over your feet so your weight does not get back, allowing your skis to shoot out from under you.       This stabilizing movement lets you focus on the safe haven of soft snow ahead and sustain movement down the hill. You will slide over that icy surface and reach the safety of good snow.

Give that positive alternate response a name. We simply use "arm." Before you know it, with practice and repeated success, ice will be replaced with arm and you will begin to feel a mastery over this extremely threatening situation.

What about steeps? We have a survival skill we call "tips up the hill" — steering our inside ski up the hill to decelerate at the end of each turn. You can call on this to control speed right from the start instead of invoking the power panic turn after you lose control.

Instead of leaning up the hill, holding each turn and struggling down, reach down the hill, with each pole touch. This will allow your energy to flow in the right direction. Don't forget: the sooner and more efficiently you start your turn, the more time you will have to finish it. It is in the finish portion of the turn where we gain control. When you hold back out of fear, your weight drops back, your skis get away from you and you lose control. Replace holding back with contact with the front of your boots. This way, you can make an immediate adjustment before things get away from you.

As you become more proficient and gain more technical knowledge, you will create your own "positive alternate responses" uniquely useful to you. You will learn to anticipate situations that provoke fear or panic. You will also learn to respond in a positive, take-charge manner; at the very least you will head off a counter-productive reaction. At best, fear may disappear altogether.

### Lighten up

How about viewing fear as respect? *You don't ski slowly — you have excellent speed control.* Good speed control allows you to carry more speed with less apprehension. *You are not a wimp — you exercise good judgment.* When you trust your judgment, you explore new horizons. You can even resort to humor: Ice becomes "loud powder." Hard snow chunks become "death cookies." Humor does not make the problem disappear but it allows us to put it in perspective and settle on a strategy.

Fear — both appropriate and inappropriate — can be managed effectively on the slopes. These techniques, combined with skill development, will help you learn a sense of well-being, confidence and mastery. If we know we can control our own destiny, we can let go of inappropriate fear. It can become a thing of the past. Without fear, we can really have fun and rediscover the joy of skiing. And we can look at our accomplishments and feel justified pride.

## Pushing through fear

In her book, *Feel the Fear and Do It Anyway* (Ballantine Books, $12), psychologist Susan Jeffers lists five truths about fear that I have learned to apply to my skiing:

• The fear will never go away as long as I continue to grow [in my skiing].

• The only way to get rid of the fear of doing something [skiing bumps] is to go out and ... do it [ski bumps].

• The only way to feel better about myself is to go out ... and do it [ski bumps].

• Not only am I going to experience fear whenever I am on unfamiliar territory, but so is everyone else [of my ability].

• Pushing through fear is less frightening than living with the underlying fear that comes from feeling helpless [being immobilized on a slope].

My daughter, Susan, credits her ability to push through fear in skiing to a time when she was 9 years old skiing with the family at Steamboat. Accidentally, we landed on a steep, no-way-out bump run called Cyclone. Crying, Susan sat down at the top and refused to move. Her father knew she was capable of skiing it. "You can sit here and cry until tears freeze to your face or ski down," he told her, matter-of-factly. "There's no other way. You can do it."

He and I followed the boys — who by then were long gone — down the first part of the run. When we looked back, Susan carefully was criss-crossing the hill, focusing on her turns, determined not to fall. She didn't.

"All of a sudden, being left behind seemed more scary than going down," she recalls. "I had to do it."

## Turn fear into energy

*Instead of working to eliminate fear, learn to turn it into energy.* In their clinics on skiing the extreme, brothers Rob and Eric DesLauriers and Dan and John Egan teach life-saving tactics prompted by the fight-or-flight response. They show how to avoid a sudden cliff or tree when skiing powder by throwing your feet and skis up as if you were jumping into a swimming pool.

This maneuver will stop you in your tracks and could save your life.

Men in the clinics catch on easily. But when I did it, it took me several tries before I got comfortable catapulting my body at will. Men learn this early in life — diving for a pass or tackling in football, flinging their bodies on the ground to pop-up a volleyball, or sliding into first base. Women gymnasts do it, but theirs is a more controlled aerial, not an indiscriminate throwing of the body!

Recently, I participated in Women's Week in Telluride. As part of the "extend-your-boundary" philosophy behind the women-teaching-women ski clinics, an optional activity was offered to the group: climbing the wall at the Peaks Hotel spa.

After watching my sons scale indoor climbing walls over the years, muscles bulging as their arms strain to reach the next handhold, I never thought I'd do that one day. Yet, by the fourth day of skiing in a supportive environment led by such vibrant women, I felt exceptionally strong and capable, physically and mentally. Next thing I knew, I was hugging a wall 30 feet above the ground. My spirits soared even higher! I had entered a new comfort zone. I was fearless! The first thing I did when I got home? Told my sons!

## Fantastic & familiar

Two "F-words" allow me to ski where it is scary — *fantastic* and *familiarity*. I will try new terrain, technique or higher speeds when conditions are fantastic — a 9 or 10 on my 1-to-10 scale of the perfect ski day.

One day in early spring at Blackcomb in the Canadian Rockies, daffodils were blooming in the village, new snow felt as soft as rabbits' fur and the royal-blue sky dazzled. The temperature, warm for skiing, hovered around 40 and the sun defined every variation in the snow. My skis were perfectly tuned and ideal for the conditions. Because I trusted the surface and my equipment, I had a confidence, almost a cockiness, in my skiing. I was boogying. Nothing to think about except lovin' life!

About midday, when I was skiing with a male friend, we stopped where a crowd of skiers was peering over a ravine. With the same spirit that propelled me all morning, I slipped over the side, methodically making one turn after another down the steep center, until I reached the runout. A good, solid run. At the bottom, I waited and waited for my friend. Twenty, 30 minutes passed.

"I couldn't make that first turn," he said when he finally showed up, the fear plain on his face.

Later, when I heard people bragging about skiing "the Saudan" (Saudan Couloir, a double black-diamond chute which has been renamed since my visit to Couloir Extreme), I realized I was lucky to have hit it on one of my fearless days!

Familiarity is easy to understand: You move more freely in darkened rooms of your home, where you are familiar with the furniture, than in a pitch-black hotel room, where moving too fast might cause you to stub your toe. In skiing, you can be more gutsy on a run you have skied before or on the kind of terrain or snow you have already experienced.

At Mammoth Mountain in California, I had to be coaxed by a patient guide into jumping off a cornice for the first time. The only way to get from where I was to where he stood was to (gulp!) get air, just as he did. I had no choice, he said. Heart pounding, hands shaking, I sucked up my knees and flew. It was so much fun, I went back again and again, each time with less fear. The more familiar it became, the more I expanded my comfort zone. Experts call this desensitization.

The same thing happened with my fear of steeps. After hiking up to and skiing down McConkey's Bowl, a precipitous drop off Jupiter Peak at Park City, Utah, I finally "got it": The feeling of letting go of a good edge set, reaching forward for my pole plant and projecting my body down the fall line. Now, whenever I ski steep runs — my favorite type of terrain — I call on those sensations and say to myself, "I know how to do this. I've done this."

It is like riding a bike — scary at first, but with practice you master the technique and dispel your fears. Learning to ski the right way, plus mileage, mileage, mileage, will do wonders for your courage.

Still, occasional fear may seep in. When my youngest son, Nick, was 17, he and I broke trail in the trees on the steep North Face of Peak 9 at Breckenridge, unable to find the run we had set out to ski. We came to a chute no wider than a tall slide in a children's playground and about as long. Nick breezed down it, but I froze.

Though not nearly as steep as other runs I'd skied, its narrow boundaries, flanked by thick trees, made me feel confined. While the chute fanned a little at the bottom, I knew I'd have to make a quick turn to avoid trees. The longer I looked at it, the more nervous I got. I opted to go around in untracked powder rather than slide down that little blip of a hill!

In 1995 I cartwheeled violently about 200 yards down a steep, bumpy chute at Lake Louise in Canada. Realizing I was hopelessly out of control, I was able to let my body go limp, like a rag doll being tossed down a staircase. This, I believe, saved me from serious harm. I suffered only bruising and a painful neck injury that a chiropractor back home fixed in three visits.

But the trauma immediately after the fall left me in such a state, I could barely muster the courage to slide my skis on the snow. Fear washed over me like a cold shower, leaving me shaking and vulnerable. For a fleeing moment, I vowed to give up skiing. But heeding my own advice, I talked myself down to the mid-mountain lodge where the ski patrol met me for a sled ride to the bottom.

My fear eventually subsided, and three days later I went heli-skiing, bruised ribs and all.

*Janet Spangler is the executive director of Woman's Ski Experience at Sugarbush, Killington and Mount Snow in Vermont; Sugarloaf and Sunday River in Maine, and Attitash*

*Bear Peak in New Hampshire. With the help of her WSE team members, Debbie Voigt, Diane Stone and Jay McGarry, and the director of women's programs at Eldora Mountain, Colo., Peggy Spangler, she offers this advice to help us work through our fears in skiing:*

"We are, all of us, anything but ordinary" — Rosemary Altea

Skiing isn't much different from the rest of our lives. It is about how we program ourselves, what we choose, how we act on choices we've made. We have the inner strength to take us wherever we want to go, whether it is down a steep, icy slope, through a mogul field, or skimming through powder up to our bellies.

### Focusing

As director of Women's Ski Experience, I do a lot of what I call "transportation skiing" — getting from point A to point C as fast as possible — from group to group throughout the day. I notice that when I have a focus my skiing improves dramatically, almost unconsciously.

For example, one day as I was skiing down a narrow, steep bump run covered with two feet of late-morning powder at Sugarbush, it occurred to me that not only was I going too fast, but I was more than slightly out of my comfort zone. This thought popped into my head: "Stop! Take a breath, evaluate and ... bail out!"

Then I remembered the woman farther down the trail who needed my help. I was on that particular run not to feed my ego (or in this case, slaughter it), but to get to an injured person. The image of her loomed larger than my comfort level, so I skied through all the powder, in and out and over the uncomfortable bumps, barely remembering to breathe. I focused on getting there *fast*, not on how I looked or felt.

Later, I realized that I had not engaged in the usual "you-idiot-you-can't-ski-this" conversation with myself. And, I also realized that though I may never voluntarily ski that trail again, I knew I could.

Another realization of "unconscious" skiing came to me one beautiful, albeit cold, afternoon at Sunday River. I was hurrying back from lunch to our meeting room on the other side of the mountain. As I flew from trail to trail, moving from the far right side of the hill to the far left, traveling over three separate mountain peaks, I felt a "Zen" connection flowing between my body, the wide-open air, and the snow in all its configurations under my skis. I was truly caressing the surface. I smiled and reveled in the experience. At the top of a steep drop-off, I glanced down at my feet as I prepared to go over the lip. What a surprise! I had forgotten to buckle my boots!

Having a focus gets you active instead of just standing on your skis. For example, take your focus off your feet and think about your hands. They should be parallel with the pitch of the hill. The steeper the slope, the more angles are created in the body when the hands mirror the steepness of the hill. In this way, you will put your skis more on edge. You will be amazed how much more secure you will feel.

Or, ski without your poles. It might be scary at first, but you will soon find your hands help you balance, naturally, without the use of "crutches" to lean on or pivot around. You will acutally enjoy the carefree feeling of being unencumbered with poles and begin to trust your feet to carry you.

A focus takes your mind off of fear, allowing you to learn new skills. There's nothing magical about it. When fear shows up, it is usually because you do not have the skills, or confidence in your skills, to ski a particular part of a slope. That's normal. As you have learned, fear is a positive emotion. It comes out to protect you and keep you safe.

### Intimidation vs. fear

There is a difference between intimidation and fear. If your progress down the hill suddenly stops (due to a slick patch of frozen granular or a sudden steep pitch in the trail), and you do not think you can go on, intimidation kicks in (funny how it just sneaks in there!). Your brain — a powerful thing — turns what may be a little intimidating into downright fearful. Fear keeps you from moving. Then, you are stuck. Only you can tap into your head to change it. You have got to review the knowledge you have in order to ski a particular run or condition. If you have learned a technique and have done it before, you can deal with intimidating situations.

Remember, fear stems from lack of skill. Intimidation causes you to question your skill. It is important to keep clear on the difference. The next time your progress is stopped, think about the last time you handled a similar situation. Repeat the action, or focus on other skills you have that will allow you to ski through intimidation.

One practice I've found helpful when I come to the top of a steep roll in the terrain is to commit myself to the pitch. I ski right over the top lip and make six turns before stopping. By then the intimidation factor is reduced to little, if any.

### Yikes!

At Women's Ski Experience we encourage you to step out of your comfort zone, the place where you most likely spend 60 percent of your ski day. In your comfort zone, you use the skills you have already perfected, ones you feel good about. This is where you feel safe and in control (and, oh, don't we love being in control!).

The catch with control is that it can prevent our body and mind from learning something new. Stepping out of control is stepping into "yikes!"

You don't need to stay in the yikes! mode long. We advocate no more than 20 percent of your ski day. And you do not need to be on a black diamond trail to get into your yikes! zone. You can achieve it on a green slope. Try skiing on only one ski. Ski only on the edge. Ski backward.

Yikes! is where the learning happens. Let's think about it from a different angle. Let's say you are an average ballroom dancer. You go to a swanky, black-tie affair and are having a blast dancing the steps you know: fox-trot, cha cha, swing.

Suddenly, Antonio Banderas appears and asks you to tango with him. You think, "Me? Yikes! I don't know how to do that!" But it's Antonio Banderas. You do not think twice about declining. So out onto the dance floor you go, allowing him to guide you through every move. You are learning to tango!

The next time you dance the tango, it may not be with Antonio, but you will dance with a renewed confidence that you would not have had if you'd stayed in your comfort zone.

The other 20 percent of your ski day you can slip into the "boring" zone. That may be where you are really comfy: at the end of a trail, the run in for lunch, waiting for a friend to catch up, or skiing green trails all day with a nervous friend. Ease in and out of boring.

OK. So what if you happen to like boring? What if you do not care if you ever experience yikes!? (Which I do not think is the case or you would not be reading this book.) What happens to your comfort zone if you stay there? It begins to shrink because you are not learning anything new. And then, after awhile, you grow uncomfortable on blue trails, and your comfort zone shrinks even more, until one day you are skiing only in the boring zone 100 percent of the time.

And then you stop skiing altogether. You give it up, pack away those ski clothes, sell that equipment. And after all your dreams!

Wouldn't you rather step momentarily into yikes! and keep learning and expanding your skills? Just for a moment ... And another moment ... and another?

### Work on the basics

Learning to deal with simple, basic fears can empower you to tackle the harder, deeper ones. Knowledge lessens fear.

• Fear of going too fast — Take instruction on how to control speed through turn shape. (See Chapter Fourteen.)

• Fear of falling — Maybe you haven't learned how to get up. Spend some time with an instructor or an experienced "faller" to find the easiest way to get back on your skis. Get familiar with less risky ways to fall (See Chapter Twelve.)

• Fear of getting lost — Carry a trail map with you at all times and know how to read it. Look for landmarks and ask directions.

• Fear of ungroomed slopes — Avoid surprises. Check the daily snow conditions and grooming reports in the base lodge and on the mountain. Some areas provide handouts you can take with you.

• Fear of cold and frostbite — Invest in good warm ski clothes and accessories. Make sure your boots fit properly and get boot heaters installed. (See Chapters Seven and Ten.) Know when to go inside.

• Fear of walking in ski boots and carrying equipment — Take an experienced skier friend aside and ask how they do it. Engage in some serious people-watching and copy what they do. It does not take strength, just finesse!

• Fear of getting on and off the lift — Ask an instructor or ski patroller if you can share a chair for some tips. For a Poma, t-bar, or rope tow, observe how others do it and ask the lift operator for help. Hint: do not sit down!

• Fear of equipment failure — You would not drive a car wondering if the brakes were safe. If you are unsure about your equipment, make sure it is ski-shop checked for safety. Learn from other sources like women's ski clinics and ski shop technicians who are willing to spend some time with you. Study this book.

• Fear of getting hit — know Your Responsibility Code (see page 195). Every knowledgeable skier lessens the possibility of skier to skier injuries.

The next time you feel a quickening of your pulse, a flip-flop in your stomach, or perspiration on your palms, embrace the sensation. You are about to experience something new and wonderful. Your comfort zone is expanding. Each time you step out of that place you call security, just for a moment, you become a stronger, more confident and skilled skier.

---

*Chapter Summary:*
This chapter shows us fear is universal. Learning to recognize, understand and deal with the paralyzing fear we feel on the slopes can help us ski better and enjoy it more.

You learned about fear-managing tactics from authors, other women skiers, Olympic racers, and instructors.

---

*For information:*
**Women's Ski Experience** — write to Janet Spangler, P.O. Box 621, Warren, VT 05674, or call (802) 583-WSE1.

**Women's Turn** — Skier Development Programs, Sugarbush Resort, R.R. 1 Box 350, Warren, Vt 05674-9993; (800) 53SUGAR.

Chapter     Fourteen

# *Black diamonds can be a girl's best friend*

> *"Steep terrain freaks me out. I get frightened before I start and feel psychologically disadvantaged."*
> — *Jill, age 42 from Colorado*

> *"I want to ski bumps smoothly, gracefully and aggressively, preferably in an expensive Descente suit and with an outrageous tan and good hair!"*
> — *Susan, age 32 from Colorado*

> *"Icy slopes make me nervous because it's difficult to cut an edge and I feel less in control."*
> — *Ghana, age 41 from Colorado*

Graceful, smooth fluid. When women in my survey described how they wanted to perform on skis, these are the words they mentioned most often. We all would like to experience these sensations on the slopes more than we do.

Such masterful moments can quickly change to Maalox moments if a soft surface turns icy, or terrain drops like a trap door, or skis sink out of sight in deep powder, or we build up pedal-to-the-metal speed. *Screech ...* and we revert back to the old reliable sophomore snowplow.

Sound familiar? Then this chapter is for you. Women ski instructors and racers share tips for skiing the hard stuff: ice, bumps, steeps, powder. They also cover running gates and skiing in control.

Notice one common theme in each of these sections: In order to climb the ski ladder to a higher ability without taking one step forward and two steps backward, you must be able to inch out of that place they call The Comfort Zone. Gradually, they want you to expand it, like breathing air into a balloon.

## Control as you go

Women in my survey said they need to feel in control to ski successfully. A veteran of 10 years on the slopes, said she still did not think she had her act together.

"When I feel in control, confident and comfortable on any terrain," she wrote, "I will be completely satisfied. Then people will look at me from the lift and say, 'Wow! That woman can ski!'"

*Maggie Loring is the director of The American Skiing Company's Perfect Turn Education program and an examiner with the eastern division of PSIA, for which she conducts women's educational events. Her tips here will help you gain the confidence you need to ski in control.*

Most women I have skied with mistake confidence for control. While we need to be in control when we negotiate the terrain, the ultimate expressions in skiing are freedom, abandon and weightlessness — not exactly feelings one would equate with control. To the contrary, it is often the *release of control* that gives us the rush, making these sensations exciting and enjoyable. How can we gain both confidence *and* control?

### Turn shape

Let us review turn shape. To make a turn, you travel across the mountain on one set of edges, and then you must get to the other set of edges to go in the opposite direction. This maneuvering can be fairly quick, producing a short, sharp direction change; it can also be gradual, producing a more drawn-out arc. The key factor is the angle at which you come out of the turn. If you exit your turn by heading across the hill directly, you will not gain or lose momentum. (Yay! in diagram below) If you angle your turn exit up the mountain, you will slow progress, which sometimes is necessary. (Sometimes) If you stop the direction change early, you end up heading more directly down the mountain and increasing speed (UhOh!).

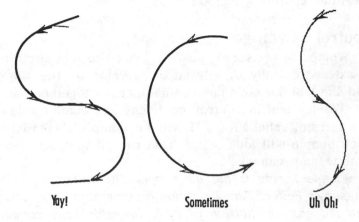

**Yay!**    **Sometimes**    **Uh Oh!**

### Vision

The confident skier chooses the path she wants in each turn. She knows when she should begin moving from one set of edges to the other by *looking ahead* a few turns. Here's an example I use in my clinics: Imagine driving a car. If you look directly down at the pavement, those little yellow lines come up very quickly, and you must swerve sharply to avoid crossing them. By looking farther down the road at those same lines, you have plenty of time to react.

It is the same in skiing. Try not to watch your feet or the snow directly in front of you. Internalize what your feet are doing and pay attention to the direction of travel. Check your vision by picking a tree or other object down the trail and ski toward it while making turns. Trust your body to do what is necessary. Practice this by making differently shaped turns on a gentle slope: speeding up, maintaining speed, and slowing momentum.

### Letting go

The second component necessary within every turn is *letting go of the old turn*. This may sound simplistic, but in reality this is what prevents many good skiers from becoming great skiers. It also prevents many women from getting much enjoyment from the sport.

Beginners and intermediates often find themselves traveling quickly toward the woods. Suddenly, they realize they need to head in the other direction. The common reaction is to cling to the old set of edges until the last possible second. By then it is too late to make a move to the new set. Their skis slide away.

Advanced skiers often experience a similar situation. The trail gets a bit slick, or an undetected bump causes a slight bounce. Again, they hang on for an extra second. All of a sudden they are off balance and trying to catch up; in other words, they are out of control.

To let go of the old turn, you must continually be moving toward the new turn in a smooth, rhythmic and progressive manner. Do not abruptly try to turn at the end of a traverse.

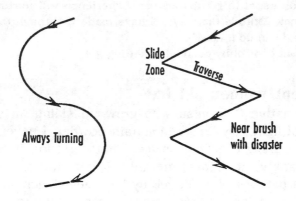

Imagine driving a car on a slippery surface. You see an obstacle you must avoid. You do not wait until you are about to hit it before turning the wheel. You turn early and as smoothly as possible so the tires do not lose their grip with the road. Do the same with the edges of your skis.

**Risk a little, gain a lot**

As you learned earlier in this book, you can gain confidence by practicing on slopes that do not threaten you. Try to vary the pitch, the line and the pace. And do not allow well-meaning friends or relatives to lead you to tougher terrain to create a breakthrough. Practice when and where *you* want. *Feel* your skis turn until you are pleasantly comfortable before you advance to more difficult spots.

When you are ready, seek out that funny feeling in the pit of your stomach. Let yourself get just a little out of control. Then go back to an easier slope to recapture the comfort zone. The key to building confidence is *losing control and getting it back.*

Risk a little at a time. This will prevent you from getting frustrated and feeling defeated.

There will always be times, even on easy slopes, when the unexpected happens, and you get that feeling in your belly. This is when confidence training comes in to play. In those moments it is important to *keep moving* and look for a spot to get it together. Experience will nurture your new attitude that says, "I have made it through this before; I can do it now!"

Gain control by confidently letting go!

## Confident women ski ice

As a native Coloradan who grew up skiing on velvet carpets of light, dry Rocky Mountain powder, I never have gotten the hang of skiing on ice. That's putting it mildly. Quite frankly, it freaks me out! I can handle a few scattered patches of hardpack by "tip-toeing" across them and averting any harsh movements, but an entire mountain of true, blue ice sends me cowering to the lodge. Skiing on the East Coast has awakened my respect for the women who can ski it!

As Mermer Blakeslee confirms, I am in good company. But hope springs eternal, and mine is renewed after reading her brilliant tips.

*Mermer, a PSIA Demo Team member and examiner, travels around the country training ski teachers, leading women's seminars, and conducting workshops on psychological issues of skiing. At Ski Windham in New York, she runs "Inside Tracks," an intensive ski seminar to enhance the mind-body connection.*

If you get scared or a bit tentative skiing on ice, join the crowd. In all levels that I teach — novices to instructors — everyone cringes and makes all sorts of grunting noises when they hear the word "ice."

Skiing on ice is like living with a teenager: You need to accept a different, looser sense of control and a lot of noise. But if you attempt it, the reward can be not only a large dose of fun but an unexpected, expanded sense of life.

Here are three easy ways to *almost* enjoy the different types of icy slopes.

### Step on it

Think of that teenager again. The first rule is do not try to argue. You will lose. Same with ice. You cannot fight it when it is ungrippable. Instead, develop what I call a cheating tactic and use the ice for what it is good for — its frictionless quality. This method works best on slopes where snow has been scraped off and pushed below patches of ice.

Ice is in cahoots with gravity pulling you down the slope. There *is* a part of every turn when you want to go down, and ice certainly helps you do that. It even turns your skis for you. But first you have to throw out some old advice: "Traverse across the ice and turn after it." That tactic is exactly *opposite* of what I explain here:

Look ahead. When you spot your icy patch (the shinier, the better), traverse across the hill toward it and ski onto the ice from the side. As soon as you feel it underneath your feet, instead of trying to grip and hold to your path, go where it wants to take you — down the hill.

With your uphill foot flat against the ice, *extend* that leg and push your body right down the hill into your next turn. You will actually push yourself away from the hill toward your new turn. Both of your skis will have no problem turning because there's no friction to hold them back. The ice does the steering for you for the first half of the turn. All you have to do is keep following the arc you just began. This is easy because you are now back in the snow at the bottom of the ice patch. Carry the arc across the hill till you feel comfortable starting a new turn.

To practice this, go on an ice hunt. Plan your track so you can start your turn right *on* the ice patch. It is actually less work than turning on soft snow.

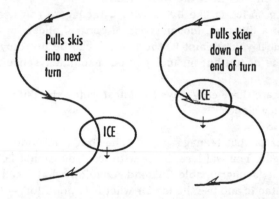

Pulls skis into next turn

ICE

Pulls skier down at end of turn

ICE

**Using the ice**                    **Fighting the ice**

When you first try this, give yourself a boost by yelling, "Now!" when you feel the ice underneath you. The loud cry works like magic. It gives you just enough spunk to overcome that moment of hesitation. Soon you will gain the confidence that this method really does work! It is all about giving up control and getting it back again.

*Follow your instincts*

If you tend to protect yourself from going downhill as soon as you feel your skis slip on an icy slope, you are following a natural instinct. But sometimes the way we grope for security creates a bigger problem.

In trying to avoid the fall line, you may instinctively swing the fist of your downhill arm across your body back toward the mountain trying to hang onto the side of it. When you do this, you become even more vulnerable and unstable. Without much friction underfoot, you can spin around 360 degrees, which is neither fun nor confidence-inspiring.

Instead, use your instincts to your advantage. When you feel that fist (and your pole handle) coming across your body blocking your next turn, try this: Focus on your pole *basket* and swing it across the hill directly below your feet. Keep it there close to the snow until you are ready to turn again. You will feel your elbow bend as your pole handle comes back to the right position.

*Move on it*

Now that you are stable, you are ready to move forward, which is the main secret to skiing ice. Think of walking on slippery pavement: Keep your center forward over your feet or they will slip out in front of you.

If icy slopes make your body freeze and hold on to a broad slide, trying desperately to avoid the next turn, try what I call the "Forget-It Turn." (Some of my teenage students dubbed it The F——It Turn.)

Tune into your downhill ski. Feel yourself gripping the edge into the snow by rolling your downhill foot onto its arch. When you feel that ski start to slide sideways, *forget* about it and switch to focusing your uphill ski. Push against the hill with your uphill foot and extend your leg and body toward your next turn.

As before, yelling out a cue word that gets you charged can help. A woman student of mine skied her best in this situation when she yelled (to herself) the teenage version. She got enough energy from that word to keep moving toward her future turn that she forgot to worry about the past!

Soon you will develop a rhythm as you roll your downhill foot, push on your uphill foot, extend toward the next turn, then roll your foot again — never going static, always moving forward.

Skiing ice will always be loud, and maybe a compromise from what you would prefer; but if you use these methods you will be surprised at the results. Not only will you be able to *ski* the trail instead of just getting down it, but you will get that rush of exhilaration that comes when you expand your limits and loosen your need for rigid control. For a moment you might even feel like ... well, you know, a teenager.

## Mogul Mavens

The number-one technique improvement listed by the women in my survey was learning to ski the bumps. "Moguls!" wrote one of the women in the survey. "I look at them and cannot decide where to go other than away!"

I used to think that way, too, until I learned to check my speed. For me that was the key to being able to ski 10 or 12 bumps fluidly instead of having to stop after three or four wildly out of control!

*Kathy Ryan is a 19-year veteran ski instructor who was one of the first to teach women's ski clinics for Women's Way at Squaw Valley in 1979. Currently, she teaches at Vail/Beaver Creek ski schools. She also serves as a senior member of SKI magazine's equipment test team.*

Maybe it was a wrong turn. Or maybe it was your love of challenge, excitement, or intensity. Or perhaps pressure from your friends and family brought you over to the bumps. Now, reality and fantasy clash. Your turns, which minutes ago felt graceful, powerful and in control, aren't. Your mood fluctuates between frustration, anger, despair and dreaded fear.

### Samurai skiing

Myamoto Mussashi, a 16th-century samurai warrior, wrote *The Book of Five Rings*. Commentary accompanying his book advises: "Flexibility is a primary consideration, and not just in the physical sense. The ability to adapt to circumstances psychologically and emotionally is crucial."

Have you considered the "ability to adapt" while skiing? You have probably been more concerned with getting down the hill gracefully and in one piece, focusing on weight transfer, pressure control, balance and edging. You believed that once you mastered these skills, you would be brilliant on skis. Versatility hasn't even been a consideration.

But making the transition from forgiving groomed terrain with a single fall line to bumped runs with converging multiple fall lines requires letting go of the old calculated ways of skiing. Your favorite turn must give way to other skiers' favorite turns — different in size and shape from yours — that form the bumps.

You will not feel comfortable while you establish new habits. But in order to move from ski hell to ski heaven, you must first pass through a zone of moderate discomfort, which I call purgatory.

Here are some activities which will not only allow you to have fun while in purgatory, but will also teach you versatility on skis.

### Rhythm change

Learn to make other skiers' favorite turns by skiing behind them. Make your turns exactly in their tracks. This will familiarize you with turn shapes and timing that are different from yours. After 10 or 20 turns, stop and talk about the differences.

Then, change the game. Turn not *where* they turn but *when*. This will help you learn to act and react without premeditation.

### Ski the "Boo"

Skiing around bamboo poles or race gates also will help create versatile skiing. Turning at designated spots compels you to vary from your memorized turn and favorite rhythm.

### Across the hill

Practice handling converging fall lines by skiing across the hill instead of down it. Look uphill before you begin this side-hill slalom exercise. As you ski the diagonal, feel a change in the rhythm of your turns created by gravity pull versus your direction of travel. Notice how the skis feel under your feet. Explore the asymmetry of the turn down the hill versus the turn up

---

the hill: The turn downhill will feel long; the turn up the fall line will feel short.

Repeat these turns — four to the right, four to the left — until you tack your way to the bottom. Reformat your judgment about the syncopated rhythm you feel. Then ski a gently bumped run. See how many times you actively need to steer the skis *up* against the obvious pull of gravity.

*Step up for early weight transfer*

On groomed, single-fall-line runs, you *passively* move to the outside ski on or before the fall line to transfer your weight. When you use this same passive weight transfer in the bumps, you feel out of control, late, wild.

This dryland exercise shows you how an *active*, early weight transfer should feel in the bumps:

On a flight of stairs, step sideways on any two stairs (you can use ski poles, but it is not necessary). Place your right foot on the higher stair, left foot on the lower. Keep your upper body and hips facing down the stair corridor.

Step up on your right leg by gradually extending, or straightening, your right knee. This move requires using your femur (thigh bone) and quadricep (large thigh muscle). With all your body weight off your left foot, balance on your right leg. Feel what it takes to be committed to a single leg.

Now gradually bend (flex) that knee until your left foot touches the lower stair. This is the "bend zee knees" or flexion that occurs during the control part of the turn. Notice how the movement is the responsibility of only one leg; the other leg just shadows the movement.

Combine this exercise with mental imagery. Imagine that you are making a right turn. Step and extend up on the left leg until you reach the center of your make-believe turn. At this point, begin dropping your weight by flexing that knee and ankle until the turn is complete.

Think of stepping up the stairs next time you are on a moderately bumped run. Step up and onto the bump to initiate your turn with dynamic weight transfer.

On steep terrain the step up becomes a step *against and away* from the hill in order to maintain your center of mass in a perpendicular position to the fall line. The only way to try this is with baptism by immersion: you must find steeper terrain.

*Timing the pole plant*

Besides being comfortable with a variety of turn shapes and keeping perpendicular to the fall line, timing of the pole plant is critical to successful bump skiing. You can create bump hell with a late pole plant.

The purpose of the pole plant is to stabilize the upper body and to create torque or twist in the body, which is a very effective turning force in the bumps. These two conditions must occur *before* each turn.

To do this, think of your pole plant as a door bell. The bell rings first, then you open the door for your guest to enter. With a properly timed pole plant, you reach out, touch your pole to the snow first, then step up and enter your turn.

Incorrect timing of the pole plant continues to be one of the most frequent sabotaging behaviors I see in aspiring bump skiers. Remember, the pole plant quiets the body, and on steeper terrain it also creates an energy which automatically starts the skis turning.

*Speed control*

*Speed is not the true way. Speed is the fastness or slowness which occurs when the rhythm is out of synchronization.* — *Mussashi*

The blocking pole plant is the secret tool used by good bump skiers for speed control. This technique positions the ski pole on an angle down the hill where the ski will eventually carve its next turn. The wrist is open to the fall line, and the muscles of the wrist, arm and shoulder are contracted, resulting in a measured pause. This not only helps to control speed, but also creates a twist in the body.

Ron Lemasters, Beaver Creek Ski School instructor, explains how this twist, or torque, works: Imagine holding with both hands a section of garden hose. Twist the hose with your lower hand, then let go. Watch how the hose automatically realigns. This same kind of torque is created when your lower body twists under your upper body, the latter of which has been stabilized by your pole plant. As you step up to the new turn, your body unwinds in a manner similar to the twisted garden hose.

### Versatility

The degree of blocking you use will vary from turn to turn, run to run. Turns made on gentle terrain require little or no blocking. Here, the pole plant is actually a pole "touch," providing merely an opportunity to rehearse doorbell-like timing.

Moderate bumps require moderate blocking, not only to initiate a turn but to keep you traveling at a comfortable pace. Bigger bumps require that you be steadfast when contracting your shoulder, arm and wrist muscles while setting the pole plant.

Mussashi versatility is key to successful bump skiing. It is time to let go, take a risk, and be flexible and versatile in the bumps by learning to do the following:

- Be comfortable with a variety of turn shapes.
- Enjoy rhythm changes.
- Initiate each turn with a dynamic weight transfer.
- Vary your body position in relationship to the changing fall line.
- Adjust the degree of angle or blocking you use with each pole plant.

Work on these new ideas and enjoy the process of learning. But don't take yourself too seriously — it is bump skiing, not world hunger!

*Donna Weinbrecht — Who can forget her grace-ful flawless skiing through the bumps, with her long blond hair flying, in her first gold-medal run at the 1992 Olympics? This Grace Kelly of skiing made an imprint on the hearts and minds of women everywhere and remains a role model to this day. The five-time World Cup mogul champion and winner of 44 World Cup titles shares her secrets on bump technique and offers words of encouragement.*

- Practice your flat-skiing skills. If you have one bad habit in the flats, it will be 10 times more exaggerated in the moguls because things happen a lot faster.

- Pick spread-out bumps, not tight ones when learning. To grasp speed control, slowly go up and over some of the bumps and feel the absorption with your legs. Practice turning up, turning down, turning in-between.
- Everything happens underneath the hips, so keep your feet underneath you. You do not want to reach with your feet because your buttocks will stay in back. A lot of women like to break at the waist, but you need to be *on top* of your skis. Let your legs come up underneath you (as you rise onto the bump), then push down (as you carve the backside), controlling your speed.
- Mogul skiers appear to be skiing on a "platform," with their knee movements in sync. Even though it looks like a platform, the knees are dynamic. It is a series of independent motions. Never ski on a "platform." If you do, your knees will be locked. When you go up, push into the turn. Do not tuck the knee.
- The pole plant in bump skiing swings out — you hit, punch, break forward with the wrist — your arms never come down. Pole plant early in bump skiing.
- The eyes are important. Reading the terrain lets you know how you want to go over it. Ski on the offense, not defense.
- Go out there and have fun! You have got to put in the miles and get feedback from yourself ... Learn why one run is better and smoother than the last. Ask yourself why you could link turns better this time — maybe you did not get in the back seat once. *You have* got to be your own best teacher. You may not always have someone else around to tell you. But do not be too critical of yourself!
- Get in classes. Work on the basics. Analyze your own runs. Learn from yourself. You cannot do the same thing over and over if you want to improve. Try to make a change.
- Observe other people who ski well. I did not have a coach — I watched competitors.

## Powder Piggy

Have you ever listened to skiers with that JSP (Just-Skied-Powder) glow on their faces talking about "face shots" like they had just seen God? What *is* it about powder skiing that gets people to spend thousands of dollars searching for untracked snow via helicopter or snowcat? And why do your powder-hound friends suddenly disappear when it starts to dump?

I used to be one of those people who wish out loud for powder but secretly hope it will not be *too* deep! Two things changed that: fat skis (I use Volant Chubbs) and a powder clinic taught by the Egan and DesLauriers brothers (of Warren Miller fame) at Grand Targhee, Wyoming. In one day I was transformed from a petrified powder pansy to a hard-core, deep-snow, knees-to-the-trees powder junkie! When I learned to relax and not fight it, the moves came naturally. They will for you, too.

*Tricia Hohl's ski instruction career spans 17 seasons and two continents. Before joining the ski pros at Aspen, she taught at Gray Rocks, Canada; Portillo and La Parva, Chile; and Sugarbush, Vermont. She's been teaching in the Aspen women's clinics for four years.*

There are two kinds of skiers on a powder day — those having the ultimate skiing experience and those hating life.

Powder skiing is a delicate dance on a fine line between conquest and surrender. Good skiers learn to caress the snow both firmly and softly at the same time. However, even skiers of moderate ability may delight in that ultimate experience as they begin to develop a technique for how to attack and how to give in. Below are some tips on how I do just that.

*Fear*

The best speed for the powder dance needs to be a little faster than the comfort zone of most skiers with limited powder experience. And that can be scary. But any powder skier will tell you it is difficult to ski deep snow slowly. Heavy snow creates resistance against the skis, and this resistance can be exhausting and frustrating. Momentum moves the skis smoothly through the snow, so that the skier can finesse, rather than muscle, her turns.

Skis disappearing under the snow adds another huge source of intimidation. To remedy this problem, try to imagine that your skis do not exist and the only things on your feet are your boots. "Ski" your boots and your skis will do whatever your feet do — regardless of whether they are visible. (If you look ahead, as you should do in all conditions, your skis should not be in your line of sight anyway!)

### The Shape of the Turn

Managing speed comes from *shaping* the turns, not from slowing down between each one by traversing across the hill. To make nice S-shaped turns, change your focus. Ski to *go* instead of to *stop*! Start the new turn earlier, cutting out the traverse. Look in the direction you want to go before you complete the turn you are in. When you mentally anticipate where you are going to go before you get there, your body will also be ready to move in the next direction. Once you pass the scary threshold of "continual" skiing, you will discover that the shape of your turn gives you the nice rhythmical controlled skiing you are looking for. It is less fatiguing, more graceful, and a lot more fun!

### Balance

A big misconception about skiing powder is that you need to lean back. Many skiers do this because they are afraid of falling forward on their face — a common and fortunately safe event in soft powder. The truth is that sitting back hinders agility and technique, and puts tremendous strain on your quads. Rather than lean back, just take care to not lean forward; balance more on the middle of your foot.

Balancing should be continual and fluid. If balance becomes a held, static position, the ability to react to constantly changing terrain and conditions diminishes.

---

Powder challenges your ability to balance so start on a slope where you feel confident. Begin by just going straight. Keep hips over the feet while extending and flexing your ankles and knees. Ankle flexion keeps the center of your body over your feet. When you are not centered, your hips will fall back behind your feet as though you were sitting on an invisible chair.

### Steering and Edging

An edged ski slices through powder on the path of least resistance. A flat ski acts like a plow pushing snow out of its path, actually creating more resistance.

To get an efficient edge, begin with shallow turns. Slowly roll both ankles or tip both ski boot shafts laterally toward the intended direction of the turn. This tips both skis onto their edges and allows the skis' design to begin making the turn for you.

Once on the edges, the arc of the turn can be tightened by gradually guiding both feet (steering) in the direction you would like the skis to go. Steering should be a *subtle* leg rotation throughout the turn, not a twisting or pivoting of the feet, nor a throwing of the hip out and around. (Save the twisting and pivoting for stopping.)

To feel the muscles used in steering the skis, lift your foot and ski off the snow. Have a friend firmly hold the ski tip in gloved hands and turn the ski inward. Feel the leg muscles used to accomplish this. Turn the ski out, and again feel which muscles are used. In every turn one leg is rotating inward and one leg is rotating outward. Both legs need to work as a team to edge and guide the skis or one ski will be left behind resulting in the classic powder fall — a half twist to a back flop. (Expect cheers and score cards from the chair lift!)

### Pressure

As your skis turn across the slope, the pressure on the skis will feel greater. To keep the skis from becoming too heavy, absorb some of this pressure by pulling your feet and lower legs up to the surface of the powder toward your center. Do this by retracting your legs (as opposed to extending or hopping). To turn back down the hill, extend your legs away and to the side while pushing the skis down into the snow.

In powder, skis float near the surface while crossing the slope and dive deeper into the snow while descending the slope. As you begin to do this pattern rhythmically, imagine that your skis are dolphins, diving and rising in the water. Be patient but determined in your practice of these movements. It is an important and elegant step in taking charge of your powder skiing.

*Rhythmic pole swing*

Swing the pole forward, mainly using your wrist while keeping both hands up and in your peripheral vision at all times. Keeping the arms and torso quiet and stable will help you balance. A smooth pole swing also helps move your center of mass forward, again enhancing balance and helping you link your turns rhythmically.

*Fat skis are friendly*

Powder magnifies your mistakes. Fat skis forgive them. They allow you to experiment freely without suffering the usual consequences. Where else in your life can you do that? Your powder experience will always be much more fun on the wide, floaty fat sticks.

*Patience*

Here is the most important rule of all for skiing powder: have patience. You will encounter lots of different types of powder. Some can be really difficult to ski, and some is unimaginably easy. Your skiing will also change, like the powder. Some days you will dance like a gazelle, while other days you will flounder like a hippo. If you take your time, relax and have fun, you will be the head dolphin before you know it.

## Step up to Steeps

Steep slopes, especially steep slopes with bumps, a.k.a. double black diamonds, present more challenge than most women want in their repertoire of skiing, according to my survey. But nothing proves more satisfying than completing a run with a steep pitch standing on your feet!

Now that I have learned to solidly dig in my downhill ski and intensify my pole plant in a steep turn, chutes and bowls top my list of favorite terrain. Whenever I want to get my heart rate up, I'll go out for a few runs down Peak Seven above my house in Breckenridge. Here is a tip: make sure the snow is fairly soft so you can set a good edge. One slip and you will not stop 'til you drop at the bottom! Been there, done that. Trust me — it is not fun!

*Leslie Glaysher has taught and coached skiing for 10 years at Whistler Resort in British Columbia, Canada. There she also teaches in Stephanie Sloan's women's clinic. Here Leslie shows us how to get the right stuff for skiing the steeps: skills and mental attutude.*

"What the hell am I doing here?"

If that sounds familiar to you, you are not alone. The "steeps," a relative term, remain a challenge to many skiers, and the answer to that question varies. Peer pressure, the desire to keep up, or even an old-fashioned navigational mistake can land you on a black-diamond run. What you do when you get there is your choice. Assuming you are not lost, the best reason for being on a tough run is because you want to be there. Do it for yourself.

Once you have committed to learning how to ski the steeps, stick with it. Mastering this new skill can be very fulfilling, but seldom comes easily or quickly. Do not let your mind fool you. Challenging your limits is the only way to expand them. Commit to the first turn and the rest will surely follow. No waffling.

After the state of mind is in order, the technical aspects of skiing must be addressed. By the time you are ready to try the steeps, you should have heard of the following concepts. Here's how to apply them to the steeps.

### Stance and balance

Weight should be centered over the arches, feet slightly apart. During a turn most of the weight should be over the downhill ski (if you do not know this already, please go back to skiing the not-so-steeps!). All the joints should be flexed, putting you in a ready, athletic position. Try to resist the natural tendency to back away from the fall line by bending your ankles so that your weight stays forward. Feel your shins on the front of your boots. Balance is not a state that you achieve, then ignore. Rather, it is a continuous series of adjustments made to sustain centering over the feet.

*Steering*

Your skis are going to go downhill, so you may as well direct them by steering your feet. It sounds easy enough, but it is amazing how many people try to cheat at this. The popular method of swinging the shoulders or hips will turn you, but on the steeps this bad habit becomes downright dangerous. Rotating in this manner leads to oversteering, causing the tails of your skis to skid out and lose edge grip. You may even end up facing back up the hill, definitely not where you want to be on a steep pitch.

You must really *look* and *reach* down the fall line. Learn to turn both feet in the direction you want your skis to go without letting the body lead or follow.

Hop-turns work well in learning this upper/ lower body separation. Practice with the zipper of your jacket facing directly down the fall line. Jump turns may make you feel uncoordinated or as if you need a new sports bra, but they become a valuable tool for dealing with super steeps (thousands of extreme skiers cannot be wrong!).

Also practice short radius turns facing down the fall line. Short turns help prevent over-rotation. The longer your skis travel across the slope, the more likely your body is to follow them.

*Edging*

On a steep pitch your downhill ski needs to grip the slope to give you something solid to balance on. The sharp edge of the ski provides that grip. From a balanced position, roll your ankles, then knees into the hill. Gradually add more edge, building pressure throughout the turn. Smoothly release the edge at the end of the turn,

---

letting your feet join your body, which is facing down the hill. Then it all happens again.

Getting a good edge is half the battle; getting off of it is the other half. Edging requires precision, including a precise boot fit. Your ski must respond immediately when you roll your foot onto its inside arch. If it does not, your ability to ski steep terrain is greatly impaired. (See Chapters Five and Seven on bootfitting.)

## Rhythm

Use your pole plants to link smooth, symmetrical turns and create a rhythm. Reach forward and down the fall line with strong, aggressive pole plants. Keep them coming. They commit you to the next turn and focus you down the hill. Repeat "plant and plant and plant and plant" to establish your timing.

The real trick is to blend all these skills so you can flow down the hill with the greatest of ease and style. Work with gravity, not against it. Take the brakes off a little and try to spread out the parts of the turn so that you do not use them all up at once. For instance, if you use all of your steering in a big hurry at the start of the turn, you leave nothing for the latter part. Get it? Aim for continuous steering, gradual edging, rhythmic pole plants with no dead spots along the way.

One other thing — do not forget to breathe!

With practice you will be able to blend all of these skills together gracefully, I promise!

### Don't let steeps give you the creeps

Snow quality and visibility can enhance or sabotage your black-diamond adventure. Do not choose a day with 30 cement-a-meters (that's how we measure it here in Whistler) of elephant snot and zero visibility to tackle the steeps.

There are varying degrees of steeps: steep, really steep, insanely steep, and are-you-out-of-your-mind steep. The latter, such as narrow chutes with exposed rocks or cliffs, are not places to be learning new skills. Pick a wide slope with a clear outrun. Corduroy cat tracks are great. This way you can practice short turns in an imaginary narrow corridor and still have room to bail out.

If you set yourself up for success with a strong mental attitude, good technical skills, safe terrain and proper conditions, you will achieve your goals. The reward is a rush of adrenaline that is completely legal and a tremendous sense of accomplishment. I highly recommend it.

Jackson Hole instructor Jamie Mackintosh says skiers should observe rules of common sense and courtesy when skiing the steeps:

• Do not stop in the middle of a pitch where you cannot be seen or where you block other skiers' lines. Ski the chute and clear it.

• Check out steep routes from the bottom before attempting to ski them. Obstacles can be hidden from above in the same way the backside of a mogul is not visible to the approaching skier. Although the chute may be free, rocks and other debris can litter the runouts.

• A fall usually results in a long slide that can pick up speed and send you careening into another skier or object. Or, you could be the target of someone sliding. Many people on steep slopes do not belong there. Keep your wits about you!

Instructors and backcountry experts will tell you to try to "arrest" your fall by swinging your legs below you and digging in the edges of your skis or boots to the snow. This works well on a smooth surface when you find yourself sliding on your stomach or back as you would on an amusement park slide. But in head-over-heels types of falls on rough, bumpy steeps you often cannot tell which way is up or down when you are hopelessly out of control. My own experience shows that letting your body go limp until you come to a stop (there has to be an end, and you can only pray it is not at the base of a rock or a tree) can help ward off more serious injury.

## Racing to improve technique

Everyone associates racing with speed and competition, two things that turn many women off in skiing. But have you ever thought of running gates to improve technique and inject a little spice in your skiing? Here a coach and two racers explain how racing can improve skiing technique for recreational skiers.

*Marti Irish has been a race coach for 15 years and competes herself in Masters cross-country and alpine ski racing. Currently, she coaches special women's clinics at the Billy Kidd Performance Center in Steamboat, Colo.*

*Brenda Buglione competed on the World Cup circuit for the U.S. Ski Team and raced on the Women's Pro Tour for six years.*

*Lisa Feinberg Densmore competed on the Women's Pro Tour from 1984 to 1990 and skis on the U. S. Masters Alpine Ski Team.*

*Marti:*

What comes to mind when someone tells you to take up racing to improve your skiing? Do you picture Olympic downhill specialist Picabo Street in her Lycra suit and crash helmet speeding down a steep and iced slope at 70 miles per hour? Does adrenaline rush through your body as you envision yourself in her boots flying off bumps at break-neck speeds?

Does becoming a ski racer even faintly resemble any goal in your ski future? Or do you recoil in fear of the very idea of alpine racing to help you ski better? Are you like so many women who are intimidated by the thought of running gates?

The common misconception that you must be a great skier to take up racing causes many women to say, "I am not a good enough skier to race." This is the most frequent comment I hear from mothers, spouses and girlfriends of participants in the Billy Kidd Performance Center.

I also hear women say, "I do not care about times. I just want to feel more confident in my free skiing."

Skiing gates to improve your skiing does not require that you be a dare-devil expert skier or even a competitive animal. If you are a parallel skier and comfortable on blue runs, you can benefit from running gates. Advanced skiers can sharpen skills for more control, confidence and finesse in the bumps, on the ice, and between the trees.

*Lisa:*

Ski racing can rekindle the challenge and excitement of the slopes. Skiers who have mastered the basics can lose interest in skiing, especially if their regular mountain is small and groomed like a carpet. But racers can ski the same trail a hundred times and still be challenged because every course is different.

### ABCs of racing

*Brenda:*

By now you know that good *balance* on your skis is a prerequisite for skiing. The *athletic stance* prepares you for quick action, and anticipates upcoming slalom gates, moguls or quick turns on the steeps.

Running slalom forces you to maintain this balanced stance — poor body position makes it nearly impossible to negotiate gates. A racer's weight must be forward and pressuring the inside edge of the downhill ski in order for it to carve the correct line around the gates. A tendency to lean back on the tails of the skis pulls weight to the heels and prevents pressure at the center of the skis.

*Marti:*

Next, avoid Z-shaped turns (sharp turns that make you skid) and emphasize *C-shaped completed* turns that have a beginning, middle and end. Your skis should feel as if they are almost going back up the hill at the end of the turn. Round turns allow the skier to gain control of speed in between turns and create energy from one turn to the next.

Energy comes from weighting the downhill ski nearly 100 percent. This bends the ski, allowing it to bow into reverse camber. Immediately, the ski rebounds or pops back, projecting you into the next turn.

*Brenda:*

Skiing gates forces you to maintain a disciplined position with no upper-body rotation. Rotating your upper body and hips causes the tails of your skis to slide and hinders the ski's ability to carve a turn.

---

**Black diamonds *can* be a girl's best friend 263**

Your upper body and hips must face down the fall-line, with your shoulders level and legs moving underneath. This counter-rotated position keeps pressure on the inside downhill edge, enhancing edge control. Racing teaches you to turn your body away from the gates, which prevents your weight from falling to the uphill ski.

*Marti:*

Ski racers want to minimize skidding and chattering — two of the scariest sensations on snow. To do this they emphasize carving smooth round turns instead of sliding. A technically correct carved turn creates speed, maintains control, requires less effort, and elicits less fear than a skidded turn.

*Brenda:*

Skiing gates forces you to make edge-to-edge turns more quickly than you would when free skiing. No matter how fast or slow you ski, in a race course you must turn when the gates dictate, instead of where you want to turn. At first, this might be difficult, but with practice you will learn how to move your feet quickly to anticipate the next turn. Developing these skills is beneficial when you need to avoid natural obstacles such as rocks, icy patches or other skiers. You will gain confidence knowing you can turn quickly and precisely to control speed or negotiate challenging terrain.

*Marti:*

Billy Kidd, world champion and Olympic silver medalist, tells the participants in his race clinics to "swing wide, turn early" in the gates. Notice how race-car drivers negotiate a corner by rounding to the outside lane, then cut back in to the inside lane to avoid skidding. Apply the same principle to turning in the gates: Ski to the outside of the turn, then cut in close below the gate to complete the turn. Most of your turn should be finished by the time you pass the gate, setting you up nice and high for the next turn.

*Brenda:*

Knowing how to change direction early in the turn helps you stay in control and keep your line when free skiing down a steep, icy slope.

*Marti:*

Always look ahead and through the course, just as you would skiing through trees. If you look right at the trees, you are sure to hit them. Get the big picture: keep the gates in your peripheral vision and turn fluidly left to right, one gate to the next. As in bump skiing, an early pole plant is crucial. Planting the pole well before the start of the turn will help you get that turn finished by the time you pass the gate.

*Brenda:*

Movements must coincide so that no motion is wasted. The pole plant should be kept to simple wrist action. Extraneous arm movement takes the weight off the downhill ski — forcing you off balance — and makes finishing a slalom course difficult. A solid pole plant in front brings the hips forward at the beginning of every turn and positions your weight where it can edge and pressure the ski. By focusing on this simplicity and using the pole plant as a timing device, you will find it easier to maintain balance and initiate turns.

*Lisa:*

Racing helps alleviate the fear factor. As your technique improves, you become more confident in a course and on the open slopes, raising your fear threshold high enough to handle any skiing.

Many women feel insecure when terrain gets steeper or rougher than their comfort level. When you ski gates, each course deteriorates a little more with each run, to slicker ice or deeper ruts. You get accustomed *gradually* to the tougher conditions during a gate-training session, instead of bouncing from a perfectly groomed slope to trouble. After running gates a while, smooth slopes in free skiing seem easy, the rugged slopes less rugged. (There's not much difference between a rut next to a gate and a trough between moguls.)

Though you may be unsure about going fast, once you have experienced a timed run such as a NASTAR course, you may find it hard not to go back to try for a personal best. Suddenly, you feel a *need* for speed!

---

*Marti:*

If speed is something you are after, racing can be a safe outlet for you. You have a license to ski as fast as you want within the controlled environment of an immaculately groomed course. It is just you and the clock. Let it all hang out. With crowded trails everywhere else, it is one of the few places you can ski with abandonment.

As in any other disciplines, practice makes perfect and sometimes can be more fun than the actual event. Training alone may appeal to many women who are not as interested in the competitive aspects of racing. In fact, not skiing against time allows you to focus on technique and strategy without pressure from the clock. A lot more learning can take place.

Feedback from a professional coach is the next helpful aid. A good coach can help you learn to read the course before you ski it and guide you in the transition from beginning skier to elite racer.

Next to a good coach, video is a terrific learning tool. Being able to see yourself on screen can be a constructive (I emphasize constructive) and immediate visual feedback for what you are trying to accomplish. Watching World Cup and pro racers also implants positive images in your mind and can transfer the right moves into your own skiing.

You can find ski racing at nearly all ski areas. Some programs move from one resort to another. Others, like NASTAR or coin-operated courses, are offered daily. Still others are single events. Costs vary.

## Adult recreational racing programs

*NASTAR* (NAtional STAndard Race) was offered at 180 ski areas in 32 states during the 1993-94 ski season, which marked NASTAR's 25th anniversary.
- Race format: Giant Slalom.
- Open to: any skier, any age, any ability.

• How it works: Racers earn gold, silver and bronze medals based on age, sex and a unique handicap system, which compares the racer's time with members of the U.S. Ski Team. State and national leaders earn awards and prizes and national winners are listed in *SKI* magazine.

• Information: World Wide Sports, 402D, AABC, Aspen, CO 81611; (970) 925-7864; FAX (970) 925-7882.

*United States Ski Association* offers two recreational racing programs:

*Masters Racing* attracts skiers who are *serious* about racing as well as former collegiate, professional and U.S. Ski Team racers.

• Race format: Slalom, Giant Slalom, Super G, Downhill.

• Open to: Ages 18 and older.

• How it works: Competitors ski in age classifications in local season-long series to qualify for national and international championship races.

*Citizens Racing;* is mostly for city folks who ski recreationally on weekends.

• Race format: Slalom, Giant Slalom.

• Open to: Ages 21 and older; all abilities.

• How it works: Participants are grouped according to age and ability. Top citizen racers from each region attend U.S. championships. The winners there represent the United States in "Citadin" competition in Europe.

For more information on USSA racing: United States Ski Association, Recreation Programs, P.O. Box 100, Park City, UT 84060; (801) 649-9090.

*Mitsubushi Motors Diamond Ski Classic* is a U.S. Recreational Ski Association program offered in six regions throughout the season to members of the association (non-members pay a small fee). It emphasizes *fun* in ski racing.

• Race format: Dual Giant Slalom

• Open to: All ages and abilities.

• How it works: Participants ski two runs in the novice, intermediate or elite class. Their best time goes toward accumulating points. Highest-point winners win a trip to the finals.

For more information: 1315 Gene Autry Way, Anaheim, CA 92805; (714) 634-1050.

*Pay-to-Race* courses operate at most major resorts.

• Race format: Dual Giant Slalom.

• Open to: All ages, all abilities.

• How it works: Buy tokens, normally for $1, at starting gate; race as many times as you want. Race times displayed at finish line after each run.

## Charity racing

Race courses continue to be successful venues for charities to raise money. Many invite a celebrity or two from the sports and entertainment fields and draw huge crowds who pay big bucks to ski with the likes of Christie Brinkley, Nicollette Sheridan and Clint Eastwood. These annual races at various resorts are fun and low-key (for most people) and usually include lots of social events and media hype.

*Jimmie Heuga's Mazda Ski Express* raises about $1 million for the Jimmie Heuga Center's medical program and research activities for multiple sclerosis. The season-long series spans 18 states, with national finals held in Vail.

• Race format: Dual Giant Slalom and four-hour marathon.

• Open to: All ages. Each three-person team must be co-ed.

• How it works: Scoring is based half on the amount of pledges raised, a quarter on vertical feet skied in the marathon, and a quarter on combined times of each team. At the finals, each member of the top fund-raising team wins a Mazda.

For more information: P.O. Box 5919, Avon, CO 81620; (800) 367-3101 or (970) 949-7172.

## Chapter Summary:

Do not freak out on the hard stuff. P.S.I.A. instructors, coaches, racers, and a world champion tell us how to turn 'em on ice, bumps, steeps, and in powder. They show us how to ski in control and how running gates improves free skiing. Finally, you will find a list of major racing venues for recre-ational skiers.

## For more information:

Billy Kidd Performance Center — 2305 Mt. Werner Circle; Steamboat Springs, CO 80487; (970) 879-6111 Ext. 543.

Chapter Fifteen

# Women to women

*"Lessons are great! They give you hints and tips to control your skis and make skiing more challenging and enjoyable. I like the self-confidence I get from this knowledge."* — Anonymous, age 35 from Colorado

*"I'd like to look smooth, in control, and happy through the moguls. Great instruction is the only way I know to get there."* — Anonymous, age 63 from New York

*"It helps to have an instructor tell me what to do instead of my husband."* — Irene, age 66, from Wisconsin

Academics are taking a second look at new research showing that boys demand, and get, teachers' attention more than girls in grade school through grad school. But remove the boys from the classroom and girls are more likely to participate in discussions, to achieve more and to hold themselves in higher self-esteem, the studies show.

The concept also has proven effective in ski schools. The trend toward all-women ski classes is snowballing in the ski industry. According to the Denver-based National Ski Areas Association, nearly half of its ski-area members now offer some type of women-only instructional program.

Chicks on Sticks, Babes on Boards, Thelma and Louise on Skis, call them what you may — participants of these clinics know a good thing when they ski it.

• Liz from Seattle explained why she enrolled in a women's ski seminar at Breckenridge: "In class I can ask questions freely because the female instructors *listen*. Men instructors do not seem to be in touch with how women feel about skiing. It (women's ski seminar) gives me confidence to ski with men back home."

• Vicky, a tennis coach from Denver, was attending her fourth women's ski clinic. "You don't have that macho thing you get in classes with men," she said.

• Ellyn, a teacher from Chicago, noticed an absence of "male-female competition and com-parison" that occurs in mixed classes.

• Stephanie, a rugby player from New York, came to a women's seminar at Copper Mountain because she found "male instructors gear their teaching toward men in coed classes — and they never address the fear factor."

Remember the differences between men's and women's approaches to skiing that we talked about in Chapter One? Men want to "Rambo" down the hill; women take it slower, concentrating more on technique. We certainly cannot forget that man on the lift who yelled "Go faster!" at the woman neatly weaving down a mogul field!

## If you like to dance, the terrain is music

All-women classes remove the pressure to ski like men. Women learn at their own pace, in their own way. Dancing with the mountain rather than attacking it becomes a unified goal. With everyone sharing the same objectives and strategies, the class becomes an ideal learning environment. It breeds success.

Telluride Ski School Director Annie Vareille Savath says all-women classes work because most women are not as confident about their athletic ability as men. "In coed classes, women tend to ski defensively, and lose quality," Vareille Savath says. "But competition on the same level pushes them to be better and builds confidence.

"We show women how to accomplish goals, how to recognize and deal with fears and to coordinate mind and body," Vareille Savath says. "What they learn skiing, they carry throughout their lives. It's better than psychotherapy."

Kristi Terzian, three-time national champion of the U.S. Ski Team, directs the Women's Ski Challenge at Park City, Utah. She says the camps are "all about attitude, perspective and fun." Terzian sets a positive tone the first evening by hosting at an informal party at her Park City home for all the women enrolled in her program.

Women's Ski Spree at Okemo Mountain Resort in Vermont promises "total immersion into the sport of alpine skiing." Director Maria Tomaselli focuses on exploring and educating the psychological and philosophical aspects of skiing. Says Tomaselli, "To teach is to touch a life forever."

The programs owe much of their success to the quality of instruction. Ski schools select the *crème de la crème* of their fully-certified women instructors who are well-versed in the latest teaching methods and equipment technology, and capable of setting examples in a non-condescending way. Their skiing definitely presents a visual, achievable model.

A few resorts still use a male instructor or two if their ski school is limited, or if, as Dave Merriam, ski school director at Stowe, Vermont, says, "We believe that (using) top coaches is important, male or female." While this might be valid in coed classes — the Ski Industries America survey shows 82 percent of women have no gender preference in ski teachers — feedback questionnaires from participants who've completed women's clinics indicate they prefer the women-taught-by-women format. The presence of even a single male is like having a "gal" go out for beers with the guys after bowling. It's just not the same!

Besides mastery of skills and building confidence, women come for the sheer fun of it. A spirit of camaraderie sets these clinics apart. The multi-day seminars can be a slumber-party-sorority-house-Girl Scout-camp rolled into one great getaway. "Let's Do Lunch" takes on a whole new meaning: Picture a sun-drenched mountaintop deck where new friends celebrate their skiing breakthroughs over a bottle of wine.

Lunch is one reason women spend nine consecutive Tuesdays at Greek Peak in New York. Ethnic cuisine with a different country featured each week is the delicious reward for a morning of learning on the mountain. Another reason is that each day offers a specific ski theme, such as shaping turns or skiing bumps.

A costume race highlights the final session of the 10-week program at Arizona Snowbowl; at Tahoe Donner in California, "field trips" to other ski areas add variety to the Wednesday clinics, as do the optional lessons in telemarking.

The experience even can be cathartic. Wendy Nevins, an instructor of women's seminars in Aspen, says emotions get caught up in our muscles. "When we begin to focus on our bodies, what's happening in our minds sometimes spills out." Then the bonding really gets tight.

A few years ago when I was in Crested Butte, Colorado, Kim Reichhelm invited me to sample one day of her four-day women's ski program, Women's Ski Adventures, in mid-session. When the class broke for lunch, Kim apologetically explained that I would not be returning for the afternoon. She said the women in the class felt that a stranger in their midst interfered with their cohesion and diluted the quality of instruction. Understanding the dynamics of these clinics, I agreed to leave peaceably.

## One-day clinics

Women's ski programs range from half-day clinics to all-inclusive, multi-day vacation packages. Some single-day workshops are held on a once-a-week schedule, such as the six-out-of-eight-week seminar hosted by Idaho's Schweitzer Mountain Resort. Others operate on a specific date, like Winter Park's Women's Early Season Clinic in December. One-day clinics vary greatly in price and length. Some offer a few hours of instruction; others run all day. Many include lunch, an après-ski party or an indoor presentation. Video analysis, an important learning tool, often is part of these lessons. Whatever you choose, be sure you know whether a lift ticket is included in the price.

Other programs, sometimes called Ladies Day, promote discounts on lift tickets, lessons and equipment rentals for women, but they do not offer women-to-women instruction. New York's Catamount ski area offers discounted lift tickets to women, free child care and free lessons in *coed* classes during the week. Kudos to them for getting women out of the house and on the mountain, but I think they're missing the point. When I asked why the ski school didn't teach women-only classes, a man in the office said, "I would not know how to do that!"

## Multi-day clinics

Multi-day sessions run from two- or three-day workshops to ski "weeks," which usually last five to six days. The longer time frame allows for more off-slope discussions of topics such as skin care, nutrition, exercise, and psychological issues like dealing with fear and building confidence. Equipment and biomechanics are popular subjects.

Among the most exclusive is Beaver Creek's Technique Weeks for Women, a complete ski vacation tailored to meet the requests of you and 24 of your hand-picked friends. The price varies according to length of stay, but includes lodging at the posh Hyatt Regency, instruction with video, lift tickets, indoor learning sessions, daily breakfasts, opening and closing dinners, and a sponsor's gift such as a Bogner sweater or duffel bag.

Participants receive a helpful Before-You-Go guide including suggestions on everything from clothes to conditioning. The ski-in, ski-out hotel features a health spa, restaurants and "ski valets" who deliver your skis and boots every morning and whisk them away at the end of the day.

Two- and three-day clinics, such as Heavenly Resort's Women's Ski Seminars, offer fewer days on the slopes but rank just as high in quality of instruction. For $350, you get three all-day lessons and lift tickets, video critique, continental breakfast, morning stretch class, lunch at different on-mountain restaurants, and an après-ski party with an equipment tech talk. Lodging is not included, but packages are available. And that Tahoe night life is optional.

With equipment such a vital component to the the whole process of learning to ski, ski-shop owners wisely have entered the teaching arena by sponsoring women's clinics at neighboring resorts. In doing so, they've built a loyal following of clients who depend on them for solid advice on equipment purchases and maintenance.

Buckman's ski shops in Pennsylvania host at Jack Frost Mountain, Hoigaard's in Minneapolis shares sponsorship with Olin skis for "Ski with the Best" at Buck Hill, and Kenny's Double Diamond in Vail has expanded its offerings to include several of Jeannie Thoren's equipment clinics.

The ski equipment company, Rossignol, presents "Skiing for Women Workshops," featuring former Olympians and World Cup medalists as guest coaches. Of course, the opportunity to demo Rossignol products makes these clinics, offered throughout the country, especially attractive. Call 802-434-7080 for current locations.

Some clinics offer optional activities such as snowboarding, snowmobiling, race clinics, cross-country and telemark skiing, heli-skiing, and (as mentioned in Chapter Thirteen) "climbing the wall" at Telluride's

Women's Week. These can be thrilling, once-in-a-lifetime adventures, or the catalyst for learning another winter sport. If you consider yourself an awesome expert skier, there's a place for you, too, in women's ski seminars. Instructors will fine-tune your skiing and provide you plenty of challenges on the most difficult terrain on the mountain — places you may never have skied. And, you will be skiing with some of the best women skiers in the world. Colorado's Ski Cooper offers a specialized clinic called Women in Powder for the "promising and progressive" woman skier. In two days (including one day of snowcat skiing) instructors avow you will be able to ski powder and enjoy it.

Are you into racing? Check out the women's camps at The Billy Kidd Performance Center in Steamboat. As you read in the previous chapter, running gates improves free skiing on the mountain as well as racing skills on the course. Each student in this program receives a "Personal Skiing Profile," one of the best and most comprehensive written evaluations I've seen in ski teaching.

Women who have never skied may need to look harder for women-only classes: many programs accept only skiers who have reached advanced-beginner or lower-intermediate level. Check this if you are just beginning to ski, or haven't skied since you began years ago, and want the advantage of learning with other women. If you cannot find one that accepts never-evers, call a small, local ski area. Because of their less intimidating size and friendly atmospheres, these areas often specialize in learn-to-ski programs and are perfect for beginning skiing. Colorado's SilverCreek Ski Area is one such place — they even initiated a women-only, beginner-only clinic as a springboard for more advanced women's programs.

Ideally, you should reserve your place in a women's ski seminar weeks or even months in advance. Call the resort and ask for the ski school. (Most North American ski resorts offering these seminars are listed with phone numbers at the end of this chapter.) Request a seminar brochure for all the information you need. Often, you or your travel agent can book everything at once: lodging, lift tickets, seminar reservation, car and equipment rentals.

## At the clinic

When you arrive, you are placed in a small class, usually no more than six women, according to your ability. (Some clinics send out questionnaires to determine your level prior to your arrival; others assess your skiing ability on the first morning.) If you find yourself in a group that skis slower than you, or one more advanced, speak with your instructor. She will be more than willing to move you to another group. Instructors bend over backward to make these experiences rewarding and *fun*.

Instruction is only as good as the instructor. Any time you are dissatisfied, complain to the ski school or clinic director. If you think there's a problem, say so early enough in the session to reap the benefits of another instructor or class.

Many of the bad instructor stories I hear involve ski classes in Europe. There, instructors do not really teach; they act more like guides who say, "Follow me," and ski off in front of the class, which is supposed to copy him. (Male instructors teach adult students; usually women are assigned only children's classes.) One California woman wrote in my survey: "In Europe, I improved radically because ski instructors are very strict and hit you with their poles!" Another recalls how her instructor skied off into the fog, never to be seen again!

Small wonder European women laud American ski schools and love the idea of women's ski clinics, which only now are beginning to take shape in Europe. I know of several: Méribel, in Les Trois Vallées in France; Châtel, also in France in the Portes du Soleil region on the border with Switzerland; and Baqueira Beret in Spain.

Women-only ski instruction began in the United States with Elissa Slanger's Women's Way, held at Squaw Valley, Calif. in 1975. Copper Mountain picked up the concept a few years later and the idea began to flourish.

Breckenridge Women Ski Seminar instructor Jan Degerberg explains one of the reasons for the seminars' success: "The approach instructors use in teaching can make it or break it for women. A 22-year-old macho kid instructor who wants to 'go for it,' teaching a nervous woman who hasn't skied in 12 years, could be a negative situation."

*Could be?*

It's always better when a woman is compatible with her instructor, Degerberg says.

For one woman, her experience at Shawnee Mountain's Ladies Day Program in Pennsylvania proved to be "much more" than just the basics. "We learned to laugh and be comfortable with ourselves on the slopes," she said. "We learned that skiing is not a muscle sport. It is a finesse sport. And we learned how to say 'no' to our significant other who approaches us with, 'Come on, honey. I *know* you can do it.'"

## The nature of learning

As a consultant in Sports Science for Copper Mountain Ski School, Neil Wolkodof knows how to get the most from ski instruction. Here he tells us the ingredients needed for making skiing improvements possible.

Lessons are not always a guarantee of learning to ski better. In fact, a lesson will provide the necessary information and techniques, *but your mental state will dictate whether the learning is effective.* In essence, if you learn *how* to learn, you can keep improving your ski techniques long after your lessons are over. Lessons and clinics tend to put people in a learning mode where change is supported but not guaranteed. In either situation, your mindset will determine the ultimate results.

The first key to learning a new skill or refining an old one is to understand the nature of learning. This is difficult to determine because studies cannot directly access the neurological pathways, but we can make some very good observations and derive some principles based on learning examples, situations and experiments.

Learning involves three phases:
- Understanding the skill.
- Practicing the skill.
- Making that skill automatic so that movements and reactions occur without conscious thinking.

Applying this model of learning to skiing will result in drastically improving your rate of learning.

**Understanding**

The understanding or *cognitive* phase of learning means getting an idea of what you are trying to accomplish. This involves knowing what you currently do in a given situation, like skiing bumps, and knowing what is optimum. You can understand information *visually* (watching the instructor), *auditorily* (listening to the description of the action and making a mental picture), or *kinesthetically* (how a movement feels). While visual information provides more details about the movement goal and intricacies, not everyone is set up to learn visually. The key is to determine your preferred style of information reception.

Many people do not learn because they do not have an image of what needs to be accomplished. If you do not have a goal or understanding, you probably won't improve. Your goal should be to pick one or two points of information that will lead to performing or improving the skill. For example, "Press on your right ski to turn left." Information should be specific.

**Practicing**

After you gain an understanding of the movement, the next phase is practicing, or the *associative* phase. This is the most critical phase because you begin to develop new motor pathways. In the case of old skills being refined, you are attempting to change or develop new muscle memory.

There are several methods you can use to make this phase effective. Learning best takes place when you slow down. In order to do this, you should pick terrain and speed that is below your normal ability. If you normally ski "black" moguls, practice on a blue run with consistent bumps to improve mogul technique. In this phase of learning, you must actively try to establish each movement. Don't think about the terrain or speed not being at your maximum ability level.

This phase reminds us that learning is active and requires a good deal of mental effort. It also shows us that the quality of the movements and not the quantity is the prime determinant of whether you begin to learn the skill. Better to make 10 good linked bump turns than 20 wrong ones. In this phase, it is good to remind yourself to do what the instructor said, such as to press or to reach. In this phase you need to link actively the desired movements with the trigger or stimulus.

### Making it automatic

Once the skill is fully learned, this approach works well. But fully developing a skill takes the *active thinking* required to associate movement with a stimulus. Once the active thinking produces the desired results, the automatic approach kicks in.

Most people feel they do not think at all during this phase, but in actuality you *are* thinking, just with different parameters. Sports thinking can be characterized as *visual* rather than verbal thinking. You simply think in pictures, use those pictures to cue actions, and go on to the next movement. You are aware and in control, just not in the same sense as when verbally thinking during the associative phase.

The biggest error most people make in the automatic phase is to think and cue information verbally rather than visually. This leads to slow and/or inaccurate movements and, sometimes, just total disaster. You can slowly enter the zone of visual thinking by taking movements you have perfected and applying them to slightly more challenging situations — steeper terrain, bigger bumps, deeper powder.

There is a time to think verbally and a time to think visually. Learning requires active, and in many cases verbal, thinking to develop new movements. In this case, a few good turns are worth many bad turns. As you evolve to the performance or the automatic mode, you must make those thinking patterns more and more visual in order to make the full transition to performance. And when you think, think positively!

---

## Chapter Summary:

Women-only ski clinics are popping up at North American ski areas in great numbers. Women say when the intimidation and competition with men is removed, they learn to ski better and, sometimes, even have more fun! These women-teaching-women classes have proven to be the ideal learning environment for women in skiing.

Neil Wolkodof offers tips on how people learn to ski.

Choose a women's ski program from the following list of more than 170 offered in North America.

# North American Ski Areas with Alpine Ski Programs for Women

This list was compiled from National Ski Areas Association and regional ski associations. With the increasing popularity of women's clinics, some may have been added to ski school offerings after this book's publication prior to the 1996-97 ski season. Many areas host clinics run by companies independent of their ski schools. Areas with an asterisk (*) offer Jeannie Thoren's equipment clinics.

## Alaska

| | |
|---|---|
| Alyeska Resort | (800) 880-3880 |
| Eaglecrest Ski Area | (907) 586-5284 |

## Arizona

| | |
|---|---|
| Arizona Snowbowl | (520) 779-1951 |
| Sunrise Park Resort | (520) 735-7669 |

## California

| | |
|---|---|
| Alpine Meadows | (800) 441-4423 |
| Bear Valley | (209) 753-2301 |
| Dodge Ridge | (209) 965-3474 |
| Donner Ski Ranch | (916) 426-3635 |
| June Mountain | (800) 832-7320 |
| Kirkwood | (800) 967-7500 |
| Mammoth Mountain | (800) 832-7320 |
| Mountain High | (619) 249-5808 |
| Mt. Shasta Ski Park | (916) 926-8600 |
| Ski Homewood | (916) 525-2992 |
| Ski Sunrise | (619) 249-6150 |
| Snow Valley | (909) 867-2751 |
| Squaw Valley | (800) 545-4350 |
| Tahoe Donner | (916) 587-9444 |

# Colorado

| | |
|---|---|
| Aspen Ski Areas | (800) 525-6200 |
| Beaver Creek | (970) 926-7800 |
| Breckenridge | (800) 789-7669 |
| Copper Mountain | (800) 458-8386 |
| Crested Butte | (800) 992-7700 |
| Eldora Mountain | (303) 440-8700 |
| Keystone | (800) 222-0188 |
| Loveland | (800) 736-3754 |
| Monarch | (800) 332-3668 |
| Powderhorn | (970) 268-5700 |
| Purgatory | (970) 247-9000 |
| SilverCreek | (800) 754-7458 |
| Ski Cooper | (719) 486-3684 |
| Steamboat | (800) 922-2722 |
| Sunlight Mountain | (970) 945-7491 |
| Telluride | (800) 525-3455 |
| *Vail | (970) 476-3239 |
| Winter Park Resort | (970) 726-1551 |
| Wolf Creek | (970) 264-5639 |

# Connecticut

| | |
|---|---|
| Mohawk Mountain | (203) 672-6100 |
| Ski Sundown | (203) 379-9851 |

# Idaho

| | |
|---|---|
| Bogus Basin | (208) 332-5100 |
| Brundage Mountain | (800) 888-7544 |
| Lookout Pass | (208) 777-7701 |
| Schweitzer Mountain Resort | (800) 831-8810 |
| *Sun Valley | (208) 622-2246 |

# Illinois

| | |
|---|---|
| Chestnut Mountain | (800) 397-1320 |

# Indiana

| | |
|---|---|
| Paoli Peaks | (812) 723-4696 |

# Iowa

| | |
|---|---|
| Mt. Crescent | (712) 545-3850 |

# Maine

| Lost Valley | (207) 784-1561 |
| Shawnee Peak | (207) 647-8444 |
| Ski Mt. Abram | (207) 875-5003 |
| Sugarloaf USA | (800) 843-5623 |
| Sunday River | (207) 824-3000 |

# Massachusetts

| Bradford Ski Area | (508) 373-0071 |
| Brodie Mountain | (413) 443-4752 |
| Butternut Basin | (413) 528-2000 |
| Jiminy Peak | (413) 738-5500 |
| Mt. Tom Ski Area | (413) 536-0516 |
| Nashoba Valley Ski Area | (508) 692-3033 |
| Wachusett Mountain | (508) 464-2300 |

# Michigan

| *Brule Mountain | (906) 265-4957 |
| Cannonsburg | (616) 874-6711 |
| *Crystal Mountain | (800) 968-7686 |
| *Hidden Valley | (810) 626-9503 |
| Indianhead Mountain Resort | (906) 229-5181 |
| Mt. Holiday ( | 616) 938-2500 |
| Mt. Holly | (810) 634-8260 |
| Nubs Nob | (616) 526-2131 |
| Otsego Ski Club | (517) 732-5181 |
| *Pine Mountain | (800) 505-7463 |
| Shanty Creek | (616) 533-8621 |
| Snow Snake Mountain | (517) 539-6583 |
| Swiss Valley | (616) 244-5635 |
| Timber Ridge | (616) 694-9949 |

# Minnesota

| Afton Alps | (612) 436-5245 |
| Andes Tower Hills | (612) 965-2455 |
| *Buck Hill | (612) 435-7174 |
| Giants Ridge | (800) 688-7669 |
| *Mount Frontenac | (800) 488-5826 |
| Powder Ridge | (800) 348-7734 |
| *Spirit Mountain | (800) 642-6377 |

| Welch Village Ski Area | (800) 421-0699 |

## Montana

| The Big Mountain | (406) 862-2909 |
| Bridger Bowl | (406) 587-2111 |
| Discovery Basin | (406) 563-2184 |
| Great Divide | (406) 449-3746 |
| Lost Trail | (406) 821-3508 |
| Marshall Mountain | (406) 258-6000 |
| Montana Snowbowl | (406) 549-9777 |
| Red Lodge Mountain | (406) 446-2610 |
| Showdown Ski Area | (406) 236-5522 |

## Nevada

| Diamond Peak Ski Resort | (702) 832-1177 |
| Heavenly | (800) 243-2836 |

## New Hampshire

| Attitash Bear Peak Cranmore | (603) 374-2368 |
| Balsams Wilderness | (800) 255-0600 |
| Gunstock | (800) 486-7862 |
| King Pine Ski Area | (603) 367-8896 |
| Loon Mountain | (603) 745-8111 |
| Mt. Sunapee | (603) 763-2356 |
| Temple Mountain | (603) 924-6949 |
| Waterville Valley | (603) 236-8311 |
| Wildcat Mountain | (800) 255-6439 |

## New Jersey

| Hidden Valley Ski Resort | (201) 764-6161 |

## New Mexico

| Pajarito Mountain | (505) 662-5725 |
| Red River Ski Area | (505) 754-2382 |
| Sandia Peak | (505) 856-6419 |
| Santa Fe Ski Area | (505) 982-4429 |
| Taos Ski Valley | (505) 776-2291 |

## New York

| Bristol Mountain | ( 716) 374-6000 |
| Gore Mountain | (518) 251-2411 |
| Greek Peak | (607) 835-6111 |

| Holiday Valley Resort | (716) 699-2345 |
|---|---|
| Hunter Mountain | (518) 263-4223 |
| *Lake Placid | (518) 946-2223 |
| Peek 'n Peak | (716) 355-4141 |
| Ski Big Birch | (914) 878-9303 |
| Ski Windham | (800) 729-4766 |
| Snow Ridge | (800) 962-8419 |

## Ohio

| Boston Mills/Brandywine | (800) 875-4241 |
|---|---|

## Oregon

| *Mt. Bachelor | (800) 829-2442 |
|---|---|
| Mt. Hood Meadows Ski Resort | (503) 337-2222 |
| Timberline | (800) 547-1406 |
| Willamette Pass | (800) 444-5030 |

## Pennsylvania

| Alpine Mountain | (717) 595-2150 |
|---|---|
| Big Boulder Ski Area | (717) 722-0100 |
| Blue Mountain | (800) 235-2226 |
| Elk Mountain | (717) 679-2611 |
| Hidden Valley | (800) 443-7544 |
| Jack Frost Mountain | (717) 443-8425 |
| Seven Springs | (800) 452-2223 |
| Shawnee Mountain | (800) 233-4218 |
| Ski Denton | (814) 435-2115 |
| Ski Liberty | (800) 829-4766 |
| Ski Roundtop | (717) 432-9631 |
| Whitetail Ski Resort | (717) 328-9400 |

## Utah

| Alta | (801) 742-3333 |
|---|---|
| Brighton | (801) 943-6070 |
| Deer Valley | (801) 645-6648 |
| Park City Ski Area | (801) 654-5423 |
| Powder Mountain | (801) 745-3772 |
| Snowbird Ski Resort | (800) 453-3000 |
| Solitude Ski Resort | (800) 748-4754 |

# Vermont

| | |
|---|---|
| Ascutney Mountain Resort | (802) 484-7711 |
| Bolton Valley | (800) 451-3220 |
| *Killington Ski Area | (800) 621-6867 |
| Mount Snow/Haystack | (800) 245-7669 |
| Okemo Mountain Resort | (802) 228-4041 |
| Smugglers' Notch | (800) 451-8752 |
| Stowe Mountain Resort | (800) 253-4754 |
| Stratton Mountain | (800) 787-2886 |
| Sugarbush | (802) 583-2381 |
| Suicide Six Ski Area | (802) 457-1666 |

# Virginia

| | |
|---|---|
| Massanutten Ski Resort | (800) 207-6277 |

# Washington

| | |
|---|---|
| 49 Degrees North | (509) 935-6649 |
| Crystal Mountain | (206) 663-2265 |
| Ski Bluewood | (509) 382-4725 |
| White Pass Ski Area | (509) 672-3131 |

# West Virginia

| | |
|---|---|
| Canaan Valley Resort | (304) 866-4121 |
| Snowshoe/Silver Creek | (304) 572-1000 |
| Timberline Four Seasons Resort | (304) 866-4801 |

# Wisconsin

| | |
|---|---|
| Alpine Valley Resort | (414) 642-7374 |
| *Cascade Mountain | (800) 992-2754 |
| *MountainTop at Grand Geneva | (800) 558-3417 |
| Mt. La Crosse Ski Area | (800) 426-3665 |
| Sunburst Ski Area | (414) 626-8404 |
| Trollhaugen Ski Area | (715) 755-2955 |
| *Wilmot Mountain | (414) 862-2301 |

# Wyoming

| | |
|---|---|
| Antelope Butte | (307) 655-9530 |
| Hogadon Ski Area | (307) 235-8499 |
| Jackson Hole Ski Resort | (307) 733-2292 |
| Snow King | (307) 733-5200 |

# Canada

**Alberta**

| | |
|---|---|
| Lake Louise Ski Area | (403) 522-3555 |

**British Columbia**

| | |
|---|---|
| Blackcomb | (604) 932-3141 |
| Grouse Mountain | (604) 984-0661 |
| Sun Peaks Resort at Tod Mt. | (604) 578-7222 |
| Whistler Mountain | (604) 932-3210 |

**Manitoba**

| | |
|---|---|
| Holiday Mountain | (204) 242-2172 |

**Newfoundland**

| | |
|---|---|
| Marble Mountain | (709) 637-7616 |

**New Brunswick**

| | |
|---|---|
| Poley Mtn. Resorts | (506) 433-3230 |

**Nova Scotia**

| | |
|---|---|
| Ski Wentworth | (902) 895-9281 |

**Ontario**

| | |
|---|---|
| Alpine Ski Club | (705) 445-0339 |
| Blue Mountain | (705) 445-0231 |
| Chicopee Ski Club | (519) 894-5610 |
| Craigleith Ski Club | (705) 445-3847 |
| Georgian Peaks Club | (519) 599-6771 |
| Glen Eden Ski Area | (905) 336-1158 |
| Horseshoe Valley | (705) 835-2790 |
| Mt. Louis-Moonstone | (705) 835-2112 |
| Searchmont Resort | (705) 781-2340 |

**Québec**

| | |
|---|---|
| Edelweiss Valley | (819) 459-2328 |
| Mont Sainte-Anne | (418) 827-4561 |
| Ski Vorlage | (819) 459-2301 |
| Tremblant | (819) 681-2000 |

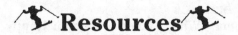

# Resources

## Books

Aburdene, Patricia and Naisbitt, John. *Megatrends for Women.* New York, Random House, 1992.

Bailey, Covert and Bishop, Lea. *The Fit or Fat Woman: Solutions for Women's Unique Concerns.* Boston, Houghton Mifflin Co. 1989.

Briles, Judith. *The Confidence Factor: How Self-Esteem Can Change Your Life.* MasterMedia Limited, 1990.

Estés, Clarissaa Pinkola. *Women Who Run with the Wolves.* New York, Ballantine Books, 1992.

Gallwey, Timothy and Kriegel, Bob, *Inner Skiing.* New York, Random House, 1977.

Gray, John. *Men Are from Mars, Women Are from Venus.* New York, Harper Collins, 1992.

Jeffers, Susan, PhD. *Feel the Fear and Do It Anyway.* New York, Ballantine Books, 1987.

Leocha, Charles. *Skiing America* and *Ski Europe,* Boston, World Leisure Corporation, 1996.

Wells, Christine. *Women, Sport, & Performance: A Physiological Perspective.* (2nd ed.) Champaign, Ill., Human Kinetics Books, 1991.

Witherell, Warren and Evrard, David. *The Athletic Skier.* Salt Lake City, Utah, 1993.

(Used in the Women's Ski Discovery segment)
DeCoursey, Doug, and Linder, Darwyn, Ph.D. *Visual skiing, The Essential Mental and Physical Skills for the Modern Skier.* New York, Doubleday, 1990.

McCluggage, Denise. *The Centered Skier.* Waitsfield, Vermont, Tempest Books, 1992.

Porter, Kay, Ph.D., and Foster, Judy. *The Mental Athlete.* New York, Ballantine Books, 1987.

## Video

Densmore, Lisa Feinberg. "BODY PREP! The Ultimate Ski Fitness Video." Hanover, N.H., Driscoll Communications, 1988.

"The Signature of Excellence." Stowe, Vt., Driscoll Communications, 1992.

Wade, Patty. "In Shape to Ski." Aspen Colo., 1993.

"ACL Awareness '96" Underhill Denter, VT, Vermont Safety Research, 1995.

## Magazine articles

Alberts, Nuna. "What Makes a Woman Happy?" *First for Women*, (December 13, 1993), p. 38.

Berger, Robert, M.D., "How To Protect Skin and Eyes on the Slopes," *Snow Country*, (March/April, 1993), p. 86. "Buyers Guide." *SKI*, (September, 1993)

Cowan, Jay. "The Selective Eye." *SKI*, (September, 1993), pp. 195-198.

"Are Composites King?" *SKI*, (September, 1993), p. 189-190.

Curtin, Irwin. "America's Top Ski Shops." *Snow Country*, (January/February, 1994), p. 54.

Fry, John. "Put Women in Charge." *Snow Country*, (November, 1993), p. 8.

Hall, Julie K. "Fiber and Fabric Guide." *Ski Tech*, (October, 1993), pull-out section. "Skiwear for Real People, *Ski Tech*, (March, 1994), pp. 42-58.

Harb, Harold. "Body Alignment Relating to Biomechanics." *The Professional Skier*, (Fall, 1993), pp. 22-26. "1 Fix for 6 Common Errors." *Snow Country*, (January/February, 1994), pp. 104-112.

Hogen, Jackson. "Take Skis for a Demo Run Before Buying." *Snow Country*, (October, 1993), p. 116.

Howden, Michael. "9 Simple Steps to a Better Backshop." *Ski Tech*, (November/December, 1993), pp. 46-47.

Irons, Dave. "Testing 101." *Ski Tech*, (November/December, 1993), pp. 26-28.

Levine, Carol. "Physiological Considerations in Teaching Women to Ski." *The Professional Skier*, (Fall, 1993), pp. 14-18.

Licksteig, Julie Ann. "Nutrition for High Altitude and the Mountain Sports," *Winter Sports Medicine.*

Masia, Seth. "Battle of the Flexes," *SKI*, (September, 1993), pp. 174-175. "Movers and Shapers," *SKI*, (September, 1993), p. 78.

Russelman, Bernadette. "Matters at Hand." *SKI*, (September, 1993), pp. 205-209.

Suplizio, Cindy and Hintermeister, Robert. "Do Anatomical and Physiological Differences Between Genders Affect Skiing?" *The Professional Skier*, (Fall, 1993), pp. 19-20, 62-63.

Ulmer, Kristen. "The Right to Ski to Die," *Skiing*, (November, 1993), p. 36, 217.

Wardlaw, Tait. "93-94 Ski Directory." *Ski Tech*, (September, 1993), pp. 40-55. "93-94 Boot & Binding Directory." *Ski Tech*, (October, 1993), pp. 55-64.

Weintraub, Anne. "Cold Comfort," *Vogue* (November, 1995), p. 256

## Newspapers

*The Denver Post,* July 18, 1994.

*USA Today,* Nov. 12, 1993; February 28, 1994.

## Reference Works

*Heart and Stroke Facts: 1996 Statistical Supplement.*
American Heart Association, Dallas, Texas, 1996.

Thomas, Dane. *Cross-Training for Expert Skiers: An
Overview.* Powder Performance Center, Crested Butte,
Colo., 1992.

*The Lazy Skier's Guide to At Home Maintenance,* Seth
Masia, Jeff Rich and Susan McCoy.

*U.S. Ski Team Alpine Training Manual.* U.S. Ski Team,
Park City, Utah, revised 1985.

*U.S. Ski Team Media Guide.* Park City, Utah, U.S. Ski
Team, 1994.

*MidLife Woman.* MidLife Women's Network,
Minneapolis, Minnesota, Vol. 3, No. 6.

# Index

---

# Other books published
# by World Leisure

- **All Terrain Skiing** by Dan Egan
  A multimedia package of ski instruction with
  a book and take-on-the-slopes weather-proof technique
  cards as one part of the package for $24.95
  Plus a video available for $29.95 when purchased separately
  or only $24.95 when purchased together with the book.

- **Great Nature Vacations With Your Kids**
  by Dorothy Jordon
  The definitive guide to nature vacations with
  your family whether traveling with infants or
  toddlers to teenagers.
  Suggestions on planning and the best tour
  operators from the "acknowledged heavy
  hitter in the field of family travel.
                                                        $9.95

- **Great Adventure Vacations With Your Kids**
  by Dorothy Jordon
  The definitive guide to adventure vacations
  with your family. From bicycling, canoeing,
  kayaking and whitewater rafting, to
  horseback riding, climbing, camping and
  fly-fishing, Dorothy Jordon fills in
  readers on the best and most family-
  friendly tour operators and
  accommodations.

                                        $9.95

• **Getting To Know You** – 365 questions and activities to enhance relationships by Jeanne McSweeney & Charles Leocha
A book of intimate questions that get right to the heart of successful relationships. $6.95

• **Getting To Know Kids in Your Life**
by Jeanne McSweeney and Charles Leocha
Interactive questions and activities to really get to know children for parents, aunts, uncles, grandparents and anyone who shares time with 3 to 7 year-olds

$6.95

• **ABCs of Life** – from women who learned the hard way
by Beca Lewis Allen
Inspired advice collected for her daughter helps women expand their lives with practical, fun and entering insights about life    $6.95

• **Cheap Dates: Boston** by Alexandra Ryan
Getting the most from Boston's myriad jazz, concert, theater, nightclub and dining adventures for the best bargain prices.    $9.95

• **Travel Rights** by Charles Leocha
The book filled with answers to travelers' difficult questions. It saves you money and makes travel more hassle-free.    $9.95

All available by calling 1-800-444-2524
or send payment plus $3.75 shipping and handling
to: World Leisure, 177 Paris St. Boston, MA 02128